An EasyGuide to
Research Design & SPSS

An EasyGuide to Research Design & SPSS

Beth M. Schwartz
Randolph College

Janie H. Wilson
Georgia Southern University

Dennis M. Goff
Randolph College

Los Angeles | London | New Delhi
Singapore | Washington DC

Los Angeles | London | New Delhi
Singapore | Washington DC

FOR INFORMATION:

SAGE Publications, Inc.
2455 Teller Road
Thousand Oaks, California 91320
E-mail: order@sagepub.com

SAGE Publications Ltd.
1 Oliver's Yard
55 City Road
London EC1Y 1SP
United Kingdom

SAGE Publications India Pvt. Ltd.
B 1/I 1 Mohan Cooperative Industrial Area
Mathura Road, New Delhi 110 044
India

SAGE Publications Asia-Pacific Pte. Ltd.
3 Church Street
#10-04 Samsung Hub
Singapore 049483

Printed in the United States of America

Library of Congress Cataloging-in-Publication Data

Schwartz, Beth M., author.

An easyguide to research design & SPSS / Beth M. Schwartz, Randolph College, Janie H. Wilson, Georgia Southern University, Dennis M. Goff, Randolph College.

pages cm
Includes bibliographical references and index.

ISBN 978-1-4522-8882-6

1. Social science—Statistical methods—Data processing.
2. Social sciences—Methodology. 3. SPSS (Computer file)
I. Wilson, Janie H., author. II. Goff, Dennis M., author.
III. Title.

HA32.S125 2015
001.4'22—dc23   2013043380

This book is printed on acid-free paper.

SFI label applies to text stock

Acquisitions Editor: Reid Hester
Editorial Assistant: Lucy Berbeo
Production Editor: David C. Felts
Copy Editor: Matt Sullivan
Typesetter: C&M Digitals (P) Ltd.
Proofreader: Lawrence W. Baker
Indexer: Wendy Allex
Cover Designer: Anupama Krishnan
Marketing Manager: Shari Countryman

14 15 16 17 18 10 9 8 7 6 5 4 3 2 1

Contents

Preface

After many years of teaching either statistics or research design, we noticed that many of our students did not make the important connection between design and analysis. Until now, students did not have a resource available that clearly makes this important connection, with most textbooks on these topics focusing on either design or analysis. We believe this lack of connection creates a disadvantage to students involved in the research process. After all, you would never consider making reservations for a vacation without first checking your bank account to see if you can cover the costs involved for the trip (and no—in this case, you can't just go into debt or rely on mom and dad to cover the cost). If you do make your vacation choice without first checking what you can really spend, you often have to start from scratch and choose a different place to go that you can afford. The same is true if you choose a design for your research without also taking into account the type of statistic you need to use to accurately test your hypotheses. Doing so might lead to a mismatch between design and analysis and could require a "do-over." We all know that often we don't have the time during the semester to start over again, and more often than not, you need to complete the assignment to pass the course. That is where this EasyGuide comes in.

In this book, we cover all the basic design and analyses that students use as undergraduates and for the most part as graduate students as well. More importantly, we bridge the gap between basic design and analysis. These are the basics, but they are indeed the most common designs and analyses that our students needed to know about when developing their research projects. We cover this material with a reader-friendly approach. Even when you are new to research design and statistical analysis, we use a more conversational tone than found in most methods and stats texts. We are not writing to impress, but rather writing to inform, keeping in mind you—our audience. That way, you don't need to be using Google or Wikipedia to find out what all the terms mean to understand what we are talking about. And, to help, we also include a glossary when there is a term that you are not familiar with. When it comes to using SPSS, we include step-by-step instructions with screenshots that illustrate exactly what we are writing about. If there are chapters that do not reach that goal, please contact us with your advice, comments, and suggestions. Of course, we would also love to hear from you when the book was your go-to guide as you were developing your design, conducting your analyses, interpreting your findings, and writing up your results section in APA style.

This EasyGuide is divided into four sections, beginning with an *Overview of Basic Design Decisions* in Chapter 1, where we discuss why the connection between design and analysis is essential. Next, in Chapter 2, we differentiate correlation from causation in relation to design and analysis. In Chapter 3, we cover the different types of variables you can include in your research and the ways to measure those variables. Then, in Chapter 4, we talk about choosing your variables, the number of variables, and the number of participants to include in your research.

In the second section of this book, *Your Basic SPSS Toolbox*, we include three chapters where we introduce the nitty-gritty of using the statistical software package called SPSS that originally stood for Statistical Package for the Social Sciences. In Chapter 5, you will read about why we use SPSS, and then we discuss how the software is structured to enter your data, how to run your statistical analyses, and how to interpret the output. Next, in Chapter 6, you will learn how to set up your data files, including specifics on how to include important details about your variables. Then, in Chapter 7, we cover how to use SPSS to run statistical analyses for all the different types of data you might include.

In the third section, *Designs, Statistics, Interpretation, and Write-Up in APA Style*, we discuss the many different types of design and the statistical analyses that follow. Each chapter in this section includes the simple to the more complex designs. We start with between-groups designs in Chapter 8, cover within-groups designs in Chapter 9, and move on to mixed designs in Chapter 10. In Chapter 11, we discuss correlations involving relationships among two and more variables. Finally, this section ends with Chapter 12, where we include details on research focused on simple frequency data, with coverage of chi-square analyses.

In the fourth and final *Summary* section of this book, we provide some important resources. In Chapter 13, you can find a chapter on making decisions about design and analysis, with three decision trees that cover most of the designs and analyses throughout this EasyGuide. Then, in Chapter 14, you will find sample results sections for each type of design where we point out the different parts of the results paragraph and the APA style necessary for most of your papers. We finish this section with a bulleted list of pieces of advice that will answer many of the common questions we've heard from our own students and colleagues over the years. When appropriate, we include the chapter number where we cover the details related to these common questions.

Using this *EasyGuide to Design & SPSS* will provide the details needed to make good choices about your design to make sure you can run statistical analyses that will answer your research question. We recognize that when you first start out learning about the research process, there are many considerations that you need to keep in mind to increase the likelihood of a successful project. By following the step-by-step procedures and visual details provided in the screenshots throughout the book, we believe you are on your way to designing, analyzing, interpreting, and communicating about your findings like an expert.

About the Authors

Beth M. Schwartz received her PhD in cognitive psychology from the State University of New York at Buffalo in 1991. Since that time, she has been on the faculty at Randolph College (formerly Randolph-Macon Woman's College) where she is currently the Thoresen Professor of Psychology, Department Chair, and Assistant Dean of the College. Dr. Schwartz's early work focused on factors that influence the accuracy of child witnesses, in particular how changes in the legal system can create a more age-appropriate interview for young children. Her current research program focuses on the scholarship of teaching and learning, examining pedagogical changes that can lead to more effective teaching and learning, and investigating the influence of honor systems on academic integrity.

In both programs of research, Dr. Schwartz focuses on providing undergraduate students with opportunities for research experience, involving students in her research program, as well as advising students interested in conducting their own investigations. As a result, many students have authored published work, presented at national conferences, and have obtained doctorate degrees. Dr. Schwartz has worked with over 1,000 students at Randolph College. She has over 100 professional presentations at conferences and is the author, co-author, and co-editor of over 20 books, book chapters, and professional articles in scholarly peer-reviewed journals. Her work has appeared in journals such as *Journal of Higher Education, Law and Human Behavior, Ethics and Behavior,* and *Journal of the Scholarship of Teaching and Learning.*

Dr. Schwartz was the founder of the Faculty Development Center at Randolph, serving as Faculty Development Coordinator from 2000 to 2007 on her campus, providing faculty with programming focused on refining teaching to become most effective in the classroom. With these programs, she helped create an environment in which discussing the scholarship of teaching and learning is a norm. In her role as Assistant Dean of the college, she continues her involvement in Scholarship of Teaching and Learning on her own campus. She is co-author of *An EasyGuide to APA Style* (2012, with Eric Landrum and Regan Gurung), *Optimizing Teaching and Learning: Catalyzing Pedagogical Research* (2009, with Regan Gurung), co-editor of *Evidenced-Based Teaching in Higher Education* (2012, with Regan Gurung), and co-editor of *Child Abuse: A Global View* (2001, with Michelle McCauley and Michele Epstein). She is a member of the American Psychological Association, a Fellow of the Society for the

Teaching of Psychology (Division 2 of APA), and a member of the Association for Psychological Science. In addition, she is currently involved in Division 2 of the American Psychological Association, recently serving as the first Associate Director for Programming of Regional Conferences, and currently serving as the Vice President of Recognitions and Awards. At Randolph College, she teaches Introduction to Psychology, Cognitive Psychology, Research Methods, Forensic Psychology, and Sensation and Perception, and a Senior Research Capstone Course. Dr. Schwartz is an award-winning teacher, earning the 2001 Randolph College Gillie A. Larew Award for Outstanding Teaching as well as the 2006 Outstanding Teaching and Mentoring Award (from AP-LS), and most recently receiving the 2013 Randolph College Katherine Graves Davidson Award for Excellence in Scholarship.

Janie H. Wilson received her PhD in experimental psychology from the University of South Carolina in 1994. Since that time, she has been teaching and conducting research at Georgia Southern University. In the classroom, Dr. Wilson specializes in teaching and learning in statistics and research methods and maintains a strong focus on involving undergraduates in her research as well as mentoring students to complete their own projects. For two decades, Dr. Wilson has taken students to conferences to present their research in the form of talks and posters, and she has published with undergraduates and graduate students as well.

Research interests include rapport in teaching based on empirical data on the first day of class, electronic communications, and interactions with students in a traditional classroom. A current project involves the development and validation of a professor–student rapport scale. Publications include a statistics textbook, *Essential Statistics*, with Pearson, as well as texts with Sage. Dr. Wilson has contributed numerous chapters to edited books, including chapters in *The Evaluation of Teaching, The Teaching of Psychology: An Empirically-Based Guide to Picking, Choosing, & Using Pedagogy* (2012), *Effective College and University Teaching* (2012), *Teaching Ethically: Challenges and Opportunities* (2012), *Best-Practices for Teaching Statistics and Research Methods in the Behavioral Sciences* (2007), and *Empirical Research in Teaching and Learning: Contributions From Social Psychology* (2011). She has co-edited several books, including *Teaching Controversial Topics in Psychology* (2012, with Dana Dunn, Regan Gurung, and Karen Naufel), *Best Practices for Technology-Enhanced Learning* (2011, with Dana Dunn, James Freeman, and Jeffrey Stowell), and a current project designed to help professors conduct and publish research in the scholarship of teaching and learning (in press, with Regan Gurung). Dr. Wilson has published in numerous journals, including *Teaching of Psychology, Journal of the Scholarship of Teaching and Learning, Journal of Classroom Interaction, College Teaching*, and *Assessment & Evaluation in Higher Education*. Finally, she has presented over 60 conference presentations, including several invited keynote addresses.

Dr. Wilson served as the American Psychological Association (APA) Program Chair for Division 2, the Society for the Teaching of Psychology (STP), as well as Program Director overseeing all programming efforts by STP. She currently serves as the Vice President of Programming for Division 2 of APA. She was honored with the College of Liberal Arts Award of Distinction in Teaching in 2003, the Georgia Southern University Award for Excellence in Contributions to Instruction in 2004–2005, the Georgia Southern University Scholarship of Teaching and Learning Award in 2012, and the Ruffin Cup award for excellence in contributions to the College of Liberal Arts and Social Sciences in 2013.

Dennis M. Goff received his PhD in experimental psychology from Virginia Tech in 1985. He has been teaching and conducting research at Randolph College (formerly Randolph-Macon Woman's College) since 1986. Dr. Goff specializes in teaching and learning in statistics and developmental psychology with a burgeoning interest in evolutionary psychology. In the past 27 years, he has mentored hundreds of senior psychology majors as they completed their independently designed research projects. In recent years, all of those seniors have presented their work at statewide conferences, and a few have earned recognition for best undergraduate research projects.

Dr. Goff's research interests have ranged widely over the course of his career. Early interests included the influence of prenatal factors on behavior in newborns. More recently, he has extended that interest to examinations of behavior in children and adults using digit-ratio as an indicator of those prenatal influences. Publications include numerous journal articles and conference presentations, many of them coauthored with his students.

Dr. Goff is a Fellow of the Association for Psychological Science. He has been recognized at Randolph by being named a Charles A. Dana Professor of Psychology and given the Gillie A. Larew Award for Teaching Excellence and the Katherine Graves Davidson Award for Excellence in Promoting the College.

SECTION I

Overview of Basic Design Decisions

In the first section, we present basic considerations for your research design. In these chapters, you will find information that helps you understand (1) the important relationship between your hypothesis, design, and statistic; (2) the need to differentiate between correlation as a design versus a statistic; (3) the different types of variables used in designs; and finally, (4) details of design such as deciding how many variables to use and how many participants to include.

Marriage—'til Death Do Us Part—Stats and Methods—Why They Belong Together

1

If you are reading this book, we are guessing that you are likely enrolled in a course that involves conducting statistical analyses, learning how to design research, or both. Regardless of the course in which you are enrolled, you clearly recognize (or soon will recognize) how important it is that you understand the connection between statistics and research methods. You have made a great choice because learning one topic without understanding its connection to the other can create problems in your research.

This book is about (1) improving your research skills, (2) building your confidence as you develop hypotheses, (3) designing your methodology to test your hypotheses, (4) choosing the appropriate statistic to analyze your data, and (5) learning how to run various statistics using **SPSS.** We provide you with step-by-step guidelines on how to conduct analyses, understand the SPSS output, determine whether you supported your prediction, and finally how to communicate your findings in **APA style.** You will find that integrating your choice of design and statistic will allow you to create sound research designs. The **hypothesis** you want to examine will be tested using a design tied to an appropriate statistic. Paying attention to this connection is key to your success in the research process.

We will go ahead and admit that the most important issue to think about first is your research question, or hypothesis. For example, suppose you suffer from headaches and want to examine ways to reduce pain. After reading journal articles (despite suffering from a headache), you come up with three options: pain medication, placebo (e.g., sugar pill), and refocusing attention. You might think (or hypothesize) that refocusing attention would not reduce pain as well as pain medication, and you are willing to bet that even a placebo would relieve pain better than simply taking your mind off the pain by focusing your attention elsewhere.

Now that you have your research hypothesis, you need to design a study to test it. You could design your study as an experiment, where you would manipulate what happens to participants. In this study, you could collect a group of people who have a headache and make them (1) take pain medication, (2) take a placebo, or (3) focus their attention on their breathing rather than the headache.

Type of Pain-Killing Method

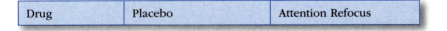

Drug	Placebo	Attention Refocus

In this particular design, you have different people in each condition. After experiencing a condition, each participant could report headache pain. We have outlined the basics of a research design. The design has a good chance of testing your hypothesis. However, unless we consider what statistic we will use after data collection, we do not know if we will gain valuable information.

One approach to this study would be to expose people to a condition and, after an hour or so, ask them if they have a headache. They would answer "yes" or "no." Imagine they all leave your laboratory, and you take the data home to analyze . . . and you have *no* idea what to do with it. When you talk with your professor about how to analyze it, you learn that yes/no answers are not all that useful as outcome measures in a study. Worse, imagine that about 75% of the people in each group answered "yes." Would you know if the pain itself was different across the three groups? Even if we found a way to analyze the data in some simple way, we would not be able to address the original hypothesis of attention refocusing not working as well as pain medication or a placebo. In this example, you would be stuck with useless data.

Back to the drawing board . . . or at least back to data collection. The design used does not test the hypothesis of interest because no statistic offers a way to analyze the data well. Results with these data will not provide any information about whether the attention refocusing was less effective than the medicine or a placebo because you only know who had a headache at the end of your study. This is why it is essential to make sure your design allows you to collect the data needed and also matches with the statistic you need to use to evaluate your hypothesis. Do not start collecting data until this connection between hypothesis, design, and statistic is checked and double-checked.

Let us look at a better match among hypothesis, design, and statistics. We will return to our three groups and assign people with headaches to either (1) take pain medication, (2) receive a placebo, or (3) refocus their attention. After an hour, we could ask all participants to rate their headache pain on a scale from 1 to 10, with higher numbers indicating more pain. With a rating scale, we obtain useful numbers that, in fact, can be analyzed with a statistic that will address your hypothesis. Later in this book, you will learn exactly how these data would be analyzed. But for now, we hope you can see that your hypothesis dictates the research design, and you must identify a statistic that will analyze your data. Failure to do this in the early phases of your research could result in trashing your data and starting over.

We Want to Help

For many years, students have taken courses in statistics followed by courses in research methodology, or vice versa. Typically, in many psychology curricula, students develop research-methods skills and statistical skills in separate courses. Do not get us wrong—instructors (including us) of these sequential courses make attempts to tie the material together in an effort to communicate how the two topics are fundamentally connected. But the three of us have spent years trying to make this connection for students through different courses, only to see students struggle. Here is the problem: After taking the introductory statistics course and the research-methods course, many students are required to take courses in which they must develop their own research and ultimately conduct original research themselves. The research question (hypothesis) dictates the research design, including types of data to collect and ultimately analyze. But without knowledge of how to analyze different types of data, you cannot make an informed decision about data collection!

To complicate matters, the majority of statistics and research-methods textbooks make few attempts to connect the two topics. Most statistics textbooks focus on the how and why of statistical analysis with just a glance at research design. This glance helps to define the statistical technique but typically does not help students see the connection between the statistic and the design. In contrast, the typical research-methods text presents the basics of design, with one chapter set aside to cover statistics. As an alternative, the author might remind students to review a statistics book and rarely explains why a particular statistic might be useful in a specific situation. To be fair, we have seen methods texts that do inform readers about the type of statistic to use when choosing a particular design, but typically, not much is offered beyond the mention of the name of the statistic.

Essentially, choosing a method without also considering the statistic would be like choosing a major in college without figuring out if you are able to take the required courses you need for that major in the time period allowed (e.g., four years). Or if you have ever tried to bake a cake, you know that it is a bad idea to start the baking process before making sure you have all the correct ingredients. Missing ingredients usually leads to a crappy cake. The same is true for research. Missing the connection between the design and the statistics leads to a crappy research project.

We offer this EasyGuide as a way to consider statistics and research methods together. You will find the text to be a valuable resource under a number of circumstances: (1) You are in your first statistics course or a research-methods course; (2) you are in an upper-level experimental course; (3) you are in a capstone course; (4) you are conducting independent research; or (5) you are beginning a masters or doctoral program. This book will be one you pick up often to review the statistics-methods connection, how to conduct SPSS analyses, how to interpret the output from your SPSS analyses, and how to write an APA-style results section.

Follow the suggestions in each chapter, with a focus on specific types of designs, and you will correctly connect your design and statistics. In the example above, with this EasyGuide in hand, you would know that the hypothesis and design of your study requires outcome data with quantity such as a rating scale or other measure with meaningful numbers. Using a better outcome variable would allow you to test your hypothesis by providing the appropriate data needed to run the statistical test.

Carefully follow the steps below to ensure that you are on your way to a successful research project.

Basic Steps of Research

1. Conduct a literature review.

2. Choose a research question and determine your hypothesis.

3. If you want to run a true experiment, choose manipulation(s) and levels of the independent variable (IV).

4. If you want to run a correlational study with specific groups of interest, choose a **pseudo-IV** and levels.

5. If you want to run a correlational study with no specific groups with an interest in whether or not two variables are related, pick variables to measure.

6. Rely on knowledge of statistics to choose appropriate variables. Your outcome variable will be called a dependent variable (DV) in some designs.

7. Make sure you know which statistic you will use when choosing variables.

8. Some statistics rely on variables with meaningful, quantifiable numbers (e.g., height and weight), and some statistics rely on variables with categories (e.g., whether people are male or female or whether they are gay, bisexual, or heterosexual, to name a few).

9. Obtain approval to conduct your study (e.g., from your professor or the **institutional review board,** depending on your school's requirements).

10. Collect data.

11. Analyze data using the statistic you chose when designing your study.

12. Present the results!

Summary

In this EasyGuide, we offer the following useful information to help with your research endeavors:

- Understanding correlation versus **causation**
- A description of the different types of measurement scales
- Information to help design your methodology
- A discussion on why and how to use SPSS
- How to create data files in SPSS
- A detailed discussion of descriptive statistics
- Using between-groups designs
- Using within-groups designs
- Using mixed-groups designs
- Conducting correlational research
- Running chi-square analyses
- Decision trees to help you connect designs with statistics
- Screenshots of SPSS data files and output files
- APA-style results sections for each type of design
- Advice on avoiding common mistakes

Throughout the Guide, when we discuss how to use SPSS to analyze your data, we include screenshots so you can follow along. Look for circles to indicate items of interest on the screenshots. We point out where to click and when to click buttons in SPSS. In addition, we include SPSS output, point out the different parts of the output, and discuss what it all means. Finally, because you are often required to take the statistical output and write a results section in APA style, we also include example results sections. The example results sections are included within the chapters, but we also included a separate chapter that points out the different parts of the APA-style results section for each type of design.

That way you can compare your results paragraph with these examples to make sure you did not leave anything out. Likewise, you can check to see if you included only the necessary information for an APA-style results section. Finally, we also included a glossary of terms, which are bolded when first introduced. We hope that by reading this EasyGuide, you can benefit from our experiences as teachers of research design and statistics.

The Two Faces of Correlation

2

You probably have heard your professor say, "**Correlation is not causation.**" Maybe the fun sound of this little ditty explains why students start repeating it with religious fervor. Such devotion to the statement would be fine except for one problem: It is a lie.

Okay, sometimes it is a lie. But at this point in your educational career, you need to know *when* that statement is a lie and when it is true. In this brief chapter, we will explain two general types of correlation—really two ways to define correlation. Make sure you grasp the distinction explained in this chapter because your ability to design and analyze a study as well as accurately interpret the results of your study depends on understanding this distinction.

Correlation as a Research Design

The first type of "correlation" defines a research design. You prepare a study based on what you want to know from the data when you are finished, so the first and most important issue to deal with is the design. If you want to know the potential relationship between number of sexual partners and number of sexually transmitted infections (STIs), you would ask people to report information on both variables based on the past 12 months. Further, in this case, since you do not manipulate people on either one of the two variables, you have a **correlational design**. In this case, *correlation is not causation!*

However, if in this study you had manipulated participants in some way, you would have an **experimental design**, for which you decide how many variables you include, how you manipulate or measure your variables, and how you will assign your participants to the conditions of your design. An experimental design is defined by manipulating at least one variable, which is called an **independent variable (IV)**.

Would it be possible to manipulate number of sexual partners? Sure, but what institutional review board (IRB) would allow you to run such a study? Instead, you would need to simply ask people to report information. Because no variable was manipulated (you did not make participants sleep with a specific number of partners as part of your study), your design would be correlational, not experimental. At the end of the study, if we found something interesting, we would be able to say that number of sexual partners and number of STIs are related. But we would not be able to say that number of sexual partners causes changes in number of STIs because we did not manipulate number of sexual partners. Although it *might* be true that number of sexual partners causes an increase in number of STIs, our design would not allow us to make such a claim.

Let us look at another example. Suppose you wanted to know if number of alcohol ounces consumed was tied to levels of inhibition. To keep things simple, we can **operationally define** inhibition using a rating scale from 1 to 10, with higher number meaning acting crazier (less inhibited). Would such a study be a correlational design or an experiment design? Well that depends. We would have to decide if we want to manipulate anything.

If we do not manipulate one of the variables, we can ask people to report number of ounces of alcohol they consumed and also ask them to rate their level of acting crazy (lack of inhibition). We could even watch people drink and interact, keeping track of number of alcohol ounces and rating their behavior. Keep in mind that watching and recording information through observation is not considered manipulation at all. With no manipulation of a variable, a meaningful outcome might indicate a relationship between amount of alcohol and inhibitions. But again, this design would not allow us to speak of cause-and-effect relationships between variables. In fact, you can even think of other variables that might explain what is really going on here. For example, alcohol and acting silly might both be tied to a third variable, such as being with rowdy friends. Maybe the presence of a bunch of rowdy friends leads us to *both* drink alcohol and act wild. So, once again, our results would allow us to discuss only the relationship between the variables, but not the cause and effect between them.

Now let us imagine that we ran a different study in which we manipulated how many ounces of alcohol participants consumed. We might give some participants 1 ounce and other participants 10 ounces. Then we could either have them rate their level of inhibition, or we could rate their inhibition by observing them. In this study, we manipulated ounces of alcohol; we had a true IV. Therefore, this type of design is experimental, not correlational. And because we manipulated a variable and measured another, we can examine cause and effect. With a significant outcome, we would know that ounces of alcohol caused changes to inhibition.

The take-home message is that a study with no manipulation of a variable is a correlational design and tells us the potential relationship between two variables.

With a correlational research design, correlation is not causation. But if a variable is manipulated, you have an experimental design, and you can examine potential cause and effect.

The statistic you run after collecting your data is a separate issue; often, you will have more than one statistic to choose from. Your goal, question, or hypothesis should remain the focus when designing a study. Now let us turn to correlation as a statistical analysis.

Correlation as a Statistic

A popular type of statistic is a correlational statistic, and the most-used correlational statistic is **Pearson's r.** In Chapter 11, we will cover Pearson's *r* in detail. Here we will explain correlation as a statistic.

For some reason and a long time ago, correlation became synonymous with Pearson's *r* analysis. To further complicate matters, often correlational designs are analyzed using correlational analysis! As an example, we can return to the study of number of sexual partners and STIs in the past 12 months. We agreed that such a study would be a correlational design because we would not be able to ethically manipulate number of sexual partners for participants. Data might end up looking like this completely fictional data set:

Number of Sex Partners	Number of STIs
1	0
2	1
2	2
3	2
3	3
5	4
7	6
9	5
10	8

Because both of these variables were free to vary (nothing was manipulated), we have many different values on each variable. In addition, the variables are both **ratio** data (see Chapter 3 for an explanation of different types of data). When data are represented by many different values like this example, and both variables are at interval or ratio level, we analyze them using Pearson's *r* correlation as our statistic of choice.

If we in fact find a **significant** Pearson's *r* value, we know the two variables are correlated in a meaningful way. A meaningful (or significant) correlation indicates that the two sets of numbers change together by more than just random chance fluctuations. Pearson's *r* will also tell us whether values on the two variables go in the same direction or opposite directions. In the sex–STI example, we can already see that the values go in the same direction. The more sexual partners people have, the more STIs they have.

Now comes the fun part: Because our *design* is correlational, we know what to say about our outcome. A correlational design means we did not manipulate a variable (an IV), and we do *not* know about a potential cause-and-effect relationship between the variables measured. After we run Pearson's *r*, we return to correlation as a research design to say, "Number of sexual partners and number of STIs are related. The more sexual partners people have in a year, the more STIs they get in a year." Though we could have also said, "The more STIs people get in a year, the more sexual partners they have in a year." Notice that we did not say anything about cause and effect or that one variable caused a change in the other; the two variables were related—due to our correlational design. The correlational statistic was used only to help us find out if anything meaningful was happening in the data set.

Summary

Correlation can refer either to a research design or a statistic. The first issue to address is your type of design, not your statistic. A correlational design means no variable was manipulated, and in that case, correlation is not causation. That is, when the study is completed, a significant result will mean that the two variables were related to each other. We will not be able to say one variable caused changes in another variable.

When correlation refers to a statistic, we often focus on Pearson's *r*. Pearson's *r* allows us to analyze the potential relationship between two variables as long as they represent interval or ratio data.

Why Your Type of Data Really Does Matter 3

Nominal, Ordinal, Interval, or Ratio

N ot all types of data are the same, and this chapter will explain why! As we discussed in Chapter 1, for any research project you need to understand the connection between your statistics and research design. An important part of that connection concerns the type of data you collect. Only some types of data will be appropriate for your research question, while others will not be useful at all. If you collect the wrong type of data you might not be able to conduct the analysis you planned. We want to help you avoid the disaster of collecting useless data!

To help you make sure the data you are collecting is suitable, we need to address a crucial component when both designing a study and choosing a statistic. We need to talk about your variables. All variables must be defined by their level or scale of measurement. If we are talking about an experiment, independent variables (IVs) and **dependent variables (DVs)** are used. You must know (and even deliberately choose!) the level of measurement for IVs and DVs. The same kind of consideration is necessary when you are planning a correlational study.

Types of measurement for variables include **nominal**, **ordinal**, **interval**, and ratio levels. Table 3.1 presents each type of data as well as examples of each and the type of statistic you can use. The type of data you use is noted in SPSS in the ***Variable View***, under the column labeled *Measure,* where you choose either Nominal, Ordinal, or Scale (i.e., interval or ratio). Chapter 6 covers how to make that choice in SPSS. In this chapter, we provide many details about each type of measurement. We will begin with advice: No matter what you want to measure as an outcome (DV), consider using either an interval or a ratio scale. As you can

Table 3.1 Each Type of Data, Corresponding Examples, and the Type of Statistic You Can Use

Types of Data/Scale of Measurement	Nominal	Ordinal	Interval	Ratio
Examples	Gender (categories of male and female)	High school class rankings	Standardized test scores (e.g., SATs, ACTs)	Balance in your checking account
	Marital status (categories of married or not)	The order that participants finished a task (i.e., first, second, third)	Temperature measured in Fahrenheit or Celsius	Exam scores (percentage correct on a test)
	Political party (categories of Democrat, Republican, Independent, etc.)	Bra cup sizes	Ratings using a scale of 1 to 7 (or any other number range) to measure opinions	Reaction time
	Hair color (categories of blonde, brunette, redhead, other)	T-shirt sizes (SM, MED, LG, XLG)	IQ scores	
		Months of the year	Personality measures	
Type of descriptive statistic to use	Mode, frequencies, and percentages	Median and range	Mean and standard deviation	Mean and standard deviation
Type of non-parametric test to use	Chi square			
Type of means test to use		Mann-Whitney-U or Wilcoxon	*t*-tests and ANOVA	*t*-tests and ANOVA
Type of correlation to use		Spearman's rho	Pearson's *r* and multiple regression	Pearson's *r* and multiple regression

see in Table 3.1, using interval or ratio scales will allow you to run the most flexible and powerful types of analysis and so likely guarantee that you will be able to test your hypotheses. Why this is the case will become obvious once you finish reading this chapter. Throughout this chapter, we include the type of statistic that is available to you given your choice of type of data collected, with more detail about each statistic in corresponding chapters. After reading this chapter, you will understand the type of measurements you can use and how you can analyze your data given that choice of measurement, which of course is how you can make sure that your data can indeed address your stated hypothesis.

Nominal Data

We will start with the simplest type of variable: nominal data. Think of nominal data as the infant of data types. Nominal variables have levels that merely name categories. Therefore, the values used for nominal scales simply represent different categories of a variable.

Examples:
- Gender (categories of male and female)
- Marital status (categories of married or not)
- Political party (categories of Democrat, Republican, Independent, etc.)
- Hair color (blonde, brunette, redhead, or other)

Imagine that the dean of your college is interested in finding out if there is a gender difference when it comes to choice of major on campus. Are females choosing certain majors more than males, or vice versa? For your dependent measure, you would assign a particular number for each major. So, you code Psychology majors with a "1," Biology majors with a "2," Modern Language majors with a "3," and so on. Notice that the values are arbitrarily assigned (i.e., any major could have been labeled with a "1"), and the numbers themselves have no real numerical value. The values simply serve as a categorization tool. Here the numbers are just nominal . . . name only.

Nominal data might even have levels that are numbers, but the numbers have no quantity. In other words, you could not meaningfully add or subtract the numbers.

Examples:
- Area code
- Number given to you to pin to your shirt for a race
- Numbers on the jerseys of baseball players
- Student ID numbers

Think about area codes for a moment. What does it tell you? Notice that the numbers used to represent these categories are not numbers in the way we typically use them. The numeral itself does not represent a frequency or amount or anything that you measured or counted. For example, if we asked you to compare area codes with someone sitting next to you in class, would those numerals tell you anything about the differences or similarities in the places that you live? No, because those numerals do not have any mathematical value. Someone with an area code of 508 does not have an area code that is greater in any meaningful way than someone with an area code of 434. The area code 508 does not mean that there is greater "area" in that region of the country compared to the "area" where the code is 434. Instead, these numbers simply represent different regions of the country. Area codes are numbers that merely represent a nominal variable.

Nominal measures present numerals that cannot be used for meaningful mathematical calculations. Think about it: Would you derive any valuable information from calculating the mean of your participants' area codes or Social Security numbers? Such calculations would be meaningless, and you can likely see why. The same constraint limits the statistical analyses you can use to test your hypothesis if you collected nominal data.

When you take a look at Table 3.1 in this chapter, you will see that nominal data only allows you to run **non-parametric tests.** For example, you can run a **chi-square analysis** with nominal data, which compares **observed frequencies** to frequencies that would be expected under the **null hypothesis**. In other words, is the observed number of items in each category different from a theoretically expected number of observations in the categories? For a more detailed discussion of using a chi square, see Chapter 12.

Ordinal Data

You might be interested in the rank order or rating of the variable you are measuring, or the sequence of events that took place, in which case you would have ordinal data. As opposed to nominal data, with ordinal data you do know that one value is greater than another. Ordinal variables have categories, just like nominal data, but the categories have a meaningful order. In fact, sometimes ordinal data are called *ranked* because the categories can be put in order or ranked.

Examples:
- Class rankings
- The order in which participants finished a task (i.e., first, second, third)
- T-shirt sizes (SM, MED, LG, XLG)
- Months of the year

When would you use this type of data? Suppose you are interested in determining if there is a relationship between birth order and high school rank. Both of these variables would generate ordinal data. With ordinal data, there are no equal differences between values. When considering birth order, the first born could be two years older than the second born, with the third sibling born six years after that. The same is true for high school rank. These ranks do not indicate that the students ranked as 1 and 2 are equally different in their GPA than students 2 and 3.

When conducting statistical analyses with ordinal data, like nominal data, you are limited to non-parametric statistics. Like nominal data, calculations like addition and subtraction with ordinal data are not meaningful. That said, you can use your ordinal data and compare medians and test the relationship between variables.

Interval Data

The range of statistical analyses that are available to us for nominal and ordinal data is limited. Nominal and ordinal data do not allow us to conduct all of the different kinds of experiments we might want to. Do not panic! **Parametric statistics** covered throughout this book require addition and only interval and ratio measures allow for addition. With interval variables, the levels have meaningful order *and* the space between each number on the scale is equal. Think about a thermometer and the markings on it that represent 10-degree intervals. Because this is an interval scale, not only do you know that 90 degrees is hotter than 80, you know that each interval on the thermometer differs by 10 degrees. That is why interval variables are named *interval* to represent these equal increments across the variable. So you could say that the difference in temperature of 80 degrees in August and 70 degrees in September is equal to the difference in temperature when comparing the 40-degree temperature in December to the 30-degree temperature in January. In both cases you have an equal difference (interval) of 10 degrees.

Here are a few examples of scales that measure interval data:

- Standardized test scores (e.g., SATs, ACTs)
- Temperature measured in Fahrenheit or Celsius
- Ratings using a scale of 1 to 7 to measure opinions
- IQ scores
- Personality measures

You also generate this type of data when using a Likert-type scale. You are likely familiar with this popular type of rating scale that asks you to indicate how much you agree or disagree with a particular statement (e.g., on a scale from 1, "strongly agree," to 7, "strongly disagree," how much do you love this new *EasyGuide for Design & SPSS*?). You have likely responded to surveys with Likert-type scales before. Think about how often we are asked to rate something or give our opinion about something. All those surveys we are asked to take to rate how user-friendly a website is, or to indicate how happy (or unhappy) we were with the service provided at a store or online are Likert-type scales.

For example, say you decide to conduct a research project to examine satisfaction of the food at different colleges. You develop a survey with questions that assess satisfaction using a rating scale. With this scale, you present numbers ranging from low to high, which represent different levels of responses to the questions. For example, you might ask participants, "How satisfied are you with the variety of choices available to eat on your campus?" with 1 representing "very satisfied" to 5 representing "very dissatisfied." Responses to these questions will tell you how satisfied students are with campus food, and you will find out if certain types of schools have students that are more satisfied than others. When using these scales, we assume there are equal intervals between the numbers on the rating scale, which is why it is often categorized as an interval scale. The responses can vary based on the question you ask. You can measure opinion (totally unacceptable to perfectly acceptable), frequency (never to a great deal), level of support (strongly oppose to strongly favor), beliefs (very untrue of what I believe to very true of what I believe), or level of familiarity (not at all familiar to extremely familiar). We can list many more, but you get the idea. This is a very useful type of measurement that can be used for many different types of dependent measures.

We feel obligated to tell you that some people would disagree with treating rating-scale data as interval data. (And yes, we could give everyone a Likert scale to tell us if they agree or disagree with treating Likert scale data as interval data.) Some would argue that it is not clear that there are equal intervals between the different numbers on the scale; for example, the difference between a neutral response and satisfied might not be the same as the difference between satisfied and very satisfied. In which case, these individuals would argue that rating scales generate ordinal data and should be treated as such. We choose to treat rating scales as interval data, and we are in the majority.

As you see in Table 3.1, when you collect interval data, you can run parametric statistics to test your hypotheses. With this type of data, you can calculate mean and standard deviation, run independent *t*-tests or any type of **analysis of variance (ANOVA)** (see Table 3.1).

Ratio Data

So far, we have described measures that provide categories, rank ordering, and equal intervals. The only missing attribute is absolute zero. For ratio data, the value of 0 equals none, zip, zilch, of that variable. In interval data, a zero represents a very low number, not the absence of what is measured. In other words, a zero on interval measures of temperature does not mean the absence of temperature, but rather a very cold day. With ratio data, zero means just that—an absence of the variable measured. Take a look at the examples of ratio variables in Table 3.1, all of which include an absolute zero point.

Examples:
- Balance in your checking account
- Exam scores (percent correct on the test)

- Age
- The number of times a person assists a stranger
- The amount of money given to a charity
- The amount of weight lost

A simple way to decide if a variable represents ratio data is to see if you can double a value. For example, height of people in feet makes sense when you double the value; a person who is six feet tall is twice as tall as one who is three feet tall. Another example is number of times people exercise in a week. Exercising 10 times a week is twice as often as exercising five times a week. Number of times exercising offers ratio data. You can only logically think of doubling examples when the scale has an absolute zero point. So always ask yourself, does the idea of doubling make sense? If it does, you have a ratio scale. If not, you likely have an interval scale.

Here is a final example for you. Suppose you were in charge of a non-profit organization (e.g., the American Cancer Society). You rely on the charitable contributions of others to sustain the operation of the organization. Your reliance on the generosity of others means you must know how to ask people for money. You might be wondering, is it better to include all the details of where the contributions are going? Or is it better to include a personal story of a single individual who benefited from contributions? With this question in mind, you would present two different types of information (your IV) to potential donors and measure the amount of contributions received (your DV) using each type of donation pitch. So, to measure your DV, you would measure amount of money donated. Money is a ratio-level variable. The amount of money donated is on a scale that includes absolute zero, since $0.00 represents none of the variable you are measuring. Remember that another way to think of a ratio variable is that a donation of $100 is twice as much as a donation of $50.

The same statistics available to you when using interval data are available to you when measuring ratio data. So if you are using a scale with an absolute zero, go ahead and run the parametric statistics, including t-tests and ANOVAs (see Table 3.1).

As a review, we include below different dependent measures. Try to determine the type of data collected for the following examples (answers are found at the end of this chapter).

- What type of data did you collect?
  - The number of times a person assists a stranger
  - Social Security numbers
  - Socioeconomic status (SES)
  - Class size
  - Political opinion poll
  - College satisfaction scale
  - Intelligence test score
  - Banking account number

In most if not all research methods courses, you covered a related and very important issue concerning measuring your variables, which we will not discuss in detail here but feel compelled to mention. Whatever type of scale you choose to measure your variable, you must be sure that this is a valid (an accurate measure of your variable) and reliable measure (a measure that will provide consistent results).

Summary

The chapters that follow will describe the match between your research question, your research design, and the appropriate statistic you should use. Once you start to dive into the details of design and statistics, you might find that you need to be sure that the data you are collecting can be analyzed using the statistic that matches your design. So, you might find yourself coming back to this chapter when you decide on the design and statistic that will best address your hypotheses. Then you can make sure that the type of data you are measuring will allow you to run the statistic that matches your design. This sounds pretty simple, but honestly, this is one of the most important initial questions to ask yourself: Self, will the data I collect allow me to run the statistic I want to run? If you answer "no" to this question, you might have a great design and an understanding of what statistic will help you answer your hypothesis, *but* with data that you cannot use for that type of statistic. In other words, you are "up a creek without a paddle."

- Answers: What type of data did you collect?
    - The number of times a person assists a stranger—ratio
    - Social Security numbers—nominal
    - Socioeconomic status (SES)—ordinal
    - Class size—ratio
    - Political opinion poll—interval
    - College satisfaction scale—interval
    - Intelligence test score—interval
    - Banking account number—nominal

To KISS (Keep It Simple Student) or to Complicate Matters

4

Whether you are a senior in a capstone research course or just a curious student in a research methods course, we are confident that at some point in your college career you will take (or have taken) a course that requires the development of a research hypothesis. This chapter provides some of the basics on how to set up the design of your research based on your hypothesis. Specifically, we will show you how to choose the number of independent variables (IVs), the number of levels for your IVs, the dependent variables (DVs) to measure, or the number of variables to include for correlational research. The designs and analyses are appropriate when you use interval and ratio data in your research (go back to Chapter 3 to learn about the different types of data.) If you are using nominal or ordinal data, take a look at Table 3.1 in Chapter 3 that includes a list of statistics to use for all types of data.

As we discussed in Chapter 1, the process of learning how to develop a good research idea was likely covered in at least one of your previous courses. A critical part of the process is formulating a workable hypothesis, one that states a specific predicted relationship between variables and one that can be tested. You will recall from our discussion in Chapters 2 and 3 that you need to make sure you include IVs that can be appropriately manipulated and dependent or predictor and outcome variables that can actually be measured. When we design an experiment or correlational research that accurately tests our prediction and supports or refutes a hypothesis, we are able to make useful contributions to the scientific literature.

Often, when we are reading the past research on our topic of interest, we come across lots of interesting studies and fascinating findings. So the problem becomes separating what we need from all of the articles and books we come across. We have seen some of our students get overwhelmed by publications and in turn struggle with how to include an appropriate number of variables. In their ambition, they often overlook the constraints on the available resources and the time frame in which they need to finish the project. We often remind our under-graduates that the project does not have to answer a lot of research questions at once. That is where the KISS (keep it simple student) comes in.

Here is what we mean by KISS. Let us say you are interested in the impact of violent video games on aggression. You read the literature that includes many inter-esting studies evaluating different types of video games, the gender of the partici-pant, the age of the participant, the amount of time the video game is played . . . and the list can go on and on. However, when it is time to propose your research and develop your hypothesis, you need to decide which variables you want to include. Of course, what variables you choose will depend on the existing literature, but your design also depends on the time frame you have to complete your research.

Here is an obvious example: If the project is assigned as a one-semester assignment, you do not want to design a study that requires you measure behav-iors over a three-year period! What changes the time needed to complete your research? In many types of research, it comes down to the number of participants you need to include. Often, the more variables you include, the more participants you likely will need to conduct your research, and often the more participants needed, and therefore the more time required to collect your data.

The last thing you want is a frantic push to collect data as the semester ends. To further complicate matters, data collection is only about half of your task. In most cases, you will also need to analyze your data, interpret your findings, and write a research paper. The more variables you include, and the more levels of your variables that you include, the more complicated your statistical analyses and, in turn, the more complicated the interpretation of those findings. All of this to say . . . KISS or you will find yourself TOOL (totally out of luck)! Next, we discuss our recommendations for both experimental and correlational research.

How Many Variables Should I Include?

For our students in an undergraduate program, we typically recommend choos-ing no more than two IVs with two levels each for their experimental research project. This elegant design yields results that are typically very easy to interpret, yet they are complicated enough to be interesting and useful. Of course, if the literature and theory justify using just one IV, then by all means include only one. However, if you are interested in examining an **interaction** between two different variables, then include two. Remember, which variables you choose to include is determined by your hypothesis, and the hypothesis you choose to test is based on previous research. Your hypothesis should be a logical extension of those past findings.

For correlational research, the issue of number of variables will have less impact on the number of participants you need and likely will have more influence on the time your participants are engaged in your research. If you choose to ask questions to record participant responses for additional predictor variables or outcomes variables, then those additional questions will take time to answer. For example, if I am interested in the relationship between frequency of playing violent video games and violent behavior, I would only need to measure two variables. However, if I add an additional predictor variable such as the degree of violence in the video games, I now need to include additional questions on my survey to measure that as well. You can imagine, participants are easier to recruit when the time commitment is shorter.

How Many Participants Should I include?

Remember that for experimental research the number of IVs you include generally influences the number of participants you test in your study. (Note: N = number of participants.) Let us take the simplest experimental design and go from there. Perhaps you are interested in studying the effectiveness of a drug on symptoms associated with depression. If you include just one type of drug and a **placebo** (your **control group** taking a sugar pill), you have two groups to compare. For now, we are sticking to the basic IV that requires **random assignment** of participants to groups. That means we assign a different group of 15 participants to each group, as illustrated in the table that follows. If we decide that you need at least 15 participants in each group, you will need a total of 30 participants (15 + 15) to run this study.

Type Drug

Drug (N = 15)	Placebo (N = 15)

However, if you add just one additional IV such as gender, now you have four groups with a 2 (type of drug) × 2 (gender) design. Now you need twice as many participants, and 15 in each condition means 60 participants total.

Type of Drug

	Drug	Placebo
Males	Males/Drug (N = 15)	Males/Placebo (N = 15)
Females	Females/Drug (N = 15)	Females/Placebo (N = 15)

In most cases, comparing two groups (i.e., drug versus placebo) will require fewer participants than when you include four groups. You need to consider not only the number of variables, but also the number of levels of those variables.

Instead of just including one dosage of drug and a placebo, you could include two different dosages of the drug along with the placebo. Of course, it would be interesting to add another type of drug to examine if the dosage changes the symptoms for your participants.

Type of Drug

	Low-Dosage Drug	High-Dosage Drug	Placebo
Males	Males/Low Dosage (N = 15)	Males/High Dosage (N = 15)	Males/Placebo (N = 15)
Females	Females/Low Dosage (N = 15)	Females/High Dosage (N = 15)	Females/Placebo (N = 15)

This is now a 3 (type of drug) × 2 (gender) design and again likely requires more participants to complete. With 15 participants in each cell, you now need to recruit 90 participants to conduct your research.

In these examples, we included 15 participants in each cell to determine how many we need to recruit. However, in most cases, larger **sample** sizes (i.e., the number of participants you include in your experiment), the more likely your results reflect true **population** values. So 15 might not be enough. If an effect exists in the larger population, a larger sample size will help you find it (i.e., a more powerful test of your hypothesis); if no effect exists in real life, you will want to know that truth too. Again, when you increase the number of partici-pants, you typically need more time and resources (e.g., money, equipment) to collect the data. So you need to select a number of participants that will provide a solid study but not cost too much time or money. The literature that provided the basis for your hypothesis can also provide some guidance for the number of participants to include to test your hypothesis. Take a look at the method section of past studies to determine how many participants past researchers included. The calculation to determine the number of participants to include in each of your groups goes beyond what we cover in this book, but there are excellent resources available that explain how to use effect size, alpha level, and power to calculate sample size (Aron, Coups, & Aron, 2013).

For correlational research, most recommend a minimum of 30 participants to test the relationship between or among your variables (a minimum of 10 for every predictor variable you include). Of course, more is better to provide a stronger test of your hypothesis. Or you could get better estimates of the number of participants that you need by using a power calculator. We recommend that you look back at your statistics textbook or get advice from a knowledgeable researcher, perhaps your instructor.

Time and money are not the only limitations on number of participants. Regardless of the size of your college, there are always limited resources when it comes to the number of participants available who will even consider participating in your research. Faculty might offer introductory students extra credit to participate in research, but students can only earn so much extra credit for any one course. Because you likely have a limited number of participants available from the participant pool, it is essential that you design an experiment that keeps your sample size to a practical minimum.

So, you get the picture: The more variables you include in an experiment, the more participants you need. This is why when you consider how many levels of your IV to include, you need to keep in mind the time and resources that even one additional IV level will require.

Now, imagine if you included more than one IV. Suppose you wanted to compare two different types of drugs. You already know that any variable must have at least two levels. That means if you include two IVs, you have four groups to compare at the very least. Using the minimum number from above, that means you will need about 60 participants to run your experiment.

How Many Independent Variables (IVs) Should I Include?

Going back to the example on video games and aggression, you could decide to include only females in your research and compare two different types of video games that vary in level of violence. This is the simplest experimental design you can use: one independent variable with just two levels.

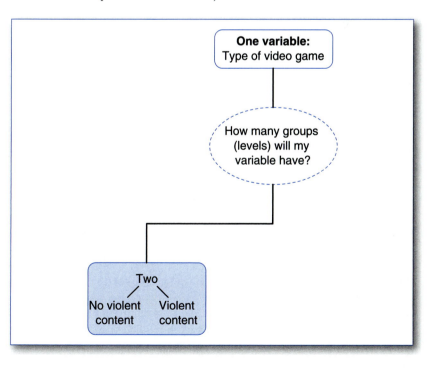

When you include two groups and you find a difference between those groups the results are easy to explain. If you manipulate one IV and find a change in your DV, then the difference in your IV is due to your manipulation. So, if you had one group play a violent video game and another group play a non-violent video game and found that participants were significantly more aggressive in the violent game condition, your finding is clear. Your statistically significant difference means that the type of game played affected the level of aggression.

Including More Than One Independent Variable (IV)

You might have noticed that most journal articles you read include more than one IV. More often, the article addresses not only the effects of a single variable on a DV, but also the interaction of the IVs on the DVs. For the example of video games, you might be interested in including gender as a second (non-manipulated) IV. Now you have a project that includes two IVs. Including both type of video game and gender allows you to examine if the type of game impacts one gender differently than the other. When you add a second variable in the mix, for example, gender, you would have two IVs, with four conditions. This is illustrated in the table below. In this case, you would have a factorial design. The four conditions are created when you combine the two levels of both variables (i.e., violence–male, violence–female, no violence–male, no violence–female.).

	Gender	
Type of Video (Violence)	Violent Male	Violent Female
	Non-Violent Male	Non-Violent Female

Again, you must decide what is most important for you to examine based on the research literature, what that literature leads you to predict, and in turn what variables to include. Consider a different example. In the case of depression and medication, you might want to include age as an additional IV to see if there is a decrease in symptoms for both young adults and seniors. Including age as an IV would provide you with the ability to examine both the impact of the medication and the effectiveness of the medication for two different age groups. Once again, you have four conditions when you combine the two levels of each IV.

	Age (of Individuals with Depression)	
Medication	Type #1 12–17 yrs	Type #1 30–35 yrs
	Type #2 12–17 yrs	Type #2 30–35 yrs

Choosing the Number of Levels of Each Variable

As discussed above, when you include more than two levels of your IV, you typically need to include more participants. However, there are times when two levels of your IV are insufficient to address the question at hand. In setting out your research design, you must first choose your independent variables, then decide how many levels to include. Once again, your review of the literature will tell you what to do. Suppose that the literature seems clear. Perhaps most researchers included two types of games and found that violent games lead to significantly more aggressive acts than non-violent games. However, your review of the literature does not address the degree of violence needed in a game to increase aggression. In other words, is it all or none, or do minimally aggressive games produce smaller increases in aggressive behavior? Under those circumstances, you would likely want to include a third level of aggressive game to further understand the relationship between type of game and level of aggression. In this case, you could include an IV with three levels (e.g., strong violence, minimal violence, no violence).

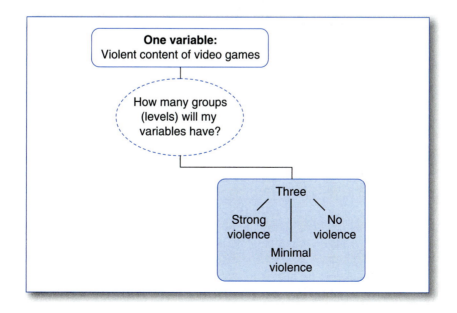

This brings us back to the "take home message" throughout this book, which is that you need to keep in mind the important relationship between your research design and the statistical analyses you run to test your hypotheses. The number of variables you choose and the number of levels you include in your design determines, in part, the statistic you need to run to test your hypothesis. The next few chapters will walk you through the connection between the design you choose (i.e., the number of variables and levels you include in your research) and the type of statistic you can run given that design. Of course, what you measure and how you measure it will also influence the analysis that is available to you; so we will move on to discuss choosing your dependent variable next.

Choosing Your Dependent Variables (DVs)

Your hypothesis will be the key to what DV you use for your research. If you predict that playing violent video games will increase aggressive thoughts, then you have identified your DV: aggressive thoughts. But if you think that playing video games will decrease pro-social behaviors, then you have to measure pro-social behaviors and not aggressive thoughts. The important word here is *measure*. The DV is what you believe will change as a result of the independent variable. To determine if there is a change in the DV, you must measure it. As discussed in Chapter 3, you need to include a DV that you can measure. This means that you can clearly state how you define the variable and how you measure the variable. In the example above, you predict a relationship between violent video games and aggressive thoughts. What will you use to measure aggressive thoughts? What are defined as aggressive thoughts? Answers to those questions are not found in the hypotheses stated. Rather, those answers can be found in the research of those who have published before you. Your review of the literature will indicate the types of DVs included in past research and the types of measurements and specific scales used to measure the variable you have chosen.

Avoiding the Un-Measurable Dependent Variables (DVs)

We will start with an example to illustrate the possibility of including DVs that you might not be able to measure. Let us say you are interested in examining the impact of childhood abuse on the number of repressed memories from childhood. For this project, one of the variables you need to measure is the number of repressed memories. So, to measure this, you decide you are going to ask your participants the following question: "Please list all repressed childhood memories." We are guessing you might see the problem with measuring this variable. By definition, it would likely be a difficult task to remember those memories that are repressed, so everyone should respond with zero recalled memories. You have set yourself up for some disappointment here. That disappointment stems from including a DV in your hypothesis that is essentially impossible to measure. For example, at this point in time, given the lack of technology to measure physiologically the memories we have stored but cannot access, we really do not have a valid measure of repressed memories. This is one example of a DV to avoid. Sure, you can ask participants to report the number of memories they believe are repressed from childhood. But ask yourself if that self-report would really be accurate. If memories are indeed repressed, are we aware that they are repressed? Not likely.

Your best bet is to include an internal or ratio scales of measurement for your DV. That way, you will be able to use most of the statistical analyses available to test your hypotheses (for more details, see Chapter 7).

How Many Dependent Variables (DVs) to Include

Your hypothesis will also indicate how many DVs you need to measure. Perhaps you predict a change in both aggressive thoughts *and* pro-social behaviors. If that is the case, you will need to measure both variables, which simply means including two different measures in your methodology. You want to be sure that all the DVs you include are indeed connected to your hypothesis and therefore need to be included in your research design. With each additional DV, you are increasing the time that each participant will have to spend participating in your research. If you include measures for both aggressive thoughts and pro-social behaviors, then both scales of measurement must be used to measure each DV separately. Clearly, this is more time consuming!

That said, collect information from participants while you have them, as long as you likely can use the data. You have captured your participant's attention. Use that time wisely. If a scale of measurement will only take an additional five minutes to fill out, and you know your participants will not get tired of participating, then collect those data! Just be sure to maintain a balance between collecting as much data as possible and the amount of time each participant will spend with you. When data collection takes too long, you lose your participant's patience, attention, and focus. If that happens, the data you collect can be worthless. Better to collect accurate data on a few important measures than to collect data on too many variables and perhaps not useful at all.

Summary

A successful research project is dependent on numerous decisions made before you start collecting and analyzing data. This emphasis in this chapter tells you to make sure that the decisions you make do not create a complicated research design that could lead to interesting findings but could also lead to failure to meet the deadline for a course, or even another semester or year in college needed to finish the project in order to graduate. That said, there are times when including a more complex design is called for. A discussion with your research advisor is our best advice here. That faculty member knows your time frame, knows the participant pool available, and typically knows how long it will take to complete the research.

SECTION II

Your Basic SPSS Toolbox

In the next section, you will learn the ins and outs of SPSS, data analysis software that will give you the ability to run your statistical analyses with ease. We discuss why we chose SPSS and then we cover all the basic details you need to know about setting up data files. You will learn about naming and labeling your variables, how to create new variables with the data you have, and, if needed, how to select only part of your data file to run analyses. In the last part of this section, we include details about descriptive statistics and the different types of data you can collect for your research. Here you will see step-by-step instructions on what you need to choose from the drop-down menus in SPSS and where to find the appropriate information from your SPSS output files.

Why SPSS and Not Other Software, Your Calculator, Fingers, or Toes 5

When your EasyGuide authors first learned statistics, we used the most advanced calculation tools available to us. Needless to say, the tools that were available to us then all have been replaced by more efficient and accurate means of conducting calculations. Even the statistical software has changed dramatically. One change is that these programs now rely on drop-down menus rather than requiring users to write computer code.

We hope when you learned statistics (or other math applications) you were taught how to use a calculator and perhaps a spreadsheet program such as Microsoft Excel. Learning how to do those calculations hopefully gave you a deeper understanding of what statistical analysis can tell us about data. However, unless you are a human calculator, you probably made errors as you worked through calculations. Some errors were easy to identify, perhaps a column of numbers that should add to 0 did not, while other errors were overlooked. Those hidden errors cascaded through your work, resulting in faulty statistics and perhaps inappropriate decisions. Further, you only worked with relatively small samples in these calculations. Imagine what it would be like to conduct one of those paper-and-pencil (and simple calculator) statistical analyses for a data set with 100 observations! You would want to make sure that all of your calculations were correct. That means you would repeat them at least twice. Very likely, the second calculation would be slightly different from the first, and you would be forced into a third or fourth or even fifth set of calculations before you were satisfied the results were correct.

Spreadsheet programs remove this nightmare of repeating calculations. Of course, you need to carefully enter all of your data in the spreadsheet for accurate calculations to follow. Next, you must insert the necessary equations for calculations in the appropriate boxes (or *cells*). Luckily, the spreadsheet software can take care of the math for you. However, even then, you really should check some of the calculations to make sure you wrote the cell formulas correctly. The advantage of using the spreadsheet over paper-and-pencil analyses is that when you catch a mistake, you can make a correction and complete the recalculations in minutes rather than hours. Remember, with this method, you still must find the appropriate equations for your calculations and write them correctly into the spreadsheet.

Data-analysis software protects us from the many possibilities for human error encountered in both paper-and-pencil and spreadsheet calculations. The computer and software store our data safely, allow us to make corrections in the data file when we find errors made during data entry, and conduct analyses again quickly. The software contains all of the formulas we might ever need, and it does not make calculation errors. In other words, data-analysis software is the most efficient and accurate calculation tool available right now.

We can rely on data-analysis software as a flexible, fairly foolproof way to analyze data, but which software should we use? We have many choices. Take a look at Wikipedia. Go ahead, we can wait. Did you notice how long the list is for that kind of software? Are they all possible options for your research? Not really. Some of the programs on the list are too specialized for general use. Some are the old fashioned kind that requires users to write computer code to make them work. Others would serve us well. We have used several programs; in fact, when we were graduate students, we were asked to learn at least two or three of them. At that time, and still today, some programs were more efficiently used for particular kinds of analyses. Now, most of the programs can handle most of the analyses we would consider using. As new versions emerged, the differences among the programs became more about look and feel than about capability and content. So which one to use?

Why We Chose SPSS

In this book we have chosen to focus on SPSS, which originally stood for Statistical Package for the Social Sciences. Our choice is based first on the generality of this software package. This program, or rather this series of linked procedures, can calculate any statistic that any undergraduate (and most graduate) students are likely to need. SPSS can produce highly advanced statistics as well, though you might need to learn some additional procedures that are beyond the scope of this book to get those analyses right. The second reason that we chose SPSS is that it is relatively easy to use. The point-and-click interface that you will see in the following chapters makes data management easy. That same interface also allows you to easily conduct most common statistical analyses without the need for any programming. The third reason that we have selected this program is that we are very familiar with it. We learned to use it early in our teaching careers and continue to use it today in the classroom, while mentoring student researchers, and for our own research. We cannot tell you how many different analyses we collectively have conducted using SPSS with our students and colleagues. Finally, this program is widely used. You will be able to find access to it in most colleges and universities and in many industries.

OK, after reading the previous paragraph you might think that we find SPSS to be flawless. As you read through the rest of this book, you will experience one thing that we see as a huge nuisance. SPSS is designed to be extremely flexible. As a result, the output for some of the procedures we will review includes a lot of "noise." For those procedures, you will see your output cluttered with a few tables of numbers that are not relevant to the analysis that you are conducting. These tables are often useful to others but not us. In the chapters that follow, we will help you to learn to identify the clutter, when you can ignore some output and even delete it from your file to eliminate the potential for confusion.

Other minor issues with the program include the names of some labels within boxes and even a couple of "descriptive" statistics that are really population estimates. These glitches will not make a lot of sense to you now. Just know that whenever we see a minor wording issue that you need to know about, we will tell you!

Finally, we need to admit that SPSS is pretty expensive. Usually, you will be able to rely on campus resources in your library or computer labs. If you wish to purchase a version of SPSS for your own use, be sure to check with faculty and others on your campus to see if your college offers an opportunity for a discounted purchase. You should also find out which statistical procedures will be included in your purchase. Some student versions will not conduct all the analyses you might need.

The Structure of SPSS

You will better understand the next chapter and much of the information that follows if you know a little bit about how SPSS is structured. You can think about the software as having three major parts.

1. The first part is where you store and manage your data. This part of the program is described in some depth in the next chapter and works much like any spreadsheet program.

2. The second part of the program actually consists of many procedures that you can use to calculate both descriptive and inferential statistics as

well as construct some graphs. In Chapters 8, 9, 10, 11, and 12, we will show you how to use many of the statistical analyses that beginning and intermediate researchers need.

3. The third part of the program produces the output or results of your analyses. A useful feature of SPSS is that you can save your output separately from your data. You will find that saving your output can save time later on when you are writing final drafts of your paper, poster, or talk. These files can be read even when you do not have access to SPSS if you download a special reader from IBM. (Search for *IBM SPSS Smartreader.*) However, you will likely find it more convenient to export your output tables to files with more widely used formats, such as Microsoft Word, Excel, or PDF documents.

Summary

We hope that you are convinced that SPSS could be a useful tool for you and that you are ready to jump in. The next chapter will introduce you to the data section of the program. In that chapter, we will give you tips for organizing your data as well as advice about how to make this section of SPSS work for you. In the following set of chapters, we will show you how to use SPSS to analyze data from many research designs that our students have used.

SPSS Data Hygiene 6

Columns, and Labels, and Values . . . Oh My!

You might think that simple intuition will guide you to a useful organization of your data. If you follow that path, you might find yourself ready to analyze your data and unable to do so. In this chapter, we offer advice to help you avoid that path and introduce you to the data section of SPSS. The data management tools in SPSS will help you to manage your data so that you will be able to (1) look back years later and still know what your data measured and (2) avoid simple calculation errors. We will show you how to enter your data, provide labels for all of your variables, and perform some simple calculations and data file manipulations.

When to Create Your Data File: Yes, Even Before Data Collection

First thing to do is set up your data file. Yes, even before you collect the first bit of data. It might sound like you are "putting the cart before the horse," but trust us; this is an important order of events. Setting up the file helps you to think about the data you are collecting and whether or not you understand how you will analyze it. And knowing you planned ahead of time will reduce your stress later. You might even avoid a panic moment when you realize you did not collect the right kind of data to answer your research question.

Second, collect your data. Unless your research is completely controlled by a computer (such as an online survey), you will likely have to record some measurements on paper. You want to plan ahead so that it is easy to transfer numbers or other data codes from that paper to the computer file. You also want to make sure that every important bit of data gets recorded and stored on paper as well as in SPSS. We have seen some disasters when this step was overlooked. The worst one was a young researcher who forgot to include a code for level of the IV for each participant! As a result, the experiment had to be conducted a second time with new participants. You can only imagine the student's reaction when she realized she had to start data collection from scratch. To avoid that type of error, you should, as a general rule, begin entering data for your study after you have tested only two or three participants. When you enter data very early in your project, you can make sure you have included methodology that provides the measures necessary to address your hypotheses. This practice, together with setting up the SPSS file before you began data collection, will avoid time-consuming mistakes.

Setting Up Your Data File

This is probably a good time to tell you that SPSS can import data from many spreadsheet programs like Microsoft Excel. If you are more comfortable typing data into one of those programs you may do that and then later import your data to SPSS. We strongly recommend that you only enter the raw data into your spreadsheet and then let SPSS perform any calculations you need. We also recommend that you follow our earlier advice and enter some data early and then import it to SPSS to assure yourself that you will be able to use the data the way that you intend.

The next screenshot shows you some data that we have entered in SPSS. We are starting out in the **Data View.**

	ParticipantID	power_group	measured_height	reported_height
16	16	.00	66.00	64.00
17	17	.00	59.00	58.00
18	18	.00	62.00	62.00
19	19	.00	65.00	65.00
20	20	.00	68.00	67.00
21	21	1.00	64.00	66.00
22	22	1.00	63.00	62.00
23	23	1.00	63.00	64.00
24	24	1.00	65.00	65.00
25	25	1.00	65.00	66.00
26	26	1.00	67.00	67.00

Each row in your data sheet should represent a single participant or subject, while each column will represent a different variable in your research project. We typically label the first column of our data file as "participant" or "ID" or "case," which helps to keep track of each participant's individual data. The data in this column is usually a number. (Notice that we are not suggesting using names because we often promise to keep data and identities of participants separate from each other!) We include the same identifier, again usually with a number that we come up with for a specific participant on every sheet of paper tied to that individual except on the informed consent form. This system allows us to find and correct errors in data entry if needed. Every now and again, after we have entered some data, we notice that a score is beyond the range of possible values for that variable. When that happens, if we code each participant's data with an identifying number, we can find the correct data sheet (with the same identifying number) and then double check all of the data that we have entered into SPSS from that form.

Before you enter any data in your file, you should label each column with a variable name. Take a careful look at the previous screenshot of a small data file from SPSS. The data set is one that we made up for an example in Chapter 10. In this research design, there are two power groups (low and high) and two dependent measures (reported height and measured height). Notice the two tabs at the bottom of the spreadsheet; one reads *Data View*, and the other *Variable View*. You will use the *Data View* to type in data and see each data point in your data file. You will use the *Variable View* to enter variable names (e.g., measured_height), perform some useful housekeeping (e.g., add labels for your independent variables), and perhaps record some notes about each variable. You get to the *Variable View* by clicking on the tab circled at the bottom of the screenshot below.

This screenshot shows what the *Variable View* looks like. Notice that the tool bars at the top of the page have not changed but that some icons (Redo, Find, Insert Case, Value Labels) are grayed out. These icons are grayed out because you can only use them in the *Data View*. It might take you a few minutes to get oriented to this different view of your data in SPSS. Part of the problem is that in *Variable View*, a row rather than a column now represents each variable. Notice that ParticipantID is in the first row of this screenshot, but it was in the first column in the *Data View*. Now look at the row of labels above (e.g., *Name, Type, Width, Decimals*, etc.) just above the information that we have entered in the white columns and rows. You will need to be aware of each of those columns in the *Variable View* for your own data, which we describe for you below.

Naming and Labeling Your Variables

The first column contains the *Name* of your variables, circled below.

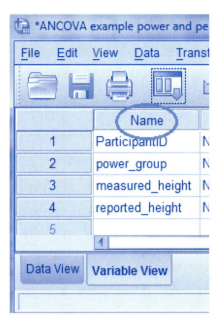

You probably have also noticed that some of our variable names look a little odd. We agree, and here is why. When SPSS was first written there were severe restrictions on how variables could be named. Many of those restrictions have been removed, but the program still does not allow a blank space in a variable name. As a result, we typically either mush words together without spaces, often creating unusual variable names. For example, you can see in the last screenshot that the first row is labeled "ParticipantID," which is not a word. And there is an underscore (_) placed within the name of the third variable for measured height (i.e., measured_height). The underscore usually indicates a space between two words, which an option rather than mushing two words together.

The second column identifies the *Type* of data for each variable.

SPSS has several data types to choose from, and you need to choose wisely. Most of your data will be numeric; however, you might also have strings or words (e.g., for text data, you might want to record comments that your participants made during the experiment).

The next column, *Width*, establishes the maximum number of digits or characters that will be displayed for that variable, and the following column, *Decimals*, sets the number of decimals places that will be displayed.

The column called *Label* can be valuable in helping you keep track of exactly how you measured something.

For example, we typically copy the exact wording for any question on a survey into this column to have that information both preserved with the data and included in output tables. You might think of putting any brief notes here that might help you to remember how you conducted this study later on. For example, "DQ scores were measured with the Bailey" or "individuals were randomly assigned to the groups." Notice that in the current example, we made a notation that *reported_height* is the "participant's estimate of their own height." This *Label* will appear on all of our output and we would not need to remember who reported the height.

The *Values* column allows you to enter text labels for specific data values. These labels help you to remember the meaning of numbers that you used to code variables. For example, we might use 0 and 1 to identify females and males in our sample. With these labels, we can make SPSS remember that we coded 0 for females and 1 for males. These labels will show up on our output, too, so that we do not have to remember which group we identified as 0 and which as 1.

Let us look at that option next. You click on the word *None* in the value column next the variable that you want to work with. The next screenshot shows you where to click to add value labels for the two power groups.

The next two screenshots show you the dialogue box that appears when you want to include labels for a variable.

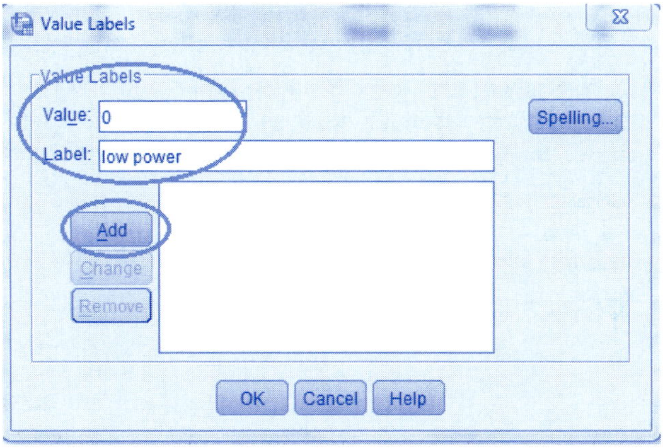

In this first box, we have entered a "0" in the *Value* box and "low power" in the *Label* box. Notice that the *Add* button is ready to be clicked. As you can see in the next screenshot, after you click the *Add* button, the value and label move down as a pair into the larger unlabeled box circled below.

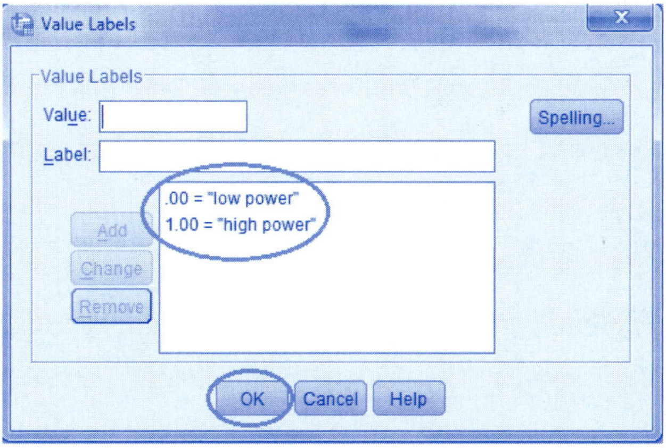

In the completed dialogue box, you can see that "0" represents the low-power group, and a value of "1" represents the high-power group. We added the "high power" label by following the same steps outlined above. Clicking on the *OK* button will take you back to your data file. You probably noticed that we used values of "0" and "1" to designate our two groups. Many researchers use those values, often using "0" to identify a control group. These two values have some added benefit if you will be doing a very advanced **Multiple Regression**

analysis; however, for any other analysis, you may use any two numbers to designate two different groups. You will notice that in this book we sometimes use "1" and "2." Of course, more value labels are needed when you have more than two groups.

Once you have entered value labels, they will appear on your output so you do not have to remember if you used "0" and "1" or "1" and "2" or which group they indicate. You may also view those labels in the *Data View*. If you switch from *Variable View* to *Data View*, at the top of the *Data View* spreadsheet, there is a row of icons. Find the icon that looks like this:

When you click that icon, you will toggle between the number and label view for any variables that have *Value Labels*. The next screenshot shows you what the labels for our power groups look like. Notice that in the *Data View* that the 0's have been replaced with the label "low power."

	ParticipantID	power_group	measured_height	reported_height
1	1	low power	68.00	68.00
2	2	low power	67.00	66.00
3	3	low power	67.00	67.00
4	4	low power	62.00	59.00
5	5	low power	73.00	71.00
6	6	low power	70.00	71.00

*ANCOVA example power and perceived height with IDs.sav [DataSet1] - IBM

File   Edit   View   Data   Transform   Analyze   Graphs   Utilities   Add

Data View   Variable View

Let us return to the *Variable View* screen.

The next column to the right of *Values*, labeled *Missing*, can be used to specify values that you will enter for missing data. You likely will not want to do that. This tool is most useful when you might have several reasons that data are missing, for example, participants refused to answer, responded "did not know," or simply left the item blank. For most of your missing data you can simply leave that cell empty in your spreadsheet. The next two columns are used to change the appearance of columns in the *Data View*. You can increase or decrease the space on the data sheet for each variable by changing *Columns*, and you can left adjust, right adjust, or center the values in the *Data View* with *Align*.

That last column, *Measure*, is really important.

You can see that power_group is a *Nominal* measure, but the other two are *Scale* measures. SPSS treats interval and ratio measures the same way and refers to them as *Scale* measures. (There is a third choice: *Ordinal*.) You can review the distinction among these different kinds of measurements in Chapter 3. Making the wrong choice here might prevent you from conducting the kind of analysis that you planned. You will make changes in the *Measure* simply by clicking on the cell and selecting the measure (e.g. *Nominal*, *Ordinal*, or *Scale*) that you want.

How to Keep Track and Remember the Details of Your Data File

This next tool will help you to remember what you did when you look at a data set that you created years ago or to understand data that other researchers have created. In the *Data View*, you will see an icon on the toolbar that looks like this:

Clicking on that icon opens a dialogue box that allows you to see all the information that has been entered about any of the variables in the file.

In the example that we have opened, you can see that the "power_group" variable's *Measurement Level* is *Nominal* and that it has the *Value Labels* we created earlier.

Now that you know how to enter your data and the information associated with it into SPSS, you are ready to consider how data can be managed with the program. For example, we will show you some tools that allow you to calculate new measures or divide your data file into parts based on groups. You should always enter every bit of data from a participant on a single row in your data file. Create as many columns as needed for each variable you measured or manipulated. After you have entered all of your data, you will be able to ask SPSS to perform any of these calculations that you need to transform or recode a variable if needed. Read on to see how this all works.

Creating New Variables in Your Data File: Transformations

There are times when you will not need to make any calculations or other changes to your data. However, there are many occasions when you will. For example, imagine that you have created a new survey to measure food preferences.

Imagine that you have asked five questions that evaluate "liking" for junk food and five questions that evaluate "liking" for healthy foods. You will likely want to combine the answers to each of those five questions to get a measure of overall preference for junk and healthy foods. You might even want to calculate the difference in the two measures to evaluate how much your participants prefer one kind of food over the other.

In SPSS, you can conduct calculations by clicking on the *Transform* drop-down menu and then choosing *Compute Variable*.

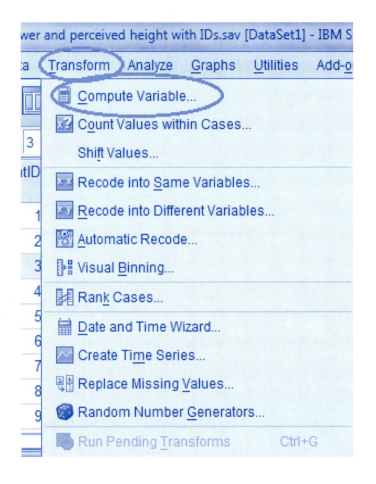

Choosing *Compute Variable* will open the following dialogue box, which allows you to set up the calculations needed to create new variables using the variables you already entered in your data file. Let us take a look at a simple example.

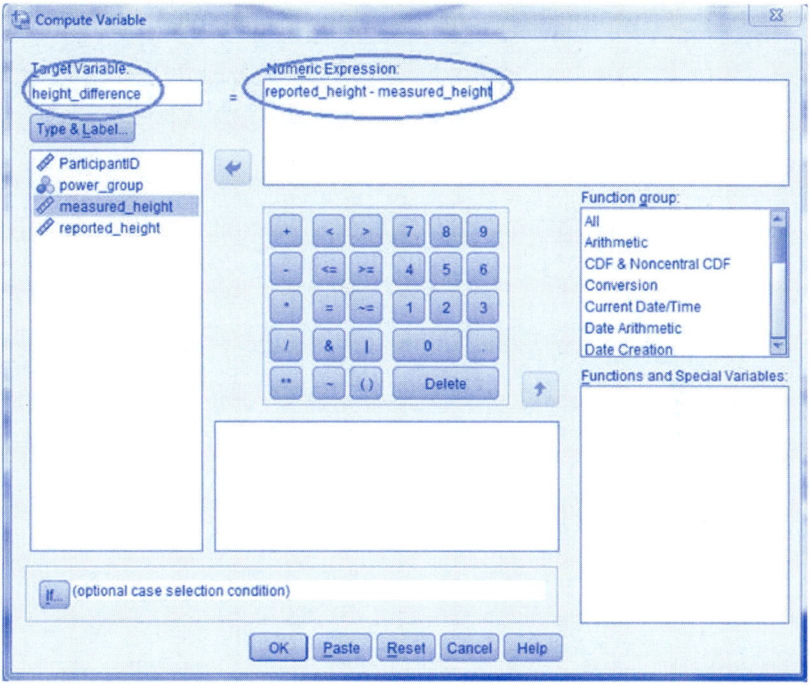

First, notice that all of the variables in your data file are listed in the large text box at the left. The box at the far right labeled *Function group* contains statistical, mathematical, and other kinds of calculations that you might need for more advanced manipulations of your data. For this example, we wanted to create a new variable measured as the difference between reported height and measured height. To calculate the difference, you must enter the name of your new variable in the box labeled *Target Variable*. We typed the name of a new variable, height_difference, in that box circled above. To calculate this new variable, we moved the names of the two variables necessary for our calculations (reported_ height and measured_height) from the list of variables over to the box labeled *Numeric Expression* (circled above). Finally, we placed a minus sign between the two variables and clicked the *OK* button. After you click the OK button, a new column will be created in your data file, and a value for that new variable will be included for each participant. The next screenshot of the data illustrates that column (circled).

	ParticipantID	power_group	measured_height	reported_height	height_difference
16	16	.00	66.00	64.00	-2.00
17	17	.00	59.00	58.00	-1.00
18	18	.00	62.00	62.00	.00
19	19	.00	65.00	65.00	.00
20	20	.00	68.00	67.00	-1.00
21	21	1.00	64.00	66.00	2.00
22	22	1.00	63.00	62.00	-1.00
23	23	1.00	63.00	64.00	1.00
24	24	1.00	65.00	65.00	.00

*ANCOVA example power and perceived height with IDs.sav [DataSet1] - IBM SPSS Statistics

File   Edit   View   Data   Transform   Analyze   Graphs   Utilities   Add-ons   Window

Data View   Variable View

Again, we recommend that you put all of your "raw" data into your SPSS data files and then use this procedure to perform any calculations that you might need on those raw scores. Following this advice will avoid calculation errors that you might make with a calculator and while retaining responses to individual items. In this example, we still have the measure of actual height and the estimated height with the additional measure of the difference between those two.

Conducting Analyses With Only Part of Your Collected Data: Split File and Select Cases

In some of your research, you will need to conduct follow-up analyses for example to examine responses within your groups to see if they are different or similar. In the example that we are working with in this chapter, we want to calculate the correlation between estimated and actual height separately in the two power groups. The *Split File* option (circled) under the *Data* drop-down menu is intuitive.

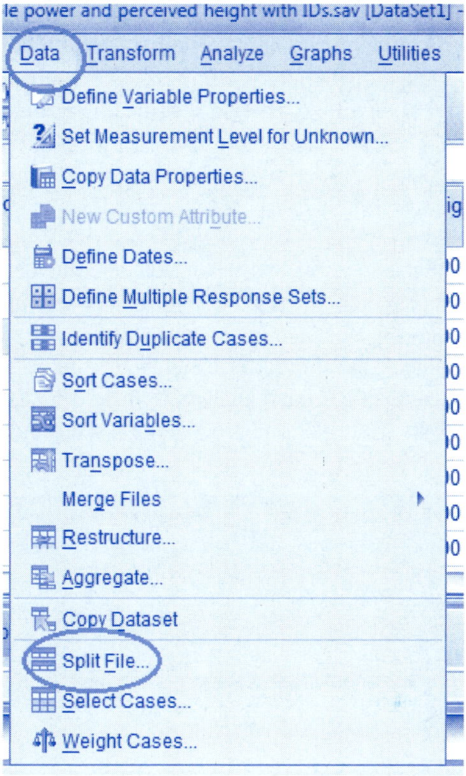

The following window appears. At this point you must then select either *Compare groups* or *Organize output by groups*. These choices can be seen near the top right of the next screenshot.

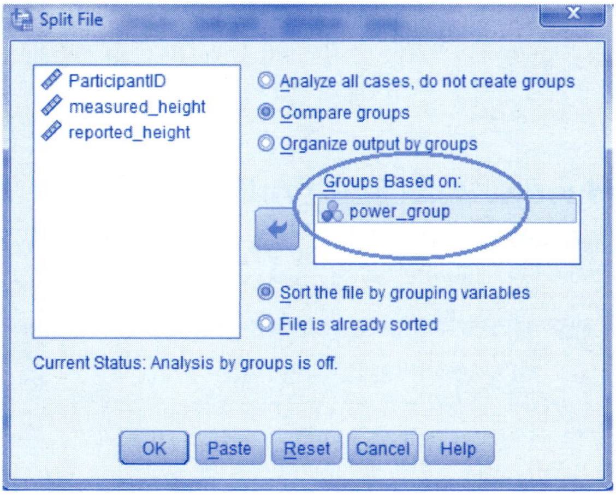

As beginning researchers, your choice here will not make much difference: select *Compare Groups*. Once you have made that selection, you will move the name of your grouping variable into the box labeled *Groups Based on*. As you can see, we selected *Compare groups* and will obtain separate analyses for our two power_groups. Click the *OK* button to return to the basic SPSS database screen. Later on, if you wish to return to analyses of your complete data file, you return to this procedure (use the *Data/Split File* dropdown menu again), this time select *Analyze all cases*.

Finally, there might be occasions when you need to eliminate some data from a file. For example, after entering all of your data, you might learn that one of the experimental groups obtained knowledge about your manipulation or you might find some outliers that should be eliminated from a second analysis. As a result, you might conduct a second analysis to make sure that the outliers did not change your results. You open the procedure by selecting *Data/Select Cases*.

Choosing *Select Cases* opens the following dialogue box. To select cases you only need to click on the *If condition is satisfied* button (see circle on next page).

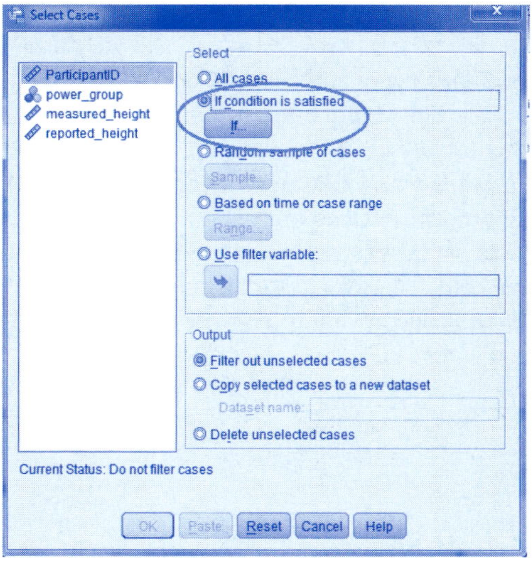

That click will open a second dialogue box illustrated in the next screen-shot. This box looks very much like the *Compute variable* dialogue box that we described earlier in this chapter. To choose certain cases, you will choose a certain variable and value of that variable and enter that in the text box at the top of the dialogue (see circle below). When that function is true, those cases will be included in further analyses. In our example, we entered "power_group = 0." If we clicked on the *Continue* button and then *OK* button in this *Select Cases: If* dialogue box below, all further analyses would include only individuals from the low power group. Again, we can later return to the *Select Cases* dialogue and select *All cases* and then analyze *all* of our data.

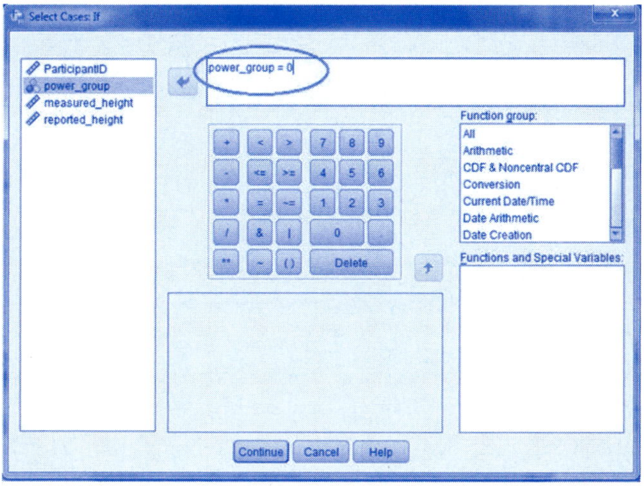

Summary

Likely, you will not need every tool that we have described in this chapter for every research project, but we hope that when you do need one of them, you will be ready with a useful bag of tricks. We are confident that if you follow our advice from this chapter, you will make your data-collecting life easier, even in your very first independent research project. You will no doubt need some practice with these tools before you become an expert, so practice away. You can find other tools that could be useful to you in the menus that we introduced here. Explore to your heart's content!

Tell Me About It 7

Descriptive Statistics

In Chapters 3 and 4, we explained the use of SPSS to analyze your research data. SPSS will do a great job with most data sets, and you will get plenty of output to share with the world. While you are writing up APA-style results sections and bragging about your data, do not forget to include the simple parts of the puzzle: **descriptive statistics**. When you describe a group of numbers, you can use values such as measures of **central tendency** (which tells you one value that best represents a data set), **variability** (representing how spread out values in a data set are), simple **frequency** (how often a value occurs in a data set), and **percentages**, to name the most popular options. We will cover which options to use to describe the four types of variables: nominal, ordinal, interval, and ratio.

Describing Nominal Data

If you have a group of values that are nominal data, you are limited in how those data can be described. With nominal data, you only have categories; you have no numbers to represent quantity. As an example, suppose you had a sample of college students and wanted to know how many had a tattoo and how many did not. The variable is whether or not someone has a tattoo, and the two levels are "no tattoo" and "tattoo." Imagine that 15 people reported having a tattoo, and 10 people reported not having one. In SPSS, we label values as 1 = no tattoo and 2 = tattoo; however, the use of 1 and 2 is arbitrary—we could use any two numbers.

Using SPSS

In the next screenshot, we went to *Variable View* and entered "no tattoo" as the variable name, and then under *Values* we entered 1 for no tattoo. Next we will click *Add*.

After clicking the *Add* button, enter a 2 for tattoo, then click *Add* again and *OK*.

In *Data View*, when we *View Value Labels*, the data would look like the following.

To describe this nominal variable, you might want to look at how often each value (tattoo or no tattoo) occurs in your sample. You could ask SPSS to provide a simple frequency for each group by clicking *Analyze, Descriptive Statistics*, then *Frequencies*.

A box will open. Move "tattoo" to the right-side box using the arrow and then click *OK*.

The output offers a simple frequency for each group as well as percentages.

With these descriptive statistics, you could begin to summarize your sample data. As an additional option, you could offer a measure of central tendency. Unfortunately, nominal data are so simple that you can only use the **mode**, which is the value that occurs most often in the data set. Although you can easily see that the mode in our fictional data set is having a tattoo, allow us to show you how to obtain the information from SPSS.

Because we were already working under *Analyze, Descriptive Statistics, Frequencies*, return to those options and click *Statistics* (circled below) on the right side of the *Frequencies* box that opens. In the next box that you see, click *Mode*.

Click *Continue* and *OK* to obtain the following output now containing the mode of 2. Keep in mind that 2 represents the tattoo group, so we know the most often occurring value is having a tattoo.

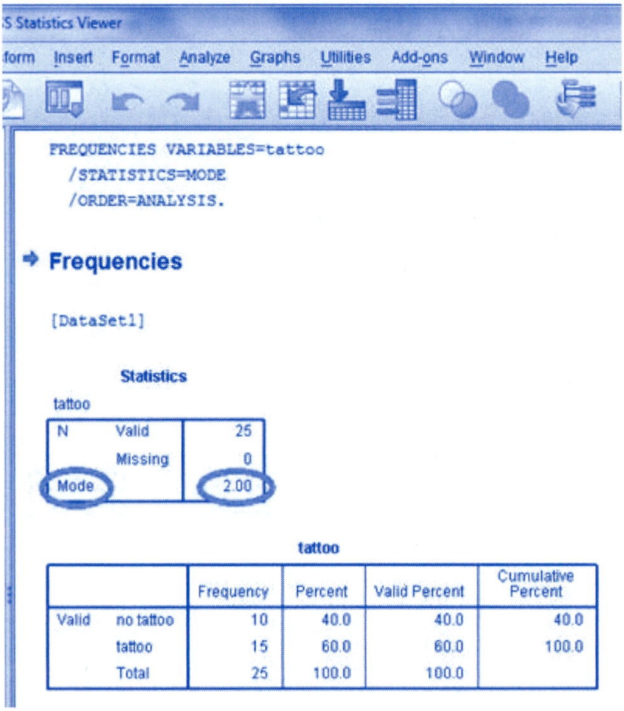

```
S Statistics Viewer
form   Insert   Format   Analyze   Graphs   Utilities   Add-ons   Window   Help

FREQUENCIES VARIABLES=tattoo
  /STATISTICS=MODE
  /ORDER=ANALYSIS.
```

➡ **Frequencies**

[DataSet1]

Statistics

tattoo

N	Valid	25
	Missing	0
Mode		2.00

tattoo

		Frequency	Percent	Valid Percent	Cumulative Percent
Valid	no tattoo	10	40.0	40.0	40.0
	tattoo	15	60.0	60.0	100.0
	Total	25	100.0	100.0	

The mode, simple frequency, and percentages are the only options that produce meaningful values with nominal data.

Describing Ordinal Data

For ordinal data, you know the values are still categories, but they also have a meaningful order. An example is rank in college: first year, sophomore, junior, and senior. Suppose we had a sample of 5 first-year, 7 sophomore, 10 junior, and 13 senior students. We can describe those data by entering values into the variable "rank" into SPSS.

Using SPSS

In *Variable View*, enter numbers and labels for *Values*. Notice in the following screenshot that 1 logically comes before 2 to represent the order of the categories correctly.

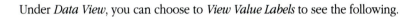

Under *Data View*, you can choose to *View Value Labels* to see the following.

Because the data now have a logical order for the categories, you have more options to describe your data. You can certainly ask for simple frequencies, and you can ask for the mode. But you can also ask for higher-level descriptive statistics. With ordinal data, the appropriate measure of central tendency is the **median,** which is the value at the 50th percentile. If you were to organize values from lowest to highest (or the reverse order), you could pick out the middle value. The good news is that SPSS will do the work for you—which is particularly helpful when you have very large data sets. In addition to a measure of central tendency, you can report a measure of variability with ordinal data. Simply report the **range**, which in this case for ordinal data will be the lowest and highest values in the sample. Click *Analyze, Descriptive Statistics, Frequencies.* Move the "rank" variable to the right side, click *Statistics,* and ask for *Median, Minimum,* and *Maximum.* A click in the boxes next to each term will allow you to choose each option.

The minimum and the maximum represent the range on this variable. Yes, you could ask for the range in SPSS, but remember that we entered values of 1, 2, 3, and 4 for the software to read. If you ask SPSS for the range, it will subtract 1 (the lowest value) from 4 (the highest value) and tell you the range is 3. As you can see, a range of "3" means nothing. For the range of ordinal data, simply report the lowest and highest values; SPSS tells you the lowest value is a 1 (which represents first-year students), and the highest value is a 4 (seniors).

```
SS Statistics Viewer
sform  Insert  Format  Analyze  Graphs  Utilities  Add-ons  Window  Help
```

```
FREQUENCIES VARIABLES=rank
  /STATISTICS=MINIMUM MAXIMUM MEDIAN
  /ORDER=ANALYSIS.
```

→ **Frequencies**

[DataSet2]

Statistics

rank

N	Valid	35
	Missing	0
Median		3.0000
Minimum		1.00
Maximum		4.00

rank

		Frequency	Percent	Valid Percent	Cumulative Percent
Valid	first-year	5	14.3	14.3	14.3
	sophomore	7	20.0	20.0	34.3
	junior	10	28.6	28.6	62.9
	senior	13	37.1	37.1	100.0
	Total	35	100.0	100.0	

From this output, you can see that the median (middle value) is a 3, which means the best value to represent this ordinal data set is juniors. And values in the data set range from first-year students to seniors. To make sense of these data, you need to remember that 1 = first-year students, 2 = sophomores, 3 = juniors, and 4 = seniors.

Describing Interval or Ratio Data

We group these final two types of data together because they both have math properties and allow math calculations when offering measures of central tendency and variability. Before we begin, we have to offer one caution: *Interval and ratio data must not have **outliers**, which are values that mathematically distort the descriptive statistics described in this section.* If you have a sample of interval or ratio data with a number (or a few numbers) that are much higher or much lower than the majority of other numbers in your data set, you must only describe your sample using the median and range just as you would with ordinal data (above). Or, you can report results both with and without the outliers, requiring that you run your analyses twice.

However, assuming you have interval or ratio data with no outliers, the appropriate measure of central tendency is the **mean (M)**, and the best measure of variability is the **standard deviation (SD)** (although some people use the standard error of the mean, which is also fine). As an example, imagine you wanted to know about ratings of happiness among your friends. Let us say that happiness is **operationalized** using a rating scale from 1 (Very Unhappy) to 10 (Very Happy), and you asked 17 of your friends to rate their happiness. The data might look like the happiness ratings below.

7 6 8 7 6 5 4 9 7

8 5 4 6 7 5 8 6

Using SPSS

We can enter the ratings into SPSS. Notice that unlike the nominal and ordinal data described above, we have no values to label because the numbers are not categories; they are simply numerical values.

	Happiness
1	7.00
2	6.00
3	8.00
4	7.00
5	6.00
6	5.00
7	4.00
8	9.00
9	7.00
10	8.00
11	5.00
12	4.00
13	6.00
14	7.00
15	5.00
16	8.00
17	6.00
18	
19	

*Untitled4 [DataSet3] - IBM SPSS

File   Edit   View   Data   Tran

18 : Happiness

You can follow the same procedure of *Analyze, Descriptive Statistics, Frequencies* that we described above. Once again, you need to move the variable to the right-side box, click *Statistics*, and ask for the *Mean* and *Standard Deviation (Std. deviation)*.

Click *Continue* and *OK* for the following output.

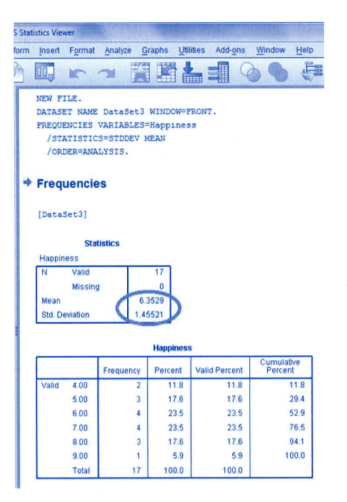

Notice that because you went through the option of *Frequencies* in SPSS, you will get simple frequencies. It is up to you whether you want to examine that frequency table. Likewise, under *Statistics* you could ask for *Mode, Median, Range, Minimum,* and *Maximum* (as well as other descriptive statistics options), but we generally focus on the mean and standard deviation when describing interval or ratio data with no obvious outliers. In this example of happiness, SPSS shows us that the average happiness rating from our friends is 6.35. (Note: For APA style, you include only two digits after the decimal point). Recall that happiness is measured on a scale from 1 to 10, with higher numbers indicating more happiness. In addition, the standard deviation tells us that most of our friends rate their happiness at 6.35, give or take 1.46 happiness points. We can even add and subtract the standard deviation of 1.46 from the mean of 6.35 to show a reader where most of the values fall. That is, most of our friends rate their happiness between 4.89 (6.35 – 1.46) and 7.81 (6.35 + 1.46).

We should note that SPSS offers a second way to get means and standard deviations. Click *Analyze*, *Descriptive Statistics*, and *Descriptives*.

Move the variable to the right, click *Options*, and notice that the default is for *Mean* and *Standard Deviation* (*Std. deviation*) to be chosen. *Minimum* and *Maximum* are also chosen by default, and we do not mind even though we usually do not report these values.

Click *Continue* and *OK* for output.

Of course, the data reported here are the same as under the *Frequencies* option, but the output is much more concise. You can use the *Descriptives* option for interval or ratio data if you would like.

Describing Data With Two Samples

In the examples we have shown you in this chapter so far, we have focused on a single group of values, a single sample. We took this approach to explain the different descriptive statistics needed for different levels of data: nominal, ordinal, interval, or ratio. But we know you probably want to run studies with two or more groups; you can think of the groups as two or more samples. Each sample will need to be described. We hope in your study, you will use an outcome measure (DV) that reaches interval or ratio level because these two higher levels of data allow math calculations and more powerful statistics. Keep in mind that your IV can be any level of data (nominal, ordinal, interval, or ratio), but your DV should be interval or ratio data whenever possible. Remember this advice when designing studies.

As an example, if you ran an experiment that involved asking people to spend 30 minutes each day for a month sitting on the couch, and later asked the same people to spend a month walking on a treadmill for 30 minutes a day, you might want to look at a ratings of happiness at the end of each month. The main question likely would be *Do people report higher levels of happiness after regularly walking on a treadmill as compared with when they sit on a couch?* Notice that the IV is nominal with two categories: couch and treadmill. Importantly, the DV in this example is happiness rating, which most researchers would consider to be interval data.

After you collect data, SPSS will conduct an analysis to address your hypothesis, and the mystery will be solved. Later chapters will give you information on how you would analyze data from such an experiment, but for now, we will focus on describing the data from two groups using descriptive statistics. Do not be concerned that the same people are tested twice; you still have two separate groups (or samples) of information based on what they were asked to do.

SPSS allows you to click a couple of options after entering your data (described below), and you will have descriptive statistics for your groups. Before we go any further, we can look at fictional data. As in our last example, happiness is operationalized with a rating scale from 1 (Very Unhappy) to 10 (Very Happy).

Couch	Treadmill
3	8
6	7
5	7
7	6
4	9
5	10
8	10
5	8

Using SPSS

In this design (the same people in both groups), we will merely enter the data into two SPSS columns so the data look like what you might write on paper. If you have forgotten how to label columns, refer to Chapter 6.

To ask SPSS for descriptive statistics on your two groups, click *Analyze*, *Descriptive Statistics*, *Descriptives* as we covered in the prior section.

In the box that opens, move the two variables over to the right under *Variable(s)* by highlighting them and clicking the arrow in the middle of the box. Then click *Options* to make sure *Mean* and *Standard Deviation* (*Std. deviation*) are checked.

Click *Continue* and *OK* to see the output page.

Notice that we now know the average happiness rating in each experimental condition. We also have a number (the standard deviation) for about how spread out those values are *within* a condition. When people sat on a couch, the average happiness rating was 5.38, give or take 1.60 happiness points on a scale from 1 to 10, with higher number indicating more happiness. On the other hand, when they worked out on a treadmill, the average happiness rating was 8.13, give or take 1.46 happiness rating points.

Summary

The descriptive statistics you choose rely on your variables' levels of measurement: nominal, ordinal, interval, or ratio. Be sure you know the level of your data before summarizing it, then describe your sample or samples with appropriate descriptive statistics.

In this book, you will learn how to write APA-style results sections for many statistical analyses, but keep in mind that you should always run descriptive statistics to describe your variables to the reader. Those descriptive statistics are included in the results section in some way. Here are some options:

- Include descriptive data into the results section.
- Refer to a table that contains descriptive data for each variable (particularly useful when you have several variables to describe).
- Refer to a figure to show descriptive data.

For all of these options, rely on SPSS output to give you the data you need to report. If you choose to create an APA-style table, refer to the APA manual for instructions or take a look at *An EasyGuide to APA Style* (Schwartz, Landrum, & Gurung, 2014). If you choose to create a figure such as a graph, see the APA manual as well as *An EasyGuide to Research Presentations* (Wilson & Schwartz, 2015). Whenever possible, offer your reader a table or figure for important results. In particular, figures provide information in an interesting format and give readers a break from reading text.

SECTION III

Designs, Statistics, Interpretation, and Write-Up in APA Style

In this section you will read about a range of inferential statistics from *t*-tests through ANOVAs and even MANOVAs, correlations, and chi-square analyses. You will find detailed guidance on how to connect specific analyses with particular research designs, how SPSS allows you to conduct various statistics, and what your results will look like in the output produced by SPSS. You will also learn about relevant output in SPSS files and which parts of those output files need to be included in an APA style results section. Lastly, we include results-section examples to illustrate how to incorporate the SPSS output in text for your research papers and presentations.

Celebrate Your Independence! 8

Between-Groups Designs

N ow that you have a burning question to ask in a scientific way, you have to decide how you will go about asking it. If the study you have in mind includes an independent variable (IV), that means you have at least two levels—otherwise it would not be a variable at all because nothing would vary. We will start with the simplest design you might have: one IV with two levels.

One IV, Two Levels

When people walk in the door of your lab or go to their computers to take an online survey, you have to be prepared for one of two options. First, you might ask different groups of people to complete each level of your IV. For example, if you want to know how long people will play a video game against a computer versus against another person in the room, you might ask some participants (group 1) to play a video game alone and ask completely different participants (group 2) to play the video game against another person sitting in the same room.

As a second option, you can ask each participant to play the game twice, playing against a computer *and* playing against another person. Although this second option does have the advantage of controlling for whether a participant is very good at the game (or really bad at it), you can probably already see potential problems. Participants might not want to devote a lot of time to your study, or they might get tired of playing the game after the first time and quit soon after starting the second game. When you repeatedly test the same people, you also run the risk of participants figuring out what you are looking for in your experiment and either giving you what you want or deliberately going against your expectation, both of which would keep you from knowing the truth.

In this chapter, we will talk about the first option: You will put different people in each of your IV levels. We call this a **between-groups design**. Although a between-groups design might mean you need more people in your study, you should still be able to find an effect if one exists in the world.

Between Groups With Two Levels of an IV

When people participate in your study, in many cases, you can manipulate what happens to them. You can control the experiences they have when they are in your "lab." This allows you to examine a potential cause-and-effect relationship between the IV and the dependent variable (DV). This also requires using a true IV, which means you do something to participants, such as asking them to play a video game with a computer or with another person. Of course, it also requires you to measure an outcome. In this example, the outcome is how long people play. Notice that you never manipulate the outcome because that would be cheating. You leave it alone and wait to see what happens.

You probably remember that an outcome is called a dependent variable (DV). Again, in the video game example, the DV is how long people play the video game.

At this point, you have one IV and one DV. One potential cause (the IV) and one effect (the DV)—one manipulated variable (the IV) and one outcome (the DV). And with a between-groups design, you have different people in the two levels of your IV. But how do you decide which people go in which group? Although the question might seem silly, it is actually important. For example, if you pick all males to play against the computer and all females to compete against another person, you will not know if differences in play time are based on the type of opponent (your IV) or the gender of the participant. Because gender completely obscures what you were truly interested in, gender is considered a **confounding variable**. A confounding variable is one that varies exactly along with the levels of your IV. In the end, a confounding variable means you have to throw your data in the trash.

As another example, suppose you asked the first 30 people who walk in the room to play against the computer and the next 30 people to play against another person. What if the first 30 people are highly motivated, early-rising, Type A people who naturally will play the game a long time? And what if the last 30 people who participate across the day are less motivated? Again, you will not be able to say whether any play-time differences are due to the experimental manipulation (computer versus in-person opponent) or differences in the type of participant who showed up early versus later on.

How do you solve this problem? The solution is simple. You **randomly assign** people to the two levels of your IV. When a participant shows up to your study (or even before the person walks in), draw one of the two IV levels from a cup. Let chance decide for you. If you are running an online experiment, randomize which level of the IV participants get when they click the link for your study. This type of random assignment is called **complete randomization**. Every participant has an equal chance of being assigned to either level of your IV.

You do not even have to worry about having the same number of participants in each IV level; chance will be on your side. Put both levels in the cup before assigning each participant to a group, and you will have a 50–50 chance of pulling each of the two conditions randomly. Random assignment also usually takes care of the many **individual differences** among all of your participants. For example, chances are slim that all the participants with video game experience will be randomly assigned to one level of your IV. Instead, video game experience is likely to be fairly equal between the two IV levels. So, voilà! These individual differences should not influence your DV. Notice that none of the individual difference variables (e.g., video game experience) vary exactly along with your IV levels. If that happened, of course we would have a confounding variable and useless data. However, variables such as video game experience *do* introduce some "noise" to the data set; variables that merely introduce some individual difference variability across conditions are called **nuisance variables** and often are part of the research process.

When using random assignment, if you want to make sure you have the same number of people in each group, you can get fancy. Put both levels in a cup, pull one level out to assign a participant, and the next participant will automatically be put in the other condition (the one still in the cup). Then return the chosen level to the cup and start over again for the third participant, and so on. This procedure is called **block randomization** because you are assigning people in blocks of IV levels before beginning with a random level again.

Regardless of whether you use complete randomization or block randomization, you will have different people in the two levels of the IV. We generally analyze such a design with a statistic called an **independent-samples *t*-test**. A ***t*-test** is used when you have one IV with two levels. It is used for simple research designs. Independent samples means you have different people in the two groups. Therefore, it makes sense that you use a statistic named *independent-samples* t-*test*. Using this design and statistic means you have one DV, or outcome.

Imagine you collected the data of time (in seconds) that people play video games against either the computer or an opponent in the room. The data you collect might look like this:

Computer Opponent	Live Opponent in the Room
620	724
540	809
232	673
478	544
723	625
602	580
577	827
598	668
543	736
510	505
640	515
390	

Using SPSS

But your SPSS data file will look different from the data table above (see Chapter 6 for a complete review on setting up a data file in SPSS). To analyze these data in SPSS, you will need to take the seconds of playing video games (under each IV level) and arrange them for the computer to read. In SPSS, the IV is defined in the first column using 1 for level 1 (computer opponent) and 2 for level 2 (live opponent). Please note that a second option is to label IV levels with 0 and 1; either approach is fine, and we use both in this book to give you options. After labeling IV levels, the DV numbers are typed into the second SPSS column labeled "Playtime," making sure that all numbers for computer-opponent times are to the right of a number 1, for the first level of the IV. All live-opponent numbers are to the right of a number 2. Like this:

Opponent	Playtime
1	620
1	540
1	232

Opponent	Playtime
1	478
1	723
1	602
1	577
1	598
1	543
1	510
1	640
1	390
2	724
2	809
2	673
2	544
2	625
2	580
2	827
2	668
2	736
2	505
2	515

In SPSS *Variable View*, enter column headings on the far left. For the "Opponent" variable, click under *Values* (which has "None" in the box on the next page and is circled). In the box that opens, put a 1 next to *Value* and "Computer" next to *Label*. Then click *Add*.

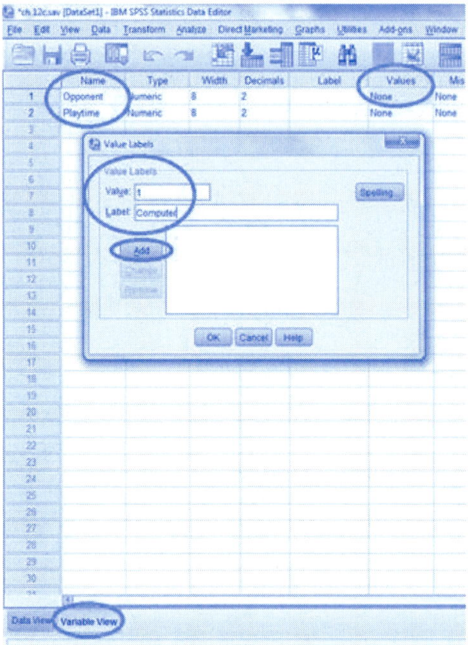

Use the same procedure for a *Value* of 2 for "Person," then click *Add* again (see screenshot below). Click *OK* and move to *Data View* by clicking the button at the bottom left of your screen.

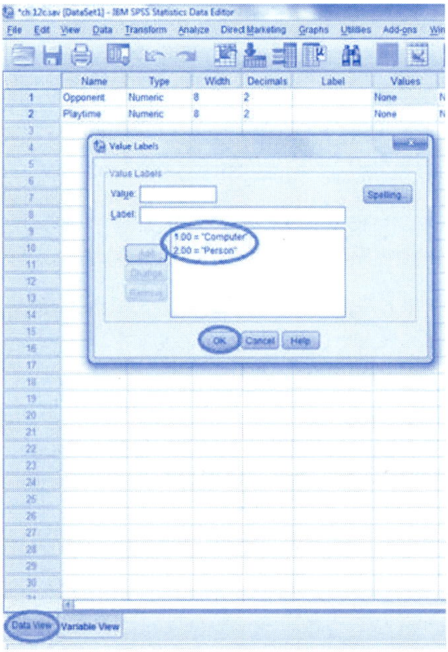

Under *Data View*, when you click *View*, then *Value Labels*, you'll see "Computer" and "Person" in the first column rather than 1 and 2. Sure, the computer needs the 1 and 2 values to process data in its tiny computer brain, but your brain can process entire words. Below is what your screen should look like when you look at the *Data View:*

	Opponent	Playtime	var	var	var
1	Computer	620.00			
2	Computer	540.00			
3	Computer	232.00			
4	Computer	478.00			
5	Computer	723.00			
6	Computer	602.00			
7	Computer	577.00			
8	Computer	598.00			
9	Computer	543.00			
10	Computer	510.00			
11	Computer	640.00			
12	Computer	390.00			
13	Person	724.00			
14	Person	809.00			
15	Person	673.00			
16	Person	544.00			
17	Person	625.00			
18	Person	580.00			
19	Person	827.00			
20	Person	668.00			
21	Person	736.00			
22	Person	505.00			
23	Person	515.00			
24					

Now that the data are entered into SPSS, you are ready to analyze the results of your experiment. This is a magical moment for most researchers. When you actually experience this moment, you will understand why we call it magical ☺. Remember, we are looking for a **significance (or *p*-value)** of .05 or less. Soon, we will click some buttons and see if we find a meaningful difference between the play times for these two groups. We will find out if people play computer games for different amounts of time when playing with a real, live person versus a computer. Here goes:

Follow the circles in the next screenshot and click *Analyze, Compare Means,* then *Independent-Samples T Test.* (The label should be *t*-test, with a lower-case *t,* but no big deal.)

In the box that opens, "Opponent" is in gray, so move it under *Grouping Variable* (i.e., your IV) using the arrow provided in the middle of box. Click *Define Groups*, then let the computer know that *Group 1* is indicated by a 1 (put a 1 in the box). The second box (*Group 2*) gets a 2. Click *Continue.*

Next, click "Playtime" to highlight it, and move it over to *Test Variable(s)* (i.e., your DV), again using the arrow in the middle. Before you click *OK*, make sure your setup looks like the screenshot below.

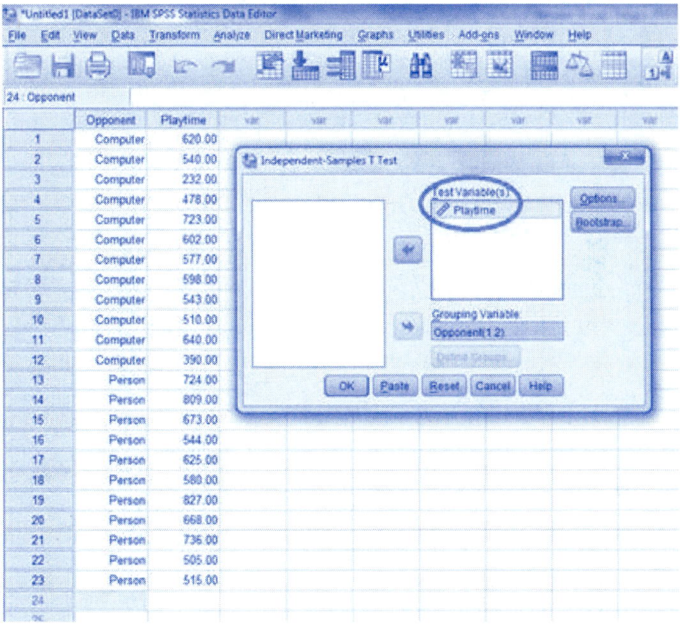

After you click *OK*, you will see your results in the form of an output file. Below is what the SPSS output file looks like. The first part of the output file to find is the significance level. Did we get the magic number of .05 or less? Can we say that our two groups differed in a meaningful way?

```
T-TEST GROUPS=Opponent(1 2)
  /MISSING=ANALYSIS
  /VARIABLES=Playtime
  /CRITERIA=CI(.95).
```

T-Test

[DataSet0]

Group Statistics

	Opponent	N	Mean	Std. Deviation	Std. Error Mean
Playtime	Computer	12	537.7500	128.10587	36.98098
	Person	11	655.0909	112.27685	33.85274

Independent Samples Test

		Levene's Test for Equality of Variances		t-test for Equality of Means						
									95% Confidence Interval of the Difference	
		F	Sig.	t	df	Sig. (2-tailed)	Mean Difference	Std. Error Difference	Lower	Upper
Playtime	Equal variances assumed	.004	.951	-2.327	21	.030	-117.34091	50.43609	-222.22851	-12.45331
	Equal variances not assumed			-2.340	20.965	.029	-117.34091	50.13563	-221.61452	-13.06729

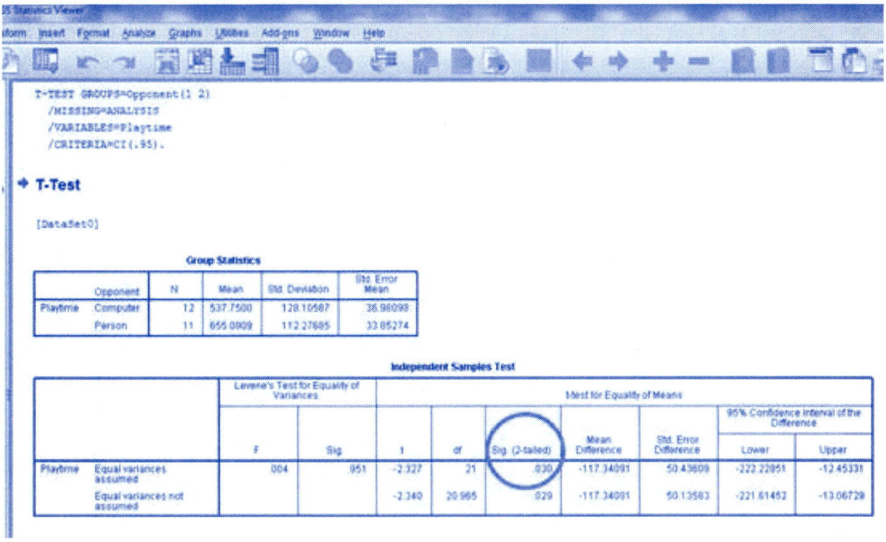

We hope you answered, "Yes!" The significance value circled (i.e., **_Sig._** **_[2-tailed]_**) was .03 across from the row labeled _Equal variance assumed_ (the top row of the table), which says the difference between the two groups was meaningful rather than just random variability in play time (DV) numbers. So, the IV, or type of interaction they experienced (person versus computer), significantly changed the DV, the number of seconds they played the game.

Before we go any further, it is always a good idea to save both of your files. You have a data file, where you entered the data, and you now have an output file, where the results of your analysis are found. Save these two files separately using whatever names will help you remember what the study is about. The default file names provided by SPSS are not very helpful when it comes to finding the file again. So, for this example, you might save the data file as "video game. sav" and the output as "video game.spv." (FYI: Those file extensions are SPSS defaults.) Later you will be able to easily find the files, open them, and either review your results or conduct additional analyses.

Now you get to share our results with the world, or at the very least you will share with your instructor who assigned this task. We will help you do that using the highly organized APA style. Your job will be to pull relevant information from your SPSS output and write an APA-style results section. Our job is to show you how.

From the independent-samples _t_-test output, you will need

- the _t_-value,
- **degrees of freedom (_df_)**,
- the significance value,
- the two group means,
- the number of participants in each group (_N_ values, although they really should be symbolized by _n_ values), and
- the variability or spread of numbers between the two groups (standard deviation is fine).

Below, we have circled relevant information from the SPSS output. Notice in the bottom table that you have a _t_-value, degrees of freedom, and a significance value on the row marked _Equal variances assumed_. This row is the correct one to use when you report data. You also have group means, standard deviations, and the number of participants per group (_n_) in the top table.

Before we look at an APA-style results section, you need to know one final piece of information. If you have a significant effect, as you do here, you will need to calculate the size of the effect. Unfortunately, SPSS does not calculate **Cohen's *d***, which is the effect-size statistic, for us. However, SPSS output does give us all the numbers we need for the calculation. Here is the basic equation for calculating Cohen's *d*:

$$d = \frac{M_{group1} - M_{group2}}{SD_{pooled}}$$

M represents a mean. $M_{group\,1}$ is the mean for group 1 (playing against the computer), and $M_{group\,2}$ is the mean for group 2 (playing against another person in the room). As a shortcut if you do not want to subtract means, SPSS gives us the numerator for the equation; it is labeled "Mean Difference" in the output table, and the value is –117.34091. The denominator of Cohen's *d* is the standard deviation (a measure of variability) across the two groups, called *standard deviation (SD) pooled*. The formula for standard deviation pooled is

$$SD_{pooled} = \frac{SE_{pooled}}{\sqrt{\dfrac{1}{N_{group1}} + \dfrac{1}{N_{group2}}}}$$

You will use values from the output to calculate SD_{pooled}. Look for the *std error difference* in the table to find 50.43609 for this example. This is what you will use for the numerator. You likely have guessed that the two values for N refer to the number of observations in each of the two groups, in this case 12 and 11. See the items circled below.

Now put all the pieces together in the formula.

$$SD_{pooled} = \frac{50.43609}{\sqrt{\frac{1}{12} + \frac{1}{11}}} = 120.94985$$

You are ready to calculate Cohen's d.

$$d = \frac{-117.34091}{120.94985} = -.970162$$

The sign of Cohen's d does not matter; think of it in terms of absolute value. In the APA-style results section below, we can remove the negative sign and simply discuss the absolute size of the effect, included as d below.

Writing an APA-Style Results Section

> ### Results
>
> We analyzed these data using an independent-samples t-test. Type of opponent affected how long people played a video game, $t(21) = -2.33$, $p = .03$, $d = .97$. Participants who played against a person in the same room played longer ($M = 655.09$ sec, $SD = 112.27$, $n = 11$) than those who competed against the computer ($M = 537.75$ sec, $SD = 128.11$, $n = 12$).

Independent-Samples *t*-Test With a Pseudo-IV

Remember that we have been discussing one IV with two levels. A true IV is a variable that you manipulate. In the study we have been discussing, we manipulated participants by asking them either to play a video game against a computer or a real person in the room. Sometimes we have a study design that looks like it has an IV and can even be analyzed using the independent-samples t-test. But it is not really a *manipulated* variable, so we are not technically allowed to call it an IV. During design and analysis, we have to call this non-manipulated variable a pseudo-IV, a fake IV, or any other name that reminds you that the variable was *not* manipulated. (Please note that when you decide to submit a manuscript for publication, you do not say you had a fake IV! If you clearly define your variables and method, the fact that you did not manipulate a variable should be clear.)

Why is an understanding of pseudo-IVs important? Because manipulation of a true IV (a real experiment) means you can learn cause and effect. Without manipulation, we cannot know cause and effect; we will only know that the two variables—the pseudo-IV and DV—are related. Look at the APA-style results section for the computer game study above. Because we had a true IV, we were allowed to tell the world that we found cause and effect. Even the APA wording reflects that. We cannot use cause–effect wording without manipulation (remember this discussion from Chapter 2).

As a completely new example, suppose we wanted to examine how long males versus females play a video game. So, in this example, we are not comparing two types of opponents (computer versus person). Instead, we are comparing males and females, which is what differentiates the two groups. The non-manipulated IV is gender, and the DV is still playing time. If we ran the study, imagine the data looked like this:

Males	Females
780	540
689	320
756	780
644	655
530	486
833	592
715	400
730	771
877	690
579	622
	561

Using SPSS

We would still lay out the data in SPSS using "Gender" in the first column, with 1 representing males and 2 representing females. And the DV numbers (Play time) will still be in the second SPSS column. To analyze these data just as the prior example, click *Analyze, Compare Means*, then *Independent-Samples T Test*. Set up your variables in the boxes that open, including labeling values of "Gender" as 1 = "Males" and 2 = "Females." After clicking *OK* and obtaining the SPSS output, pull relevant numbers (see numbers circled in the next screenshot) to write your APA-style results section. You will notice that we have reached the magical significance number of $p < .05$ again, so we know males and females truly differ in the amount of time they play computer games.

Here is the one *big* difference: When you write your APA results, do not say gender *caused* playtime to vary. Only say gender *related* to length of time people played video games. After pulling relevant SPSS output, and calculating Cohen's *d* using the formula discussed earlier, below is what the results section looks like for the pseudo-IV.

Writing an APA-Style Results Section

Results

We analyzed these data using an independent-samples *t*-test. Gender of participant related to how long people played a video game, $t(19) = 2.32, p = .03$, $d = 1.01$. Male participants played longer ($M = 713.30$ sec, $SD = 107.86$, $n = 10$) than female participants ($M = 583.36$ sec, $SD = 143.80$, $n = 11$).

Between Groups With More Than Two Levels of an IV

A *t*-test is reserved for a simple research design with one IV (or pseudo-IV) having two levels. But often, you will want to conduct a study with more than two levels of the IV. For example, you might want to examine three types of videogame opponents: the computer, a person in the room playing, and a person playing from a remote location. With three IV levels, you cannot analyze data using a *t*-test; you must use an analysis called ANOVA (or analysis of variance). Keep in mind that a between-groups design always involves different people in the IV levels. And if you are manipulating people (have a true IV), you will still want to randomly assign people to IV levels.

After running the study, your data might look like this on paper:

Computer Opponent	In-Person Opponent	Remote-Location Opponent
620	724	655
540	809	792
232	673	765
478	544	879
723	625	634
602	580	778
577	827	671
598	668	804
543	736	732
510	505	420
640	515	510
390		814
		788

Using SPSS

Data layout in SPSS would be very similar to the independent-samples *t*-test, but instead of 1 and 2 representing levels, you will need 1, 2, and 3 to represent all three levels in the first column. Of course you will identify the labels as "Computer," "Person," and "Remote" rather than view mere numbers in the first column.

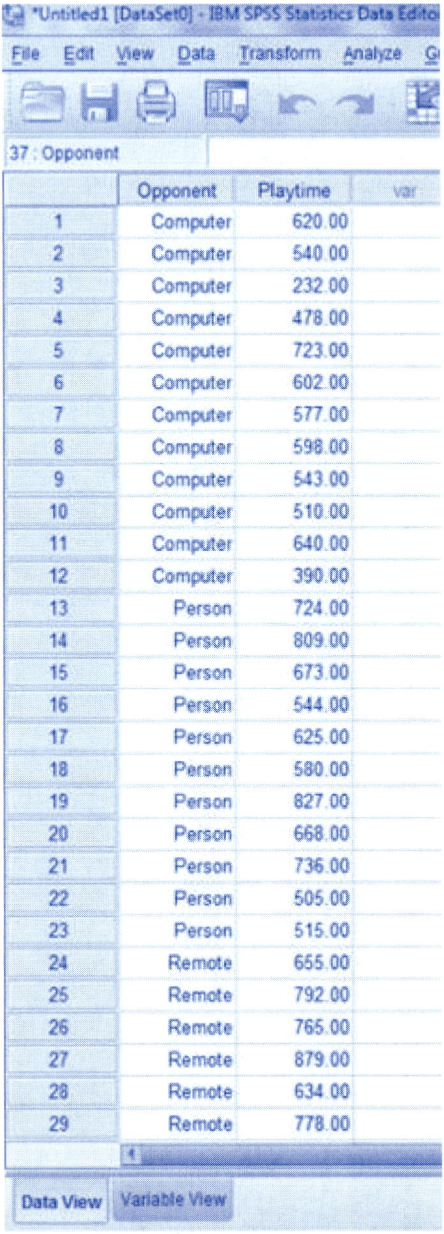
*Untitled1 [DataSet0] - IBM SPSS Statistics Data Edito
File Edit View Data Transform Analyze G
37 : Opponent
Opponent Playtime var
1 Computer 620.00
2 Computer 540.00
3 Computer 232.00
4 Computer 478.00
5 Computer 723.00
6 Computer 602.00
7 Computer 577.00
8 Computer 598.00
9 Computer 543.00
10 Computer 510.00
11 Computer 640.00
12 Computer 390.00
13 Person 724.00
14 Person 809.00
15 Person 673.00
16 Person 544.00
17 Person 625.00
18 Person 580.00
19 Person 827.00
20 Person 668.00
21 Person 736.00
22 Person 505.00
23 Person 515.00
24 Remote 655.00
25 Remote 792.00
26 Remote 765.00
27 Remote 879.00
28 Remote 634.00
29 Remote 778.00
Data View
Variable View

To analyze the data and look for that important significance value, the next screenshot points out what to choose to analyze your data. Simply click *Analyze*, *General Linear Model*, and *Univariate*.

When the box opens, your two variables will be on the left. Move "Opponent" to *Fixed Factor(s)* on the right as shown below. Click "Playtime" to highlight the variable, and move it over to *Dependent Variable*.

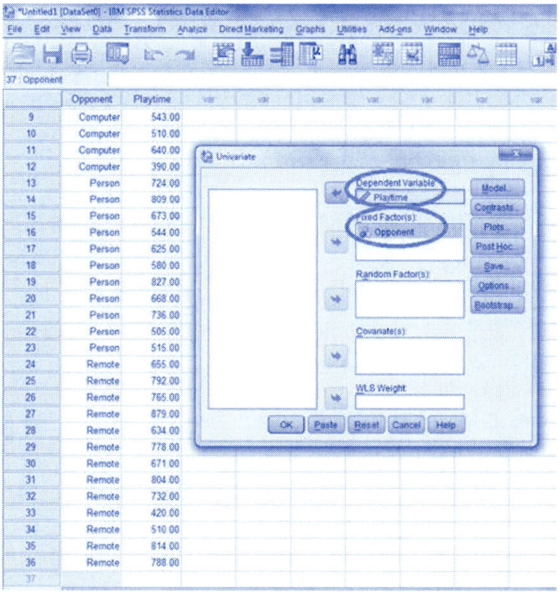

Click *Options*, highlight "Opponent," and move it from the left to under *Display Means for* on the right as shown below. On the lower half of the box, click *Descriptive Statistics* and *Estimates of effect size.*

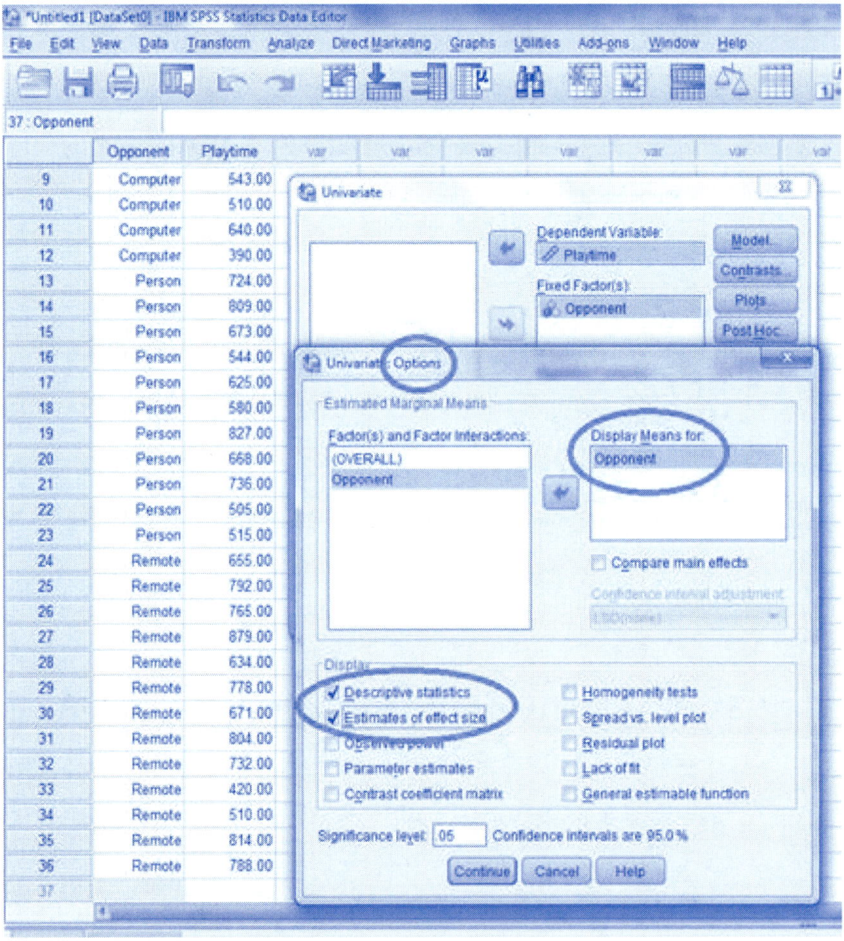

Click *Continue*. Finally, click *OK* to view output. Although you will not have these nice circles to point out particular information on your output, it should generally look like this:

➜ Univariate Analysis of Variance

[DataSet1] C:\Users\jhwilson\Desktop\EasyGuideStatsMethods\Ch 9 anova.sav

Between-Subjects Factors

		Value Label	N
Opponent	1.00	Computer	12
	2.00	Person	11
	3.00	Remote	13

Descriptive Statistics

Dependent Variable: Playtime

Opponent	Mean	Std. Deviation	N
Computer	537.7500	128.10587	12
Person	655.0909	112.27685	11
Remote	710.9231	130.24494	13
Total	639.1389	141.72086	36

Tests of Between-Subjects Effects

Dependent Variable: Playtime

Source	Type III Sum of Squares	df	Mean Square	F	Sig.	Partial Eta Squared
Corrected Model	192820.223ª	2	96410.112	6.236	.005	.274
Intercept	14429996.54	1	14429996.54	933.435	.000	.966
Opponent	192820.223	2	96410.112	6.236	.005	.274
Error	510148.082	33	15459.033			
Total	15271185.00	36				
Corrected Total	702968.306	35				

a. R Squared = .274 (Adjusted R Squared = .230)

Estimated Marginal Means

Opponent

The significance value (*Sig.*) found on the *Tests of Between-Subjects Effects table* is less than .05 (in fact, it is less than .01).

Notice we circled the relevant information for you. You need

- the *F*-value (similar to a *t*-value),
- *df* (two numbers in this analysis),
- the significance value,
- three group means,
- the number of participants in each group (*N* values), and
- three group standard deviations.

A significant effect means that your groups differ. When you had only two groups (with the *t*-test), you certainly knew which two differed. But in the current study, you have three groups. At this point, you only know that at least two of them differ from each other. However, you do not know *which* group means differ from each other. No problem, since SPSS can conduct another test to use only when you have a significant ANOVA outcome; you know that at least two groups are different when compared to each other. SPSS offers ***post hoc* tests** to see where specific effects are.

After you have a significant ANOVA, conduct *post hoc* tests by again opening your main box (*Analyze, General Linear Model, Univariate*), then click *Post Hoc* at the right of the box. Move "Opponent" to the right, under *Post Hoc Tests for*, then click ***Tukey*** in the bottom half of the box for a conservative test to see which group means differ from each other in a meaningful way. When your ***post hoc* analysis** is set up like the one below, click *Continue*.

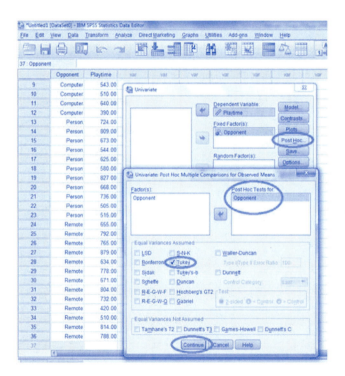

We should tell you that it is OK to set up both the ANOVA and *post hoc* analyses in SPSS when you are ready to analyze a data set. You do not have to first run the ANOVA, examine the output, then go back and run *post hoc* tests if the ANOVA value is significant. But be careful! If you want to go ahead and run the *post hoc* tests, do not even look at them if your ANOVA is not significant! An ANOVA that fails to find significance means *no* groups differ from each other; it makes no logical sense to then conduct *post hoc* tests to see *which* means differ from each other.

Your *post hoc* output should look like this:

Estimated Marginal Means

Opponent

Dependent Variable Playtime

Opponent	Mean	Std. Error	95% Confidence Interval	
			Lower Bound	Upper Bound
Computer	537.750	35.892	464.727	610.773
Person	655.091	37.488	578.821	731.361
Remote	710.923	34.484	640.765	781.082

Post Hoc Tests

Opponent

Multiple Comparisons

Playtime
Tukey HSD

(I) Opponent	(J) Opponent	Mean Difference (I-J)	Std. Error	Sig.	95% Confidence Interval	
					Lower Bound	Upper Bound
Computer	Person	-117.3409	51.90009	.076	-244.6931	10.0112
	Remote	-173.1731*	49.77358	.004	-295.3072	-51.0389
Person	Computer	117.3409	51.90009	.076	-10.0112	244.6931
	Remote	-55.8322	50.93646	.523	-180.8198	69.1554
Remote	Computer	173.1731*	49.77358	.004	51.0389	295.3072
	Person	55.8322	50.93646	.523	-69.1554	180.8198

Based on observed means.
The error term is Mean Square(Error) = 15459.033.
*. The mean difference is significant at the .05 level.

Homogeneous Subsets

Playtime

Because the ANOVA was already set up, the output will start with the overall ANOVA again, followed by *post hoc* comparisons of group means (*Multiple Comparisons*). On the first row, "Computer" and "Person" have been compared. Look at the top *Sig.* value that is circled and has a value greater than .05. We now know that "Computer" and "Person" groups failed to differ in a meaningful way. Next, look at the second *Sig.* value that compares the "Computer" and "Remote" groups; a *Sig.* value (*p*-value) of .004 indicates a meaningful difference between those two groups. Now notice that the third row compares "Person" and "Computer," but we already looked at that comparison on the first row. Skip it and move on to the fourth row—a comparison of "Person" and "Remote." This is the third and final unique comparison among the three group means. With a significance value of .523, the two groups did not differ from each other.

The only remaining task is to write your results in APA style. You will need the circled items from the ANOVA and from follow-up *post hoc* analyses. Because you had a true IV (you manipulated people), you can use cause–effect language in your results section. Finally, you will need to report the effect size using **partial eta squared (η^2)**. Partial η^2 also has a longer name, *proportion of variance accounted for*. It essentially tells you how much of the variance in your data set "is associated with" or "can be explained by" the different levels of your between groups factor. If eta squared is .5 then we could explain 50% of the variance in the DV by knowing about the between groups factor. Look at your original ANOVA output table to locate effect size to the right of *Sig.*

Writing an APA-Style Results Section

Results

We used a one-way, between-groups ANOVA to analyze these data. Tukey's *post hoc* comparisons examined differences between groups ($p <$ .05). Type of opponent affected how long participants played a video game, $F(2, 33) = 6.24$, $p < .01$, $\eta^2 = .27$. Participants who played against another person from a remote location played longer ($M = 710.92$, $SD = 130.24$, $n = 13$) than participants who played against the computer ($M = 537.75$, $SD = 128.11$, $n = 12$). No other group means differed ($p > .05$).

In this example, we included a true IV; we manipulated people to either play against the computer or another person who is present or absent (three IV levels). But, remember that you cannot use cause–effect language if you decide to use a pseudo-IV, one that you would not manipulate. A true experiment and IV require manipulation. Imagine measuring time people play video games based on year in college: first year, sophomore, junior, or senior. You would not manipulate year in college, but the data could be analyzed using the between-groups ANOVA described above. Data entry, analysis, and SPSS output would be the same. The only difference would be in writing an APA-style results section. You would have to be careful to avoid cause–effect language and say year in college related to time spent playing video games.

Summary

In this chapter, we covered between-groups designs, defined by different people in the groups or levels. Between-groups designs include the independent-samples *t*-test and the one-way, between-groups ANOVA. In either type of analysis, you can choose to manipulate a variable (IV) or leave it free to vary (pseudo-IV), and then measure an outcome (DV). If you manipulate a variable, you should randomly assign participants to the IV conditions. If a *t*-test provides a significant outcome, you know which two groups differ because you only compare two groups in a *t*-test. However, a significant ANOVA requires *post hoc* tests because you will not know which pairs of means differ from each other across three or more conditions. When you know details of your *t*-test or ANOVA result, APA-style writing allows you to share your work with others.

Everybody Plays! 9

Repeated-Measures Designs

In Chapter 8, you learned about research designs that rely on observing different groups of participants. There is another group of research designs that allows you to test the same people more than once; they are called **repeated-measures designs**. When you use these designs, each person experiences every level of the IV. For example, you might want to measure how fast your participants can type when they are working in the presence of other people or alone, a social facilitation effect. You have a choice about how to manipulate this variable. You could randomly assign half of your participants to each of two groups (a between-groups design described in Chapter 8). Or you could ask all of your participants to type the same passage as fast as they can under each of the two conditions, which would be a repeated-measures design.

There are a number of reasons why you might choose to use a repeated-measures design. The major advantage of testing the same people twice is that you prevent the range of individual differences from affecting your outcome. In this case, the baseline speed of typing for each person will be the same in each experimental condition. It is not possible to accidently assign all of the fast typists to one condition or the other because they are represented in both conditions. Therefore, using repeated-measures prevents the accidental confound between social condition and natural typing speed. Another way to think about this is that with a repeated-measures design, you start off equalizing typing speed in the two conditions then see if you can alter it by manipulating the social condition within the same person. When individuals serve as their own controls in this way, we are guaranteed to start with the same distribution of individual differences in each condition, that is, the same range of typing speeds as well as the same number of slow and fast typists.

As you might imagine, comparing a person's performance in one condition to the same person's performance in another situation is more powerful than making comparisons across different groups of participants. Remember that

statistical power is the probability of rejecting the null hypothesis when the **research hypothesis** is true. We want statistical power to be as high as possible. A repeated-measures research design makes it more likely that you will support your research hypothesis if it is true. As a result, a small difference in typing time between the two conditions based on being watched or not is more likely to be statistically significant.

This design is so powerful that you might wonder why we would use any other type of design. Unfortunately, some drawbacks do exist. You probably learned about **carry-over effects** in a research methods course. In our typing example, we might expect that practice with typing in the first condition will speed up typing in the second. If all of your participants typed alone first and then typed with others second, the practice effect would be confounded with social condition. If you find a difference in the two conditions, you would not know if it was caused by the order of the conditions (i.e., typing alone followed by typing with others) or the social conditions. However, we sometimes can control for practice effects by **counterbalancing** the IV conditions; half of the participants type alone first and then with others, and the other half type with others first then alone. To make sure that order does not influence our results, we can simply include order as an additional IV when we analyze our data. The design for this analysis is presented in Chapter 10.

Of course, sometimes you cannot counterbalance the IV conditions. For example, imagine that we want to test the effectiveness of a "new miracle cure" for Parkinson's disease. We cannot give half of our participants the "new miracle cure" first and then give those same patients a placebo, particularly if the cure worked! Even if the cure was reversible, it would not be ethical to withdraw the drug and return our participants to their debilitated state. In such a situation, we can still use a repeated-measures design and measure symptoms pre-"cure" and post. While not ideal, there are times when we might not have an alternative to this **quasi-experimental design**.

Repeated-measures designs offer the same range of designs as between-groups designs, including two or more IVs (or pseudo-IV) and two or more levels of each. Just as we did in Chapter 8, we will go through examples starting with the simplest and moving on to a powerful and complex design.

One Independent Variable (IV) With Two Levels

The simplest repeated-measures design is represented by the "typing" example included in the previous section. In this design, you would have one IV (how many were present while our participants were typing) with two levels (either some people or none). Of course, you need to arrange for all participants to experience both levels of the IV. In this case, we ask all of our participants to type two similar documents, one alone and a second in the company of five other people. To control for carry-over effects, we could randomly assign participants to either type alone or in the company of others first. So half of the participants would type alone first and the other half would type in the company of others first. You would use a **paired-samples *t*-test** to analyze your data for a mean difference in typing time (your DV) between the two conditions. Notice that in this analysis, we do not bother with testing the order of conditions as a second IV. We just accepted that any additional variability from order of testing has equally affected both groups because we counterbalanced order. However, we want you to know that we could use the mixed design described in Chapter 10 to make sure that order of the social conditions did not affect typing time.

Let us take a look at what might happen if we actually conducted the social facilitation experiment that is described above. We will bring a group of participants into the lab. Half of them would type the passage while alone first and then a second time while in the presence of others; the other half of our participants would experience the experimental conditions in the opposite order. This design has one IV with two levels (social and alone) with a single DV (typing time).

Using SPSS

The SPSS data file for this analysis needs three columns.

	participant	social	alone
1	1	8.8378	8.7612
2	2	6.2585	12.0690
3	3	13.4608	4.2736
4	4	5.2016	11.1782
5	5	10.2835	16.6501
6	6	7.2070	8.6693
7	7	13.2737	12.3902
8	8	12.5799	15.1734
9	9	12.6185	12.0614
10	10	2.0417	-.7057
11	11	2.4041	-1.0230
12	12	11.0941	11.2655
13	13	11.1855	17.2368

In this screenshot, the first column identifies participants (remember that this identification can be used to correct errors that we might find during data entry), the second column includes the social condition typing times in seconds, and the third column includes the alone condition typing times in seconds. We select the analysis by clicking on *Analyze, Compare Means*, then *Paired-Samples T-Test*.

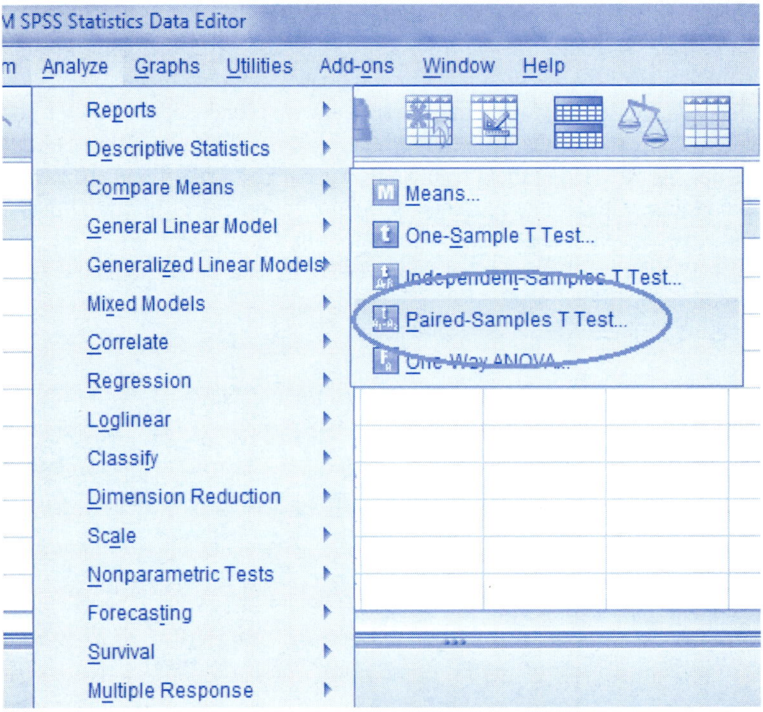

The following dialogue box will open. The next screenshot shows you the box labeled *Paired Variables*. All of our variables are listed in the left-hand box as you see them here.

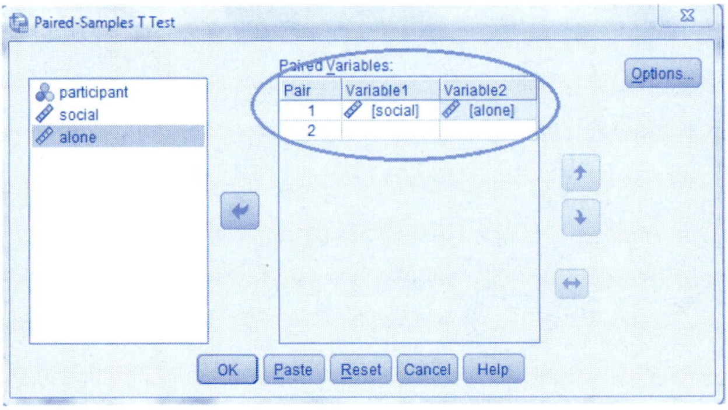

In this screenshot, we moved the variable names over to the columns labeled *Variable1* and *Variable2*. Only the row for Pair 1 is completed, but we could have included more pairs if we had additional hypotheses to test. When SPSS calculates this *t*-test, it will first subtract the scores on Variable2 from the scores on Variable1; that order determines the sign of the *t*-test. We only need to click the *OK* button to run the analysis. SPSS does its magic and produces the following tables in the output window.

T-Test

[DataSet1] C:\Users\dgoff\Dropbox\easy design and analysis\SPSS files\typing time tTest.sav

Paired Samples Statistics

		Mean	N	Std. Deviation	Std. Error Mean
Pair 1	social	8.957963	20	3.9839632	.8908412
	alone	10.144754	20	5.3577544	1.1980303

Paired Samples Correlations

		N	Correlation	Sig.
Pair 1	social & alone	20	.328	.158

Paired Samples Test

		Paired Differences							
					95% Confidence Interval of the Difference				
		Mean	Std. Deviation	Std. Error Mean	Lower	Upper	t	df	Sig. (2-tailed)
Pair 1	social - alone	-1.1867907	5.5305880	1.2366771	-3.7751855	1.4016041	-.960	19	.349

The output includes three tables. The first table presents descriptive statistics as well as a summary of the design. You can see that we had one IV (social or alone) with two levels. You can also see that we had 20 observations, and the DV mean for the social condition was lower (they typed faster) than the DV mean in the alone condition. You will also notice that SPSS reports two measures of variability for our measures. The standard deviation (SD) is labeled *Std. Deviation* and the **standard error (SE)** is labeled ***Std. Error Mean***. We typically use SD as our descriptive statistic for variability. There are times when SE might be preferred. You should ask your professor which is best for your data. We will use the descriptive statistics in this first table when we summarize our results in APA style.

The next table in the output reports the correlation between confidence reported before and after participation. Unless you have a hypothesis about the correlation between these two variables you will not need this value when summarizing results from this analysis.

The third table is the most important because it presents the values for *t*, *df*, and *p*. These values allow us to make our decision about whether or not to accept our hypothesis. In this case you can see that $t = -.96$, $df = 19$, and $p = .349$. Notice that SPSS does not directly identify *p*; rather, it labels the value *Sig. (2-tailed)*. When the value of *p* is less than (or equal to) .05, we can reject the null hypothesis and know we discovered something meaningful. We had a

one-tailed test here (check a statistics textbook for more information on one-versus **two-tailed test**), we expected that typing in the company of others would reduce typing time, so we should adjust the value that SPSS reported for p by dividing it by 2, so $p = .349 / 2 = .18$. In this case .18 is greater than .05, so we cannot conclude that there is a difference in typing time based on whether participants typed alone or in the company of others.

We have one last problem here; APA style requires us to present an **effect size** statistic, and the SPSS output file does not include this information. The appropriate effect size statistic for a paired-samples t-test is Cohen's d. If you remember calculating effect size in the previous chapter, you will notice the formula is different here. Fortunately, the SPSS output supplies the values we need for an easy calculation of that statistic. Here is the equation:

$$d = \frac{Mean_{difference}}{SD_{difference}}.$$

The $Mean_{difference}$ and $SD_{difference}$ are the first two values included in the *Paired samples test* table. So we can calculate

$$d = \frac{-1.87}{5.53} \text{ or } -.34.$$

Now we can put the relevant output together in an APA style summary.

Writing an APA-Style Results Section

Results

In this study, we used a paired-samples t-test to evaluate differences in typing time in a social and alone condition. We found that typing time was slower in the alone condition ($M = 10.14$ sec, $SD = 5.36$, $n = 20$), compared to the social condition ($M = 8.96$ sec, $SD = 3.98$, $n = 20$). However, this small increase was not statistically significant, $t(19) = -.96$, $p = .18$, $d = -.34$.

In this example, we were unable to reject the null hypothesis because our observed value for p was greater than .05, so our result is inconclusive. We used an online power calculator to check the power for this "experiment" and found that it was low, only .43. That means we only had a 43% chance of rejecting the null hypothesis if our research hypothesis was correct. With a medium effect size of $-.34$, we are inclined to repeat this experiment with more participants to see if we can reject the null hypothesis when we have more power.

Expanding the Number of Levels
for Your Independent Variable (IV)

You learned in Chapter 8 that the between-groups design can be expanded beyond two groups, so you will not be surprised to find that the repeated-measures design can be expanded, too. As you think about your ideas for research projects, you probably imagine IVs with more than two levels. For example, you might want to know if people really can taste a difference among brands of bottled water. You could choose to test three (or more) brands using a repeated-measures design, asking the same people to taste all brands in your study. In this case, you would have a **one-way repeated-measures design**, and your IV would have three levels. Your hypothesis might be that there is a difference in tastes across brands. It is very convenient that this design statement translates directly to a description of your analysis, a **one-way within-groups ANOVA**.

Of course, if you executed this experiment, you would take precautions to control carry-over effects, perhaps randomly deciding the order of waters to taste for each of the participants in your experiment. The need to control for those carry-over effects is one limitation on how many levels you might use for your IV. Imagine controlling for carry-over effects for an IV with 15 levels. Worse than that, imagine being a participant in an experiment with 15 experimental conditions! Who would do that? We expect that both participants and experimenters would run out of patience long before all of the data were collected. If all of the data were ever collected, it would be a nightmare trying to interpret the differences among so many levels of any IV. So always keep in mind that there are practical limits to the number of levels that you might include for any IV.

Here is an example of a repeated-measures design with more than two levels in the IV, a one-way repeated-measures design. It is likely that you encountered the Stroop effect in Introduction to Psychology. The Stroop effect occurs when we ask a participant to respond quickly to a stimulus that presents two cognitive processes interfering with each other. We have automatic processes that we know very well and require little attention, such as reading, and we have controlled processes that involve behaviors that require more attention, in this case naming colors. The classic Stroop experiment has three conditions. Participants are asked to read a color name presented in a matching color (e.g., Blue in a blue font) and type the color name as quickly as possible; in a second condition, they type the name of a color patch (no text) as fast as they can; in a third condition, participants type the color font of a word when the color of the ink is different (e.g., Blue in a red font). Our DV is typing speed. The first two conditions serve as control conditions for the third. We use the first two to measure how fast individuals can type the names of the ink color without the interference of a non-matching text. Since people type at different speeds, this experiment is best conducted as a repeated-measures design. That way we do not have to account for differences in typing speed between the different groups. We have one IV with three levels in this design, so the one-way, repeated-measures ANOVA is the appropriate analysis. It allows us to compare the means from three levels of a single factor when all participants experienced all three levels.

Using SPSS

In this experiment, we would present participants with each of the experimental conditions in a random order. Remember, the random order controls for carry-over effects in the three conditions. For our typing time analysis, the SPSS data file must have at least three columns, one for each of the experimental conditions. We called our experimental conditions Name (color names presented in matching font colors), Patch (color patches without names), and Stroop (font colors mismatched with the color names). Our DV is typing time so we labeled each column with the name of the condition combined with the name of the DV resulting in NameTypingTime, PatchTypingTime, and StroopTypingTime. Each row represents one participant's responses. We do not have a column for IDs because we did not have to enter these data by typing them. The computer does that for us. Here is what the data look like.

	NameTypingTime	PatchTypingTime	StroopTypingTime	var	var
1	50.23400	37.625	50.08200		
2	40.44900	39.671	44.12500		
3	33.29600	31.375	32.68700		
4	30.05800	31.402	38.79600		
5	34.03100	32.812	36.70300		

stroop data.sav [DataSet1] - IBM SPSS Statistics Data Editor

File Edit View Data Transform Analyze Graphs Utilities Add-ons Window Help

To conduct the repeated-measures ANOVA you must choose *Analyze, General Linear Model*, then *Repeated Measures*.

Next, the following dialogue box opens. You use this box to name your IV and tell SPSS how many levels your IV has.

In this screenshot, we have already done that. We typed "conditions" in the box labeled *Within-Subject Factor Name* and "3" in the box labeled *Number of Levels*. When those boxes were filled, we clicked the *Add* button to move the combination into the next text box as illustrated in the following screenshot.

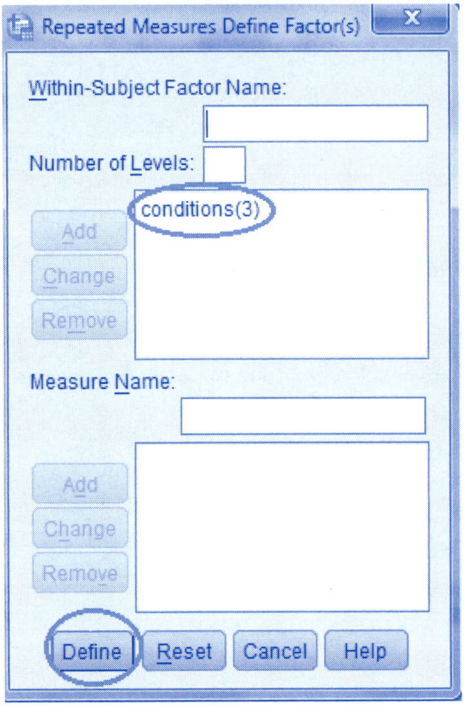

When you click the *Define* button, the following dialogue box appears.

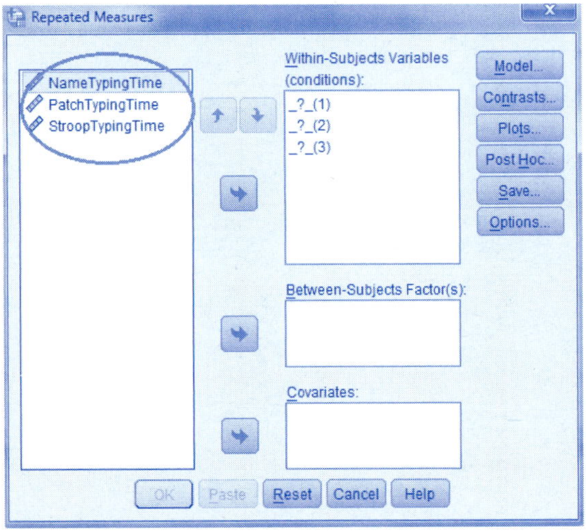

As you can see here, the names for all of the variables in your data file will appear in the box at the left of the dialogue box. You would move the variables' names that you need for this analysis over to the box on the right. You do that by clicking on each variable's name and using the arrow to move it to the other box. In some designs, the order that you move those names will make a difference so be careful.

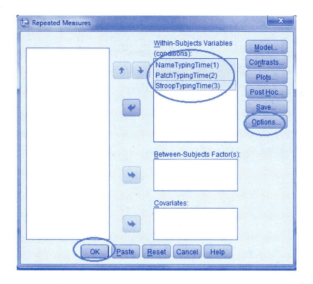

As you can see in this screenshot, we moved the names for each of our typing time variables over to the blank spaces that were created in the box on the right of the dialogue box. Some of the *Options* will be useful so we need to click on that button next. Clicking that button will open the following dialogue box.

You might find the number of options a bit overwhelming. As you scan through the list, you might ask yourself, "Have I ever heard of that? Do I know what it does?" If the answer to both questions is "no," then you should ignore that option. Here are the important exceptions. You know what descriptive statistics are (see Chapter 7 for a review); you will need the mean and standard deviation when you write your results in APA style. You also know that whenever you conduct a test of significance you need to report effect size for a significant effect. You also know that if you get a significant *F*-ratio you will need to compare differences among the three levels for your IV. So, we clicked on *Descriptive statistics* and *Estimates of effect size*. We also moved the name for our IV (conditions) into the box labeled *Display Means*. This option will conduct a *post hoc* test of the differences in the means from the three levels of conditions. After all, we want to know not only that there is a difference among the three means, but also which means are different from one another. After we moved that label, we clicked the box beside *Compare main effects*. The next screen shows you the options for the *Confidence interval adjustment*.

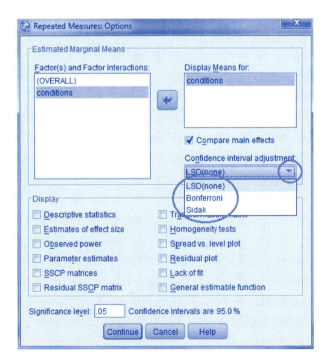

You will find three choices for *post hoc* tests in that *Confidence interval adjustment* drop-down menu, the other two are *Bonferroni* and *Sidak*. We chose *LSD(none)* from the drop-down menu for *Confidence interval adjustment*. LSD stands for "least squared differences." These are all called **pairwise comparisons**. Ask your professor or another experienced researchers which of the three is the best one for you to use. Once we make our choice, we then click on the *Continue* button and then the *OK* button. SPSS will do its magic.

You might find this screenshot of the first output section for the repeated-measures ANOVA a bit overwhelming, but take a deep breath and look it over.

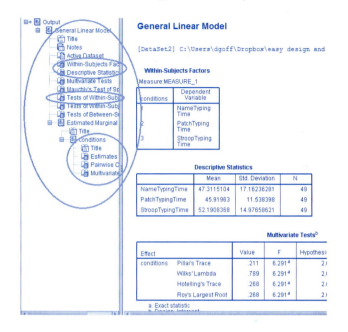

In the left-hand part of the screen, you see a list of all the labels, tables, and stuff that SPSS produces (circled above). We count nine tables, and that is a lot, but no need to look at all nine. When you think about the results of an analysis of variance, you probably imagine one ANOVA table. So why does SPSS produce so many tables? The procedure can be used for many different advanced analyses, so it produces tables for all possible uses of this type of analysis. You need only four tables to understand the basic analysis (*Within-Subjects Factors*, *Descriptive Statistics*, *Tests of Within-Subjects Effects*, and *Pairwise Comparisons*).

We will start with the Within-Subjects Factors table and Descriptive Statistics table.

Within-Subjects Factors

Measure:MEASURE_1

conditions	Dependent Variable
1	NameTyping Time
2	PatchTyping Time
3	StroopTyping Time

Descriptive Statistics

	Mean	Std. Deviation	N
NameTypingTime	47.3115104	17.16236281	49
PatchTypingTime	45.91963	11.538398	49
StroopTypingTime	52.1908368	14.97658621	49

Our first tables are visible in the screenshot above. Notice that the first table simply tells you that your IV has three levels; SPSS conveniently named them 1, 2, and 3. The first level is the Name typing time, the second is the Patch typing time, and the third is the Stroop typing time. You should always look at this table to be sure that your analysis includes the variables that you planned. The next table of descriptive statistics gives you the means and standard deviations as well as sample size for each of the three experimental conditions. You likely need those when you report your results. Until you have studied some more advanced statistics, you can ignore the *Multivariate Tests and Mauchly's Test of Sphericity* tables.

Next, let us take a look at the table for the *Tests of Within-Subjects Effects*. This screenshot presents an ANOVA table that is not too different for those you might have seen in your statistics textbook.

Tests of Within-Subjects Effects

Measure:MEASURE_1

Source		Type III Sum of Squares	df	Mean Square	F	Sig.	Partial Eta Squared
Conditions	Sphericity Assumed	1062.861	2	531.431	5.354	.006	.100
	Greenhouse-Geisser	1062.861	1.881	565.004	5.354	.007	.100
	Huynh-Feldt	1062.861	1.955	543.576	5.354	.007	.100
	Lower-bound	1062.861	1.000	1062.861	5.354	.025	.100
Error(conditions)	Sphericity Assumed	9529.493	96	99.266			
	Greenhouse-Geisser	9529.493	90.296	105.537			
	Huynh-Feldt	9529.493	93.855	101.534			
	Lower-bound	9529.493	48.000	198.531			

If you made these calculations with a calculator, you would create a table that looks like this:

Source	SS	df	F
Condition	1062.26	2	5.35
Error	9529.49	96	

In this output table, you can find columns for Source, *Type III Sum of Squares* (*SS*), *df*, *MS*, *F*, *p*, and η^2 (partial eta squared, an indication of effect size) and rows for your IV (labeled "conditions") and error. You know from looking at SPSS output in other chapters and earlier in this chapter that SPSS likes to label *p* as *Sig*.

Most of the time the rows labeled *Sphericity Assumed* will provide an accurate analysis of your data and can be used when reporting your results. If you are curious about what that all means, you can read about it in an advanced statistics textbook. If you are like us, as soon as you find this table, you will start scanning the column labeled *Sig.* to see if your value for p is less than .05. It is a lot like opening a birthday present because you are anticipating something wonderful. In this case, you will find that $p = .006$, which is less than .05 and allows us to reject the null hypothesis. In other words, we accept the research hypothesis that there is a difference in typing time for the three conditions. Next, we need to look at the *post hoc* analysis to see which specific pairs of conditions are meaningfully different from each other.

The *Pairwise Comparisons* table is the best place to look for specific differences.

Pairwise Comparisons

Measure:MEASURE_1

(I) conditions	(J) conditions	Mean Difference (I-J)	Std. Error	Sig.[a]	95% Confidence Interval for Difference[a]	
					Lower Bound	Upper Bound
1 Name	2 Patch	1.392	2.036	.497	-2.702	5.485
	3 Stroop	-4.879*	2.210	.032	-9.322	-.436
2	1	-1.392	2.036	.497	-5.485	2.702
	3	-6.271*	1.768	.001	-9.827	-2.716
3	1	4.879*	2.210	.032	.436	9.322
	2	6.271*	1.768	.001	2.716	9.827

Based on estimated marginal means

a. Adjustment for multiple comparisons: Least Significant Difference (equivalent to no adjustments).

*. The mean difference is significant at the .05 level.

First, remember that our experimental conditions have been labeled 1, 2, and 3 by SPSS. We added some labels to this table to show you that 1 is the typing time for the Name condition, 2 is the typing time for the Patch condition, and 3 is the typing time for the Stroop condition. Second, remember that those first two conditions are control conditions. This is important because we only hypothesized that typing would take longer in the Stroop condition than in the two control conditions. So when we look at this *Pairwise Comparisons* table, we hope to see a significant difference between condition 3 and 1, and between condition 3 and 2. We circled those comparisons above.

You probably already noticed that this table presents much more information than we need. As its name implies, it provides a systematic comparison of *all* possible combinations of conditions. To complicate things further, it presents each of those combinations twice. So you will find condition 1 compared with condition 2 and then, further into the table, condition 2 compared with condition 1. Once again, the circles in the previous screenshot indicate the *p* values for ourcritical comparisons: 1 (Name) with 3 (Stroop), and 2 (Patch) with 3 (Stroop). Looking at those comparisons, we see that typing-time in the "Stroop" condition was significantly slower than in the Name condition with a *Mean Differences* of –4.879 seconds (remember that *Sig.* means *p*) $p = .032$. When you look at the row for "2" the *Mean Difference* in typing time was –6.271 seconds, with a standard error of 1.768 and $p = .001$. We are therefore safe in concluding that it took significantly longer to type answers in the Stroop condition than in the color-patch condition.

Writing an APA-Style Results Section

Below is how you would report these findings in APA style.

Results

Using a one-way repeated-measures ANOVA, we found significant differences in typing time among the three experimental conditions, $F(2, 96) = 5.35$, $p = .006$, $\eta^2 = .10$. *Post hoc* analysis illustrated that typing in the Stroop condition ($M = 52.19$ sec, $SD = 14.98$, $n = 49$) was in fact slower than in either the name ($p = .032$), ($M = 47.31$ sec, $SD = 17.16$, $n = 49$), or patch ($p = .001$) conditions ($M = 45.92$ sec, $SD = 11.54$, $n = 49$).

The results section tells you that the experiment produced the results we predicted. The section first reports the overall result of the ANOVA and then *post hoc* comparisons among the critical conditions. Typing time was significantly slower in the Stroop condition than in either the Name or Patch conditions. You can also see that mean typing time was similar in the two control conditions (47.31 and 45.92 seconds), but those conditions were not compared because we did not have a hypothesis about them.

Adding Another Factor: Within-Subjects Factorial Designs

Just as with between-groups designs, you can move beyond one IV with several levels. You can design a study with two or more IVs (with at least two levels each, of course). If you include two repeated-measures IVs, you must make sure that your participants experience all possible combinations of both of the variables. The result is a **repeated-measures factorial design**; the appropriate analysis is a **factorial repeated-measures ANOVA**.

Imagine that you want to open a new restaurant and your signature dish will be chili. Do you think that having a fire (with some smoke odor in the room) will affect your patrons' appreciation of your chili? How about if the chili is spicy hot? Here is how you can find out. First, make a big batch of mild chili, divide it in half, and add a few habañero peppers to the second half. There is your first IV, spicy or not. Next, you need to invite a group of volunteer tasters to the new restaurant on two different nights. On one night, you should have a wood fire burning in the fireplace, the second night should be smoke free. Flip a coin to determine if you will have your fire on the first or second night. There is your second IV, smoke present or not. Finally, ask your volunteer tasters to taste each of the two kinds of chili on each night. Be sure to counterbalance the spicy condition to control for carry-over effects. This will make sure that not everyone will taste the four different types of chili in the same order. The next table shows you the design for these manipulations. Notice that the rows represent the spiciness manipulation, the columns the presence of smoke, and the cells the combination of those two manipulations.

	Smoke	Alone
Spicy	Spicy with Smoke	Spicy without Smoke
Not-spicy	Not-spicy with Smoke	Not-spicy without Smoke

You could ask participants to rate the taste for each bowl of chili from 1 (worst I ever tasted) to 10 (best I ever tasted). This taste rating serves as your DV. A convenient thing about the repeated-measures design is that you only need to have a few volunteer tasters because they will taste all four combinations, and you still have a good chance of detecting an effect if one exists. Remember that individual differences in appreciation for chili will remain exactly the same across all conditions because the same participants will rate the chili in all four conditions.

For example, if Regina is not a huge fan of chili, her ratings might be low across all conditions, and any slight differences in her ratings would be due purely to the manipulations of your study. That is the biggest advantage of using a repeated-measures design.

A really nice aspect of the **factorial design** is that you get to test not two, but three hypotheses at once. You will be able to tell if people liked the spicy or mild chili better. You will be able to tell if smelling smoke while tasting chili increased appreciation for the taste of your chili. Finally, you will be able to tell if those two factors combined to affect people's ratings. When that happens, we call the result an *interaction effect*. Perhaps when smelling the smoke, people liked the spicy chili much more than the mild chili, but without the smell of smoke, both types of chili were rated the same. Now, you will have a really good idea of how to make your restaurant a success. We would use a factorial repeated-measures ANOVA to evaluate these effects.

So let us see how this might turn out. You recognize the design described here as a 2 (spicy) × 2 (smoke) factorial design. Both variables are manipulated as repeated measures, so we have a **factorial within-groups design**. Analysis of data in this design is best served (pun intended) with a factorial ANOVA (analysis of variance) for correlated groups. With this analysis, we will be able to evaluate three hypotheses: (1) Spiciness will change how much people like our chili; (2) smoke will change how much people like our chili; and (3) smoke and spiciness will combine to affect how much people like our chili. Take a second look at the third hypotheses, our proposed interaction effect. It proposes that people might respond differently to our spicy and mild chili in the presence of the smell of smoke. In other words, how much each chili is appreciated could be changed by the absence or presence of the smell of smoke. That is an example of a predicted interaction.

Using SPSS

We again turn to SPSS to analyze the data using a factorial repeated-measures ANOVA. This screenshot shows a section of our data file. For this analysis, we need four columns of data; each one represents a different cell in the 2 (spicy) × 2 (smoke) design.

You can see columns for taste ratings of spicy_smokey, spicy_alone, notspicy_smokey, and notspicy_alone. As you likely have guessed from the column labeled ID, each row represents one individual's taste ratings of all four possible combinations.

We begin this analysis just as we did the simple repeated-measures ANOVA. Select *Analyze, General Linear Model*, then *Repeated Measures* as seen in the next screenshot.

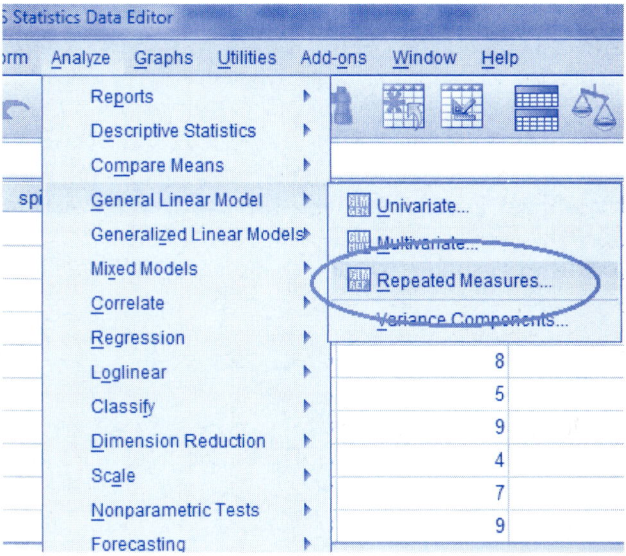

That click will open the dialogue box presented in the next figure.

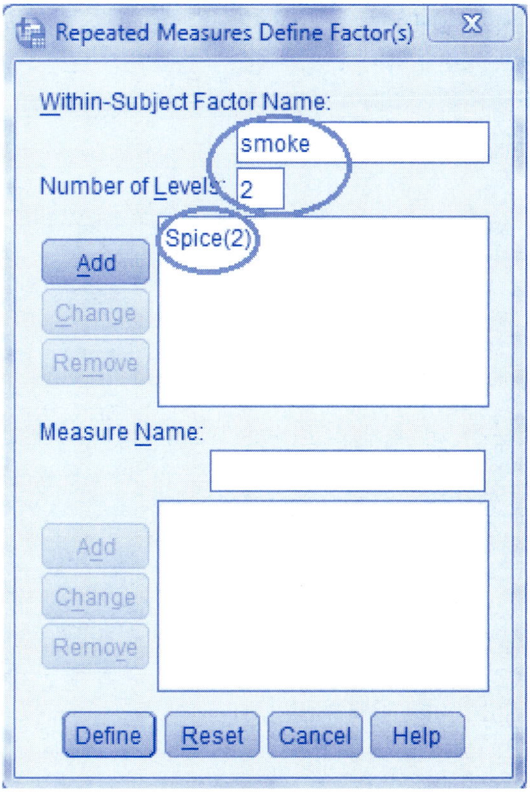

As you have seen before, when this dialogue box opens up, it is completely blank. It takes two steps to produce the design. In this screenshot, we are halfway through the process of defining our design. In the first step, we typed "Spice" in the *Within-Subject Factor Name* box and "2" in the *Number of Levels* box, and clicked the *Add* button. That moved "Spice(2)" into the box; you see it circled in the screenshot. You see that we have now typed "smoke" in the *Within-Subject Factor Name* box and "2" in the *Number of Levels* box, and are ready to click the *Add* button.

The next screenshot shows what the dialogue box looks like after that click.

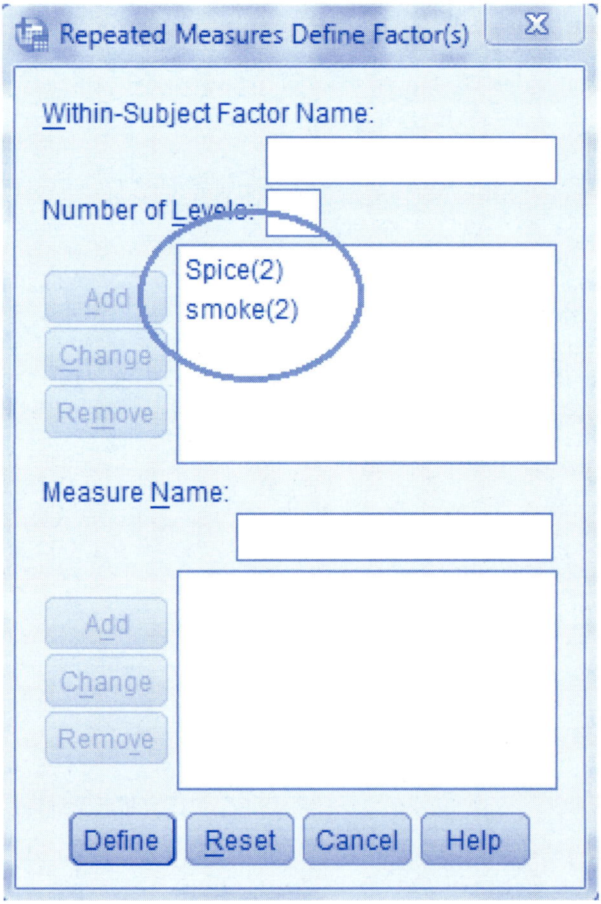

Next we click on the *Define* button, which opens the *Repeated Measures* dialogue box. The next screenshot shows you what the *Repeated Measures* dialogue box looks like when it first opens.

All of our conditions are listed in the box at left of the screen. We need to move those names into the *Within-Subjects Variables (Spice, smoke)* text box. It is very important to pay attention to the order in which you move those condition names to the right. If you move the names over in the wrong order, your analysis will be a mess. Take a careful look at the labels above the *Within-Subjects Variables (Spice, smoke)* box. Notice that it includes the names we created in the opening dialogue *(Spice and smoke)*. Now look at the notation that follows the name of the first condition in the box. A design table will help you see exactly what is going on.

The next table presents our 2 × 2 design with the SPSS notation and condition names in their proper cells.

	Smoke (1)	Alone (2)
Spicy (1)	(1,1) Spicy_Smoke	(1,2) Spicy_Alone
Notspicy (2)	(2,1) Notspicy_smoke	(2,2) Notspicy_Alone

Now that you can see which condition should go in each cell you can also see how the notation matches the condition names. So we should have Spicy_Smoke in the cell labeled (1,1), Spicy_Alone in the cell labeled (1,2), and so on. The numbers in parentheses after the name tell us that we have entered this as a condition in the proper cell for our design. Here is what the completed dialogue box should look like.

We always take more than a moment to make sure that our condition names match this notation. Once you are satisfied that the condition names have been placed properly, you should click the *Options* button to open the next dialogue box.

You saw this dialogue box earlier in the chapter. Again, we have clicked on the options for *Descriptive statistics* and *Estimates of effect size*. You might also consider clicking on the *Observed power* option. We also moved the names for each of our IVs and the interaction into the box labeled *Display Means for* and then we clicked the *Continue* button. Next, we clicked on the *OK* button in the main dialogue box, then waited patiently for SPSS to produce the results. In its exuberance, SPSS gives us the same number of less-than-useful tables in this analysis as it did in the one-way. Here again, we will focus on the tables that you need to interpret these results. The next screenshot presents the output tree or outline for this analysis.

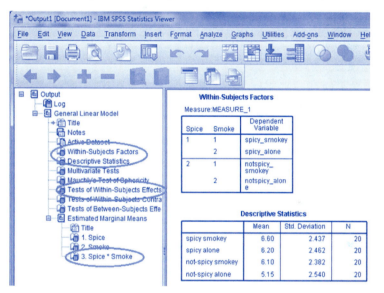

Even we sometimes feel overwhelmed when we look at the list of tables SPSS produces for this analysis. Often we simply start our review of the output by deleting some of the tables that we do not need; as examples, the *Mulivariate Tests* and *Mauchley's Test of Sphericity* can be deleted. Let us focus on the tables you do need and how to interpret them, the names for those tables are circled in the screenshot of our output.

Within-Subjects Factors

Measure:MEASURE_1

Spice	Smoke	Dependent Variable
1	1	spicy_smokey
	2	spicy_alone
2	1	notspicy_smokey
	2	notspicy_alone

First, you should always look carefully at the *Within-Subjects Factors* table. This table can tell you if you entered your design correctly when you started the *Repeated Measures* procedure. In this example, we know we did because the circled labels match up with the names we placed in our design table three pages back. We wanted two levels for Spice and two levels for Smoke, and we can see that in the left-hand column in the following figure. Most importantly, you can see that the names for our DVs match up with those levels! The next table in the output presents the means and standard deviations for our conditions.

Descriptive Statistics

	Mean	Std. Deviation	N
spicy smokey	6.60	2.437	20
spicy alone	6.20	2.462	20
not-spicy smokey	6.10	2.382	20
not-spicy alone	5.15	2.540	20

It is a good idea to review this table to see if the means and standard deviations are within the range that you expect based on previous research and your memory for how people responded in your experiment. You will see the means again in another table later in the output, and we will need them when we report our results in APA style.

Remember, we will skip the next two tables (*Mauchly's Test of Sphericity* and *Multivariate Tests*) in the output. The *Multivariate Tests* are used for a different research design. (See Chapter 10 for an example of that design and analysis.) That brings us to the test of *Within-Subjects Effects* table. This one is the most important output tables and includes the crucial results of our analysis of variance.

Tests of Within-Subjects Effects

Measure:MEASURE_1

Source		Type III Sum of Squares	df	Mean Square	F	Sig.	Partial Eta Squared
Spice	Sphericity Assumed	12.012	1	12.012	39.780	.000	.677
	Greenhouse-Geisser	12.012	1.000	12.012	39.780	.000	.677
	Huynh-Feldt	12.012	1.000	12.012	39.780	.000	.677
	Lower-bound	12.012	1.000	12.012	39.780	.000	.677
Error(Spice)	Sphericity Assumed	5.738	19	.302			
	Greenhouse-Geisser	5.738	19.000	.302			
	Huynh-Feldt	5.738	19.000	.302			
	Lower-bound	5.738	19.000	.302			
Smoke	Sphericity Assumed	9.112	1	9.112	47.598	.000	.715
	Greenhouse-Geisser	9.112	1.000	9.112	47.598	.000	.715
	Huynh-Feldt	9.112	1.000	9.112	47.598	.000	.715
	Lower-bound	9.112	1.000	9.112	47.598	.000	.715
Error(Smoke)	Sphericity Assumed	3.637	19	.191			
	Greenhouse-Geisser	3.637	19.000	.191			
	Huynh-Feldt	3.637	19.000	.191			
	Lower-bound	3.637	19.000	.191			
Spice * Smoke	Sphericity Assumed	1.513	1	1.513	6.782	.017	.263
	Greenhouse-Geisser	1.513	1.000	1.513	6.782	.017	.263
	Huynh-Feldt	1.513	1.000	1.513	6.782	.017	.263
	Lower-bound	1.513	1.000	1.513	6.782	.017	.263
Error(Spice*Smoke)	Sphericity Assumed	4.238	19	.223			
	Greenhouse-Geisser	4.238	19.000	.223			
	Huynh-Feldt	4.238	19.000	.223			
	Lower-bound	4.238	19.000	.223			

Take a moment to look at the labels in the left-hand column. SPSS has produced a pair of rows for both of the IVs and the interaction. You will notice that each of our IVs (e.g., *Spice* and *Smoke*) are paired with an error below it (e.g., *Error(Spice)* and *Error(Smoke)*). Now look at the next column of labels; you see that four labels repeat for each row in the table. We will focus on the rows labeled *Sphericity Assumed*. Again, the other rows are related to an advanced topic that is beyond the scope of this text. By this time you are familiar with the labels for the remaining columns in this table. They identify *SS, df, Mean Square, F, p*, and η^2. To see if there were any significant effects, we look down the column labeled *Sig.* to find our *p* values that are less than the .05 cutoff. In this case, we find that two of the values are in fact less than .001 (reported by SPSS as .000) and that the interaction has *p* = .017! So, we can conclude that there were significant differences in how much our volunteer tasters liked our chili based on the amount of spice, smoke, and the interaction of those two variables.

Now we want to look at the means representing each of those effects. We will look at the table or Spice first.

1. Spice

Measure:MEASURE_1

Spice	Mean	Std. Error	95% Confidence Interval	
			Lower Bound	Upper Bound
1	6.400	.545	5.260	7.540
2	5.625	.544	4.486	6.764

From the table labeled *Spice* we see that they liked the spicy chili, *M* = 6.4, better than the not spicy, *M* = 5.6. You can also find the 95% confidence intervals in case you need to report those or use them in construction of a figure. The next table presents the results for the effect of Smoke.

2. Smoke

Measure:MEASURE_1

Smoke	Mean	Std. Error	95% Confidence Interval	
			Lower Bound	Upper Bound
1	6.350	.533	5.234	7.466
2	5.675	.553	4.518	6.832

In the table labeled *Smoke* we find that the presence of smoke enhanced how much our volunteer tasters liked our chili, *M* = 6.3, compared to when it was tasted without smoke, *M* = 5.7. We must be careful in interpreting these two main effects because the interaction effect suggests a slightly more nuanced interpretation. The next table presents the descriptive statistics for that interaction.

3. Spice * Smoke

Measure:MEASURE_1

Spice	Smoke	Mean	Std. Error	95% Confidence Interval	
				Lower Bound	Upper Bound
1	1	6.600	.545	5.460	7.740
	2	6.200	.551	5.048	7.352
2	1	6.100	.533	4.985	7.215
	2	5.150	.568	3.961	6.339

This final table presents our interaction. We wish that someone could teach SPSS to produce output for factorial designs in APA style. It would save us time and make it easier to interpret the output. Since no one has done that we will have to work with the interaction table that is produced for us. You might need to take a moment to look back at the first table in this output to find out what the "1" and "2" under *Spice* and *Smoke* mean. Let's put the means for our four conditions in a design table like the one on page 117.

	Smoke	Alone
Spicy	6.60	6.20
Not-spicy	6.10	5.15

With that in mind, you might be able to see you can recast these means into an APA-style graph. We went ahead and did that using Microsoft **Excel** to produce the graph included here. Showing you how we did that is beyond the scope of this book. Finally, we will put this all into an APA-style summary.

Writing an APA-Style Results Section

Results

We used a 2(spice) × 2(smoke) within-subjects ANOVA on taste ratings for our soon to be world famous chili. Participants rated the spicy chili ($M = 6.4$, $SD = 2.4$, $n = 20$) significantly more tasty than the mild ($M = 5.6$, $SD = 2.4$, $n = 20$), $F(1, 19) = 39.78$, $p < .001$, $\eta^2 = .68$. They also significantly preferred the taste of both spice levels of chili when tasting with smoke in the air, $F(1, 19) = 47.60$, $p < .001$, $\eta^2 = .71$. Most important, the two variables interacted to effect taste ratings, $F(1, 19) = 6.78$, $p < .001$, $\eta^2 = .26$. We present the mean taste ratings, with 95% confidence intervals, for this interaction between spice and smoke in Figure 1. Our *post hoc* analyses showed that our participants liked both spicy and mild chili significantly more when they were tasted in the presence of smoke; however, the presence of smoke had a stronger effect for the mild chili.

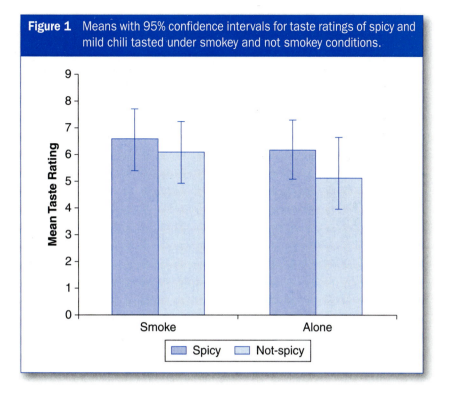

Figure 1 Means with 95% confidence intervals for taste ratings of spicy and mild chili tasted under smokey and not smokey conditions.

You should note that in our APA-style summary, we do not tell our readers how we conducted the *post hoc* analyses to evaluate our interaction. In this case, we conducted two paired-samples *t*-tests. (This statistical test is the first one described in this chapter.) The first compared taste ratings of our spicy chili with and without smoke in the air. The second compared taste ratings of our mild chili with and without smoke in the air. Our general finding is that smoke has a stronger effect on appreciation for the milder chili.

Based on this analysis, we would open our restaurant and serve both kinds of chili, but tell our customers that they are likely to enjoy the spicy chili more than the mild. We would have a wood-burning fireplace or oven so that people would enjoy our chili more but especially the mild version.

Summary

So, at this point, you should know how to conduct the statistical analyses that are most commonly used for data collected in repeated-measures designs, starting with simple two-level designs and ending with factorial design. Remember that each of these can be expanded to include more levels or more variables. In the next chapter, you can learn about the analysis of data collected in some more complicated research designs.

Complicating Matters 10

Advanced Research Designs

A s you saw in Chapter 4, we always advise our students who are first mastering the research process is to keep it simple. But, despite our strongest recommendations, our students' ideas sometimes require complex designs—and the complicated analyses that go with them. In this chapter, we cover the three most common types of designs that go beyond using a completely between-groups design or completely repeated-measures design

First, imagine you are interested in seeing if there is a difference in the number of comments to Facebook posts for males and females for both pictures and status updates. In this case, gender is a between-groups variable, while pictures and status updates represent two levels of a repeated-measures variable. Because one variable is between and the other repeated-measures, we call this a **mixed design**. Number of Facebook posts is the dependent variable. Or, perhaps you are interested in measuring a number of different responses (DVs) to three kinds of movies (as our IV); as a result, your design and analysis becomes a bit more complicated. You might choose to examine comedies, horror movies, and romantic movies and measure different types of responses, such as heart rate, blood pressure, and a self-report rating of interest in the movie. Finally, imagine we think that college students will respond to an alcohol placebo differently when they drink the placebo alone versus drinking the placebo in a group. You can see that the IV is whether or not people are alone when they drink the fake alcohol. Student responses to the drink such as how drunk they act (e.g., loudness of conversations) would be the DV. However, we might be worried that previous experience with alcohol will interfere with student responses to the placebo. In this case, previous experience with alcohol could potentially influence our findings. So, we could measure alcohol experience to control the influence of this

125

variable by analyzing the influence of this potential **covariate**. All three of these higher-level designs can be addressed with extensions or modifications of the factorial research design that we covered in Chapters 8 and 9. Below, we discuss in more detail each of these three types of designs.

Mixed Designs: One Between Variable and One Repeated-Measures Variable

The first higher-level design is called a mixed design because it is a combination of the between- and repeated-measures designs. In other words, you must have at least two IVs in a mixed design. More importantly, it is called mixed because one of those IVs must be a between-groups variable and another a repeated-measures variable. This design is very similar to the other factorial designs, those involving more than one IV we covered earlier in the book (see Chapter 9). You might wonder why anyone would choose to use this design if it is more complex. We will tell you why. Just like the repeated-measures design, the mixed design increases the probability that we will reject the null hypothesis when the research hypothesis is true. In other words, it increases power. That happens because participants are serving as their own controls, and as a result, the variance produced by individual differences among participants has less effect on the value of our statistics. You will remember that this is an advantage when it comes to finding a statistically significant finding, making it more likely that your *p*-value will be less than .05. Just like the factorial designs discussed in Chapters 8 and 9, a mixed design allows us to examine the individual effects of each IV, which you will remember are called *main effects*. It also reveals how those two variables together might impact your DV. This is known as testing for an interaction among your IVs, something you simply cannot do when testing two IVs in two separate experiments.

Let us look at an example of a mixed design. Imagine that there is some reason to believe there might be a difference in distractibility of young male and female drivers. Obviously, gender would be a between-groups variable because a person cannot be both male and female! Gender is a **non-manipulated (pseudo) IV**, and in this example, we have two levels of that variable (although keep in mind that many variables can have more than two levels). For this research, we will gain access to a driving simulator and ask our drivers to complete two similar driving challenges. In one of those challenges, the drivers will complete the course without any obvious distractions. In the second, the drivers will talk on the phone with the researcher while they maneuver in the driving simulator. All participants will "drive the course" both with *and* without the distractions. The outcome, or DV, will be a measure of stopping distance in an emergency situation—a virtual deer running into the virtual road.

So, with the two variables just described, we have a 2 (gender) × 2 (driving condition) mixed design with driving condition as a repeated-measures variable. Notice that we have kept this factorial design as simple as possible by including only two IVs (one is a non-manipulated (pseudo) independent variable) and limiting those variables to two levels each. When your research questions demand it, the mixed design can be expanded to include more IVs (manipulated or pseudo), or more levels of either of the IVs. For example, we could have included a third "distraction" group with music as a distraction, making this a 2 (gender) × 3 (driving condition) mixed design.

Data with one between-groups variable and one repeated-measures variable is called a mixed design. Such a design should be analyzed with a mixed-model analysis of variance (ANOVA). Just like the design, the analysis is a combination of a simple between-groups analysis and a simple repeated-measures analysis with the advantage of testing an interaction between the IVs.

Now, let us take a look at a design where we include that third driving condition. When we include the driving condition of music-distraction, we now have a 3 (driving conditions) × 2 (sex) mixed design with driving condition manipulated within groups. All participants would complete the course under each of the three conditions. (Yes, of course, we imagine counterbalancing our conditions to control for possible carry-over effects described in Chapter 9.) Notice that our description of the mixed design includes naming the variable that is manipulated within groups. That additional information is important to indicate because remember in a mixed design any of the variables could be varied either between groups or within groups.

Using SPSS

Some of the data from our created data set is shown in the next SPSS screenshot. For this data file, we needed to include five columns.

	participant	sex	control	phone	music	va
1	1	0	55	98	59	
2	2	0	34	83	37	
3	3	0	57	116	67	
4	4	0	50	110	47	
5	5	0	60	115	64	
6	6	0	57	105	61	
7	7	0	53	98	58	
8	8	0	33	102	39	
9	9	0	47	110	52	
10	10	0	48	96	53	
11	11	1	40	89	43	
12	12	1	61	102	66	
13	13	1	37	75	43	

The first column is for the participant identifier so we can look back at our original datasheets if needed. The second column identifies the sex of our participants (0 = "Female" and 1 = "Male"). The next three columns are for our DV, the stopping distance in feet for each of our three driving conditions ("control" = undistracted, "phone" = talking on the phone, and "music" = music playing on the "car" stereo).

The mixed-model ANOVA is conducted with the same SPSS procedure that we use for the within-subjects ANOVA. The procedure is described in detail in Chapter 9. You will use the same series of mouse clicks to open the procedure: click on *Analyze, General Linear, Model*, then *Repeated Measures.*

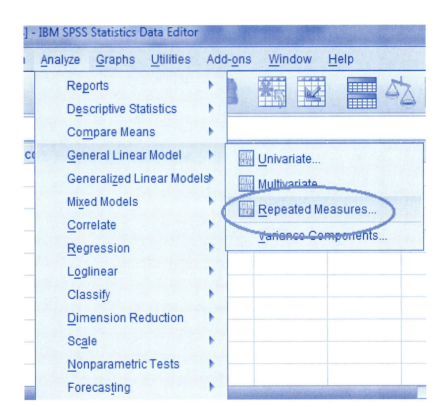

The first dialogue box for the *Repeated Measures* procedure is shown in the following screenshot.

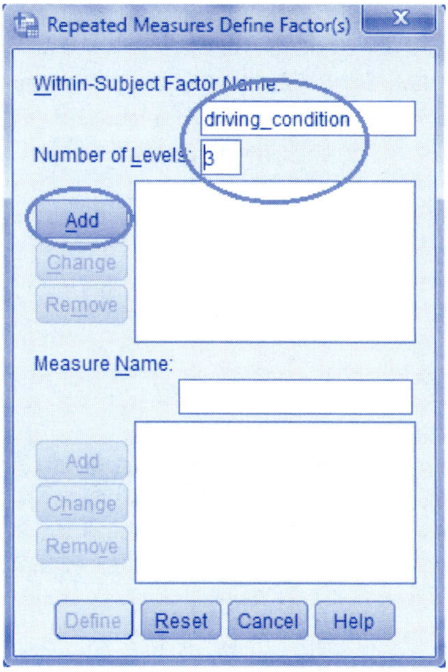

In Chapter 9, you learned how to set up the within-subjects part of this analysis. We typed "driving_condition" in the *Within-Subject Factor Name* text box, "3" in the *Number of Levels* box, and then clicked the *Add* button. The result is shown in the next screenshot.

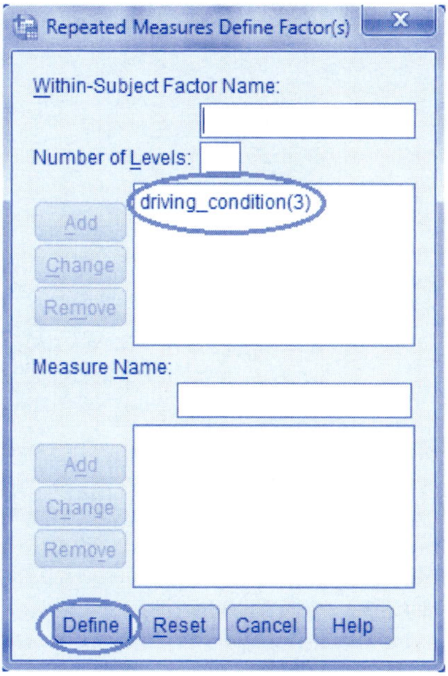

You can see how the dialogue box changed when we clicked the *Add* button. A click on the *Define* button will open the following dialogue box.

The next screenshot shows the dialogue box before we move our variables.

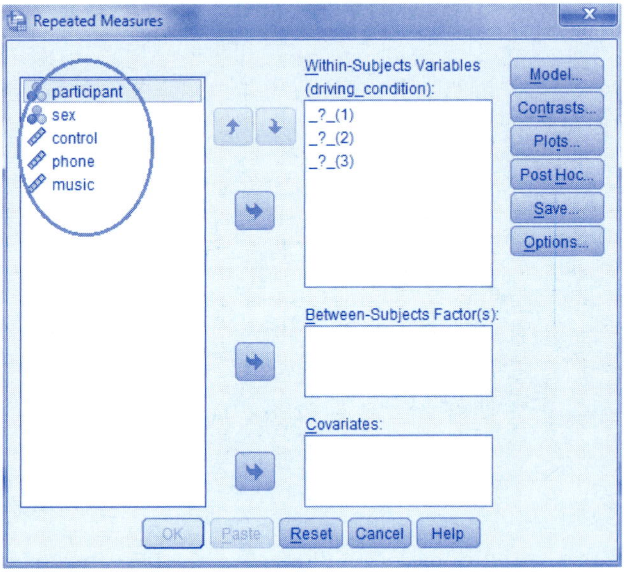

Notice that all of our variable names are listed in the textbox at left. The next screenshot shows you how this dialogue box looks after we have moved the three levels of driving conditions to the *Within-Subjects Variables* box.

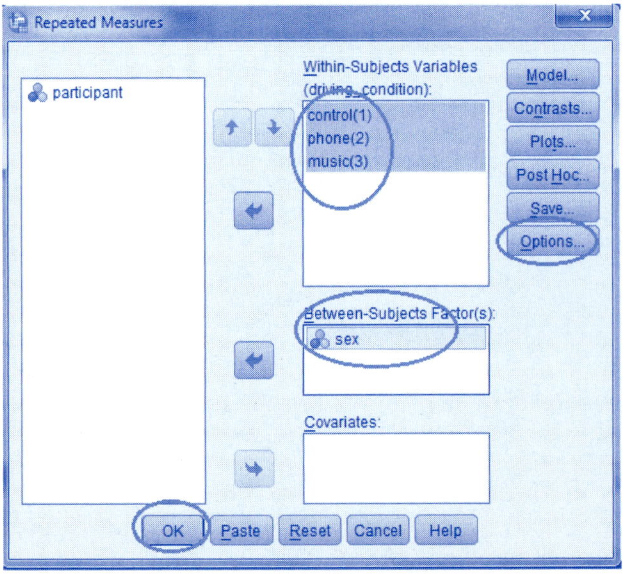

Notice that we moved the conditions of our within-subjects variable to the numbers listed in the middle top box. In this case, the numbering of the conditions does not make a difference, that is, "control" as 1, "phone" as 2, and "music" as 3. However, the order could make a difference for some advanced analyses not covered in this book, so you should always think about that order before you move the variable names. The variable name "sex" that was our between-groups variable was moved into the *Between-Subjects Factor(s)* box. This procedure has useful Options that were described in Chapter 9. To use them you click on the *Options* button (circled above) and open the following dialogue box.

We selected the same options here, *Descriptive statistics* and *Estimates of effect size*, to get SPSS to calculate the descriptive statistics and effect size for us. We also moved the names for each of our IVs and for the interaction into the *Display Means for* box. Finally, we selected the *LSD* (least squared differences) option in case we get a significant main effect for driving condition. This option will produce a *post hoc* analysis and allow us to see if there are specific differences for stopping distance among the three levels of driving condition. Including the sex and the interaction between driving condition and sex in the *Display Means* box will produce tables of descriptive statistics for each main effect and the interaction. To make SPSS work its magic you click on the *Continue* button and then on the *OK* button in the main dialogue box.

Wait a few seconds and you will see an even longer output file than some of those that we described in Chapter 9. When you look carefully, you will realize that there is one additional table in this output that is useful while the same less-than-useful tables also appear ☺.

We have circled the names of the tables that you will need to examine to present the results of this analysis. In the next few pages, we review each of those tables and show you where to find the critical information in each.

The *Within-Subjects Factors* table appears first and shows you that SPSS has assigned the number 1 to the control condition, 2 to the phone condition, and 3 to the music condition.

Within-Subjects Factors

Measure:MEASURE_1

driving_condition	Dependent Variable
1	control
2	phone
3	music

We will need to use those numbers when we interpret the descriptive statistics for driving condition.

The *Between-Subjects Factors* table simply reminds us that we had two levels of sex in our dataset, Female and Male, and that we had 10 participants in each group.

Between-Subjects Factors		Value Label	N
sex	0	Female	10
	1	Male	10

You can find the means and standard deviations for the main effect of driving condition and the interaction effect in the *Descriptive Statistics* tables.

Descriptive Statistics

	sex	Mean	Std. Deviation	N
control	Female	49.40	9.348	10
	Male	45.80	10.401	10
	Total	47.60	9.800	20
phone	Female	103.30	10.078	10
	Male	94.00	13.408	10
	Total	98.65	12.491	20
music	Female	53.70	10.144	10
	Male	51.30	11.719	10
	Total	52.50	10.739	20

We have circled the means for each of the driving conditions to help you see where they can be found. We will use these values later when we report our results. At a first glance, it looks like there is a substantial difference in mean stopping distances among the three conditions (control = 47.6 ft., phone = 98.65 ft., and music = 52.5 ft.). The interaction effect is difficult to see in this table. We can see that females in the control condition stopped in an average of 49.4 ft., while males stopped in an average of 45.8 ft. We need to compare that difference to the phone condition when females stopped in an average of 103.3 ft. and males in an average of 94 ft. We know! It is hard to track those differences in your head. So, when we present our results, we will need an APA-style table or a graph to present the interaction.

Continuing with our interpretation of the output tables, again, we will ignore the tables that are not circled in the output tree, for example, *Multivariate Tests* and *Mauchley's Test of Sphericity*. Take a moment to look at the *Tests of Within-Subjects Effects* table presented in the next screenshot.

Tests of Within-Subjects Effects

Measure:MEASURE_1

Source		Type III Sum of Squares	df	Mean Square	F	Sig.	Partial Eta Squared
driving_condition	Sphericity Assumed	31732.900	2	15866.450	579.381	.000	.970
	Greenhouse-Geisser	31732.900	1.200	26452.578	579.381	.000	.970
	Huynh-Feldt	31732.900	1.309	24241.444	579.381	.000	.970
	Lower-bound	31732.900	1.000	31732.900	579.381	.000	.970
driving_condition * sex	Sphericity Assumed	135.900	2	67.950	2.481	.098	.121
	Greenhouse-Geisser	135.900	1.200	113.286	2.481	.126	.121
	Huynh-Feldt	135.900	1.309	103.817	2.481	.122	.121
	Lower-bound	135.900	1.000	135.900	2.481	.133	.121
Error(driving_condition)	Sphericity Assumed	985.867	36	27.385			
	Greenhouse-Geisser	985.867	21.593	45.657			
	Huynh-Feldt	985.867	23.563	41.840			
	Lower-bound	985.867	18.000	54.770			

You can see that this table has the same "extra information" that we found for within-subjects ANOVAs in Chapter 9. Again here, we will use only the top rows labeled as *Sphericity Assumed* (circled above). Once you ignore the extra rows you can see a standard ANOVA table (look back at Chapter 9 for an example). We have one row for the driving condition effect, one for the interaction of driving and sex, and one for error. Looking down the column labeled *Sig.*, we find that there is a significant difference among the three driving conditions ($p < .001$), and we see that the interaction is not statistically significant ($p = .098$). We have circled the values for our effect-size statistics for both the driving conditions, $\eta^2 = .97$, and interaction, $\eta^2 = .12$. We hope that you are now asking yourself something like, "Well, where is the test for the difference between male and female drivers?" That effect appears in a separate table labeled *Tests of Between-Subjects Effects*. Take a look at the next screenshot and see if we found a difference between males and females.

Tests of Between-Subjects Effects

Measure:MEASURE_1
Transformed Variable:Average

Source	Type III Sum of Squares	df	Mean Square	F	Sig.	Partial Eta Squared
Intercept	263343.750	1	263343.750	866.827	.000	.980
sex	390.150	1	390.150	1.284	.272	.067
Error	5468.433	18	303.802			

You likely noticed that this ANOVA table has an extra row labeled *Intercept*. You can ignore this row. You can find the *p*-value for the difference between female and male drivers in the usual place, the row labeled *sex* and the column labeled *Sig.*, and find that the difference between the two groups is not statistically significant ($p = .272$). The value for η^2 appears in the column just to the right of our value for *Sig.*, in this case .067.

Take a moment to think about what we have found in these last tables. We did not find a significant interaction or main effect for sex in stopping distance; however, we did find a significant difference among the three driving conditions. To understand these results, our primary focus will be on the means for the driving conditions, but we also need to look at the means for the interaction.

The next table shows the means with standard errors and 95% **confidence intervals** for each of the driving effects. The newest guidelines for APA style strongly recommend reporting of confidence intervals, so your instructor might require that you include them in your reports. Most researchers interpret confidence intervals as the range of values that are 95% likely to include the true population mean. When you look at the next screenshot, you will see that the confidence interval for the control condition is 42.95 to 52.24 ft. So we expect, with 95% confidence, that the population mean for stopping distance falls between those values.

Estimates

Measure:MEASURE_1

driving_condition	Mean	Std. Error	95% Confidence Interval	
			Lower Bound	Upper Bound
1	47.600	2.211	42.955	52.245
2	98.650	2.652	93.078	104.222
3	52.500	2.451	47.351	57.649

These values tell the story of the main effect that most interests us in this analysis. You can see that driving condition "2" produced the longest stopping distance. That is what we expected; now, we need to see if this stopping distance is different from the control condition. Do you remember what that "2" represents? If you have forgotten, you can look back at the *Within-Subjects Factors* table on page 132 and see that it represents the phone condition. We are also interested in seeing if it takes longer to stop when talking on the phone or listening to music.

The *Pairwise Comparisons* table will give us that information. We are very happy! Scan down the column labeled *Sig.* and see if any of those values are less than .05.

Pairwise Comparisons

Measure:MEASURE_1

(I) driving_condition	(J) driving_condition	Mean Difference (I-J)	Std. Error	Sig.[a]	95% Confidence Interval for Difference[a]	
					Lower Bound	Upper Bound
1 control	2 phone	-51.050*	1.967	.000	-55.182	-46.918
	3 music	-4.900*	.708	.000	-6.388	-3.412
2	1	51.050*	1.967	.000	46.918	55.182
	3	46.150*	1.961	.000	42.030	50.270
3	1	4.900*	.708	.000	3.412	6.388
	2	-46.150*	1.961	.000	-50.270	-42.030

Based on estimated marginal means

*. The mean difference is significant at the .05 level.
a. Adjustment for multiple comparisons: Least Significant Difference (equivalent to no adjustments).

They all are less than .05, so we know that stopping distance in each of the driving conditions differed from the other conditions. You remember from Chapter 9 that there is some repetition in this table. We added some labels to the following screenshot (that would not be included in your actual SPSS output) to help you see how the numbers and driving conditions are related, and circled only the values that we need to consider to compare differences in the means for condition 1 (control) and 2 (phone), 1 (control) and 3 (music), and 2 (phone) and 3 (music).

As you can see in the next table called *Estimates*, there was very little difference between mean differences in stopping distances between females and males.

Estimates

Measure:MEASURE_1

sex	Mean	Std. Error	95% Confidence Interval	
			Lower Bound	Upper Bound
Female	68.800	3.182	62.114	75.486
Male	63.700	3.182	57.014	70.386

This *Estimates* table is the only place that we can find the means for any between-groups **main effects**. When reporting your results, you might need to report the standard deviation. Unfortunately, this table provides only the standard error and **95% confidence intervals** for measures of variability in those groups. Luckily, you can calculate standard deviation easily with the following equation.

$$SD = SE * \sqrt{N}$$

For this output, we have an unusual situation because the standard errors for both groups are the same: 3.182. We had 10 males and 10 females in our groups. So, $SD = 3.182 * \sqrt{10} = 10.06$ for both groups.

The next table shows the means with standard errors and 95% confidence intervals for the interaction between driving condition and sex of the driver. You do not need to conduct any calculations to find the standard deviations for the means presented on this table. You can find the SDs in the *Descriptive Statistics* table on page 133.

3. sex * driving_condition

Measure:MEASURE_1

sex	driving_condition	Mean	Std. Error	95% Confidence Interval	
				Lower Bound	Upper Bound
Female	1	49.400	3.127	42.831	55.969
	2	103.300	3.751	95.420	111.180
	3	53.700	3.466	46.418	60.982
Male	1	45.800	3.127	39.231	52.369
	2	94.000	3.751	86.120	101.880
	3	51.300	3.466	44.018	58.582

You can see the same pattern of stopping distance differences for the three driving conditions between males and females. For example, in the control condition, females stopped in an average of 49.4 ft. compared to 45.8 ft. for the males, a difference of 3.6 ft.; while in the music condition, the difference was 53.7 – 51.3 ft., or 2.6 ft. This pattern of similar differences explains why we did not find a significant interaction effect. We are ready to put this all together in an APA-style results section.

Writing an APA-Style Results Section

Results

We conducted a 2 (sex) × 3 (driving conditions) mixed-model ANOVA on stopping distance in a simulated driving emergency. Driving conditions served as the within-groups variable. There was a significant difference among the three driving conditions, $F(2, 36) = 579.38$, $p < .01$, $\eta^2 = .97$. As expected, the stopping distance in the phone condition was the longest ($M = 98.65$ ft, $SD = 12.49$, $n = 20$), followed by stopping distance in the music condition ($M = 52.50$ ft, $SD = 10.74$, $n = 20$), and finally the shortest stopping distance was found in the control condition ($M = 47.60$ ft, $SD = 9.8$, $n = 20$). Post hoc analyses showed that all three of these means differed from each other, $p < .001$. Females and males did not differ reliably from each other, $F(1, 18) = 1.28$, $p = .24$, $\eta^2 = .067$. Further, there was not a significant interaction between driving condition and sex, $F(2, 36) = 2.48$, $p = .10$, $\eta^2 = .12$.

These results would provide an interesting discussion. We found that driving condition affected stopping distance. In particular, talking on the phone extended stopping distance quite a bit, perhaps enough to cause an accident. Even listening to music extended stopping distance over the undistracted condition. As we expected, there were no significant differences in stopping distances for females and males. The lack of a significant interaction tells us that the males and females in our sample did not seem to differ in how distracted they were by listening to music or talking on the phone. Based on these findings, perhaps you might want to conduct another study to measure not only stopping distance, but also the number of errors made while driving under the three different driving conditions. The next complex design allows us to measure multiple DVs in a single research project.

A Multivariate Design: Measuring It All Including More Than One Dependent Variable in Your Design

Now, we turn to a design in which you can measure multiple dependent measures, a **multivariate design**. Imagine that we want to examine emotional responses to two stimuli: violent and non-violent video games. We will randomly assign our participants to one of two groups, and each will play the assigned video game for 30 minutes. After 20 minutes, we will measure our participants' emotional responses. You know how hard it is to measure emotional responses, so we plan to take multiple measures: blood pressure, heart rate, pressure on the game controller, and a verbal measure of "excitement." By using all of these DVs, we will get a more valid measure of the underlying construct, emotion. By using multiple measures, we also increase the chance that we will not overlook an important effect of our manipulation. If we measured only one dependent measure, this would be an example of a simple one-way, between-groups design. You will remember from Chapter 8 that we could use a *t*-test to analyze the difference between the two groups. When we include multiple dependent variables, we do not conduct four separate analyses (one for each DV) because this would increase the probability of reporting that we found an interesting result that was not real. Instead, we use a multivariate design in which we conduct a combined analysis of all of the DVs in one analysis. The general test of the whole darn design tells us if *any* of the four dependent measures yielded a meaningful difference between the two groups.

Even though we are using a few DVs, the design is pretty simple. We have a one-way, between-groups multivariate design; the IV has only two levels—the four DVs make it "multivariate." The multivariate design is just as flexible as the factorial research design. The multivariate design could be combined with any kind of factorial design when you need more than one IV. Again, we recommend that you keep your design as simple as possible while still being able to answer your research question. If possible, think in terms of one IV with several levels, or two IVs with two levels each. Then, use a few DVs as outcome measures. We find that even in our own work, simpler designs yield analyses that are much easier to interpret.

A multivariate design, with multiple DVs, is tested with a special type of analysis of variance typically referred to as a **MANOVA (multivariate analysis of variance)**. The SPSS output produced by this analysis is longer than other ANOVA output. That happens because the initial analysis considers all of the DVs at once, and then follow-up analyses present the results for each individual DV. As a result, our students often find the output intimidating at first, but with a little practice, you will find it easy to navigate. The trick is to evaluate that initial analysis first and *then* interpret the individual ANOVAs for each dependent variable as needed. Let us take a look at an example of this type of design.

A student of ours was interested in the development of bargaining behavior among children. She asked children of various ages to play the Dictator Game with marshmallows. In this game, children were given 10 marshmallows and asked to divide them between themselves and one other player. They could keep and give away as many as they wanted. There was one catch; if the other player rejected the offer, then the two children playing the game would not get to keep any marshmallows. With age as a non-manipulated IV, the question was whether the bargaining behavior changed between ages 3 and 12. This game is typically played only once with adults; however, our student wanted to offer the children a second chance to make an offer after they thought about the fewest number of marshmallows they would accept from the other player. As a result, the student had three DVs: number of marshmallows in the first offer, smallest number of marshmallows that would be acceptable, and number of marshmallows in the second offer. The design of the experiment is a simple between-groups design with three levels for age (3–5 years, 6–9 years, and 10–12 years). The inclusion of three closely related DVs makes the design a multivariate between-groups design. The appropriate analysis for this design is a MANOVA.

Using SPSS

The next screenshot shows you what the data file looks like for this analysis. In this case, we need at least four columns: One identifies the three age groups (3–5 years, 6–9 years, and 10–12 years), a second contains the number of marshmallows in the first offer, a third the smallest number of marshmallows that was deemed acceptable, and a fourth the number in the second offer.

So we have one column for the IV (i.e., the age group) and one column for each of the three DVs. To conduct this analysis you would click *Analyze, General Linear Model*, then *Multivariate*.

That sequence opens the following dialogue box. The next screenshot shows you the dialogue box that we use to move the variable names to the appropriate boxes to indicate the DV and IV.

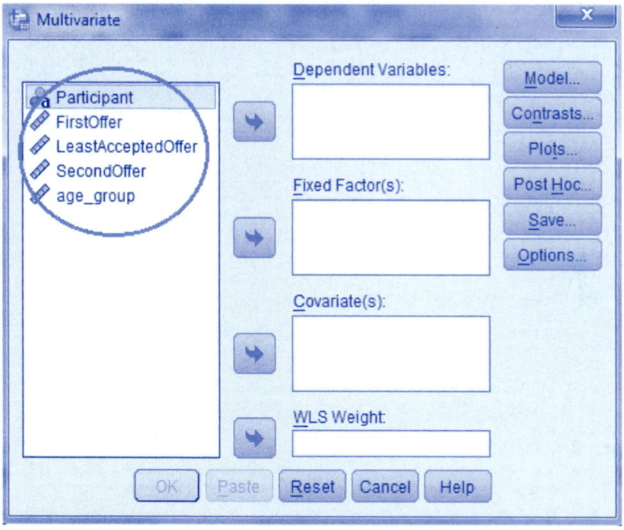

When the dialogue first opens, all of our variable names are in the box at the left of the screen. The DVs, "First Offer," "Least Acceptable Offer," and "Second Offer," will be moved into the *Dependent Variables* box using the arrow. Then "age_group" will be moved into the *Fixed Factor(s)* box. Note that SPSS calls the IVs in this type of design the Fixed Factors. The next screenshot shows what the completed dialogue box looks like.

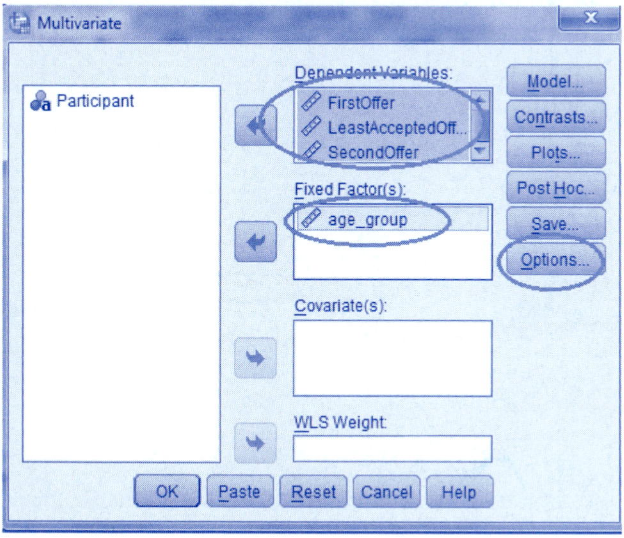

Next, we clicked on the *Options* button to open the following dialogue box.

In this box, as usual, we selected *Descriptive statistics* and *Estimates of effect size*. If we wanted confidence intervals or standard errors, we would have moved our grouping variable ("age_group") into the *Display Means for* box. Then we clicked on the *Continue* button. That took us back to the original dialogue box.

Our IV has three levels, so we anticipate needing a *post hoc* test to evaluate possible differences between the age groups. We clicked the *Post Hoc* button to open the following dialogue box.

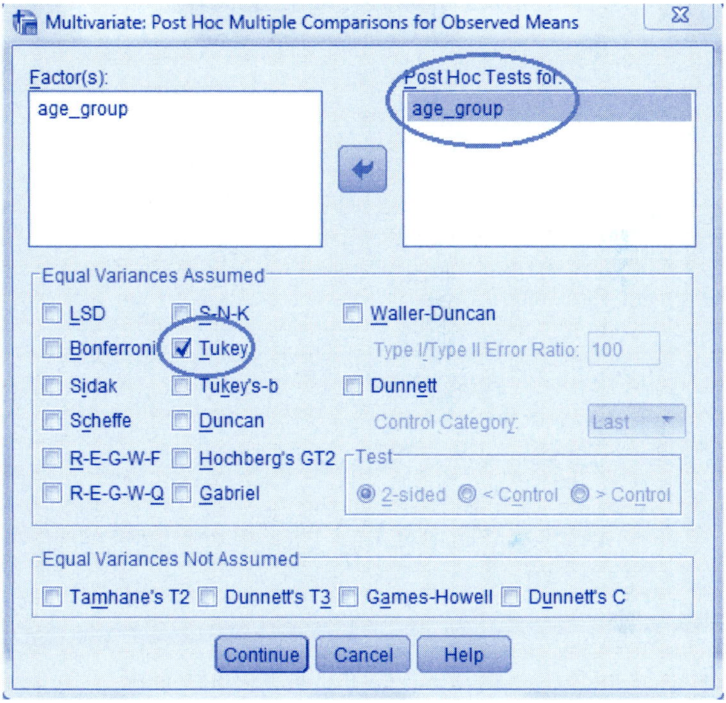

In this dialogue, we moved the name of our IV ("age_group") into the "*Post Hoc Tests for*" box and selected *Tukey*. Notice that there are many possible *post hoc* analyses. You should consult with a professor or an experienced researcher to get advice about which of these is the best for your research project. That advice should be obtained before you collect your data, if possible, but certainly before you start your analyses. We choose Tukey as an acceptably conservative test of possible differences among these three age groups. Next, we clicked on the *Continue* button and then the *OK* button in the original dialogue box to tell SPSS to conduct the analysis.

The output for this procedure is very well organized. Unlike some of the other examples in this chapter that use the *General Linear Model* procedure, for this one, we will use almost all of the tables. The following screenshot shows you the list of tables in the output.

The *Between-Subjects Factors* is the first table in the output.

Between-Subjects Factors

		Value Label	N
age_group	.00	3 - 5	14
	1.00	6 - 9	13
	2.00	10 - 12	10

The column to the far right labeled *N* tells us that there were 14 children in the 3–5 age group, 13 in the 6–9 age group, and 10 in the 10–12 age group. We always check these numbers against our other records to make sure that data from all of our participants are included in the analysis and that there are no extra data. The next table does just what its name indicates; it presents the *Descriptive Statistics*. Take a look at the way the means, standard deviations, and *N*s are grouped in this table.

Descriptive Statistics

	age_group	Mean	Std. Deviation	N
FirstOffer	3 - 5	3.0714	1.26881	14
	6 - 9	5.4615	2.25889	13
	10 - 12	4.3000	1.56702	10
	Total	4.2432	1.99172	37
LeastAcceptedOffer	3 - 5	1.3571	1.33631	14
	6 - 9	2.5385	2.47034	13
	10 - 12	2.7000	1.56702	10
	Total	2.1351	1.91721	37
SecondOffer	3 - 5	4.5000	2.17503	14
	6 - 9	5.6923	2.01596	13
	10 - 12	4.3000	1.15950	10
	Total	4.8649	1.94597	37

You can easily find the average number of marshmallows offered by each age group in the first and second trials, as well as the least acceptable offer. The SPSS table also presents the overall means for each dependent variable, labeled as *Total* (circled above). So, for example, we find that when ignoring the age group, children made an average first offer of 4.2 marshmallows and a second offer of 4.9 marshmallows.

The *Multivariate Tests* table is next in the SPSS output. It is a little harder to read because it includes more information than we typically need. At first glance it looks a little like an ANOVA table, but the format of columns and rows is not quite familiar because it includes several choices for multivariate statistics and two columns for degrees of freedom associated with each.

Multivariate Tests[c]

Effect		Value	F	Hypothesis df	Error df	Sig.	Partial Eta Squared
Intercept	Pillai's Trace	.937	158.730[a]	3.000	32.000	.000	.937
	Wilks' Lambda	.063	158.730[a]	3.000	32.000	.000	.937
	Hotelling's Trace	14.881	158.730[a]	3.000	32.000	.000	.937
	Roy's Largest Root	14.881	158.730[a]	3.000	32.000	.000	.937
age_group	Pillai's Trace	.522	3.887	6.000	66.000	.002	.261
	Wilks' Lambda	.508	4.301[a]	6.000	64.000	.001	.287
	Hotelling's Trace	.910	4.701	6.000	62.000	.001	.313
	Roy's Largest Root	.839	9.231[b]	3.000	33.000	.000	.456

a. Exact statistic

b. The statistic is an upper bound on F that yields a lower bound on the significance level.

c. Design: Intercept + age_group

You can ignore all of the rows in the box labeled *Intercept*. Start by looking at the second group of rows, labeled "age_group," which presents the multivariate evaluation of differences between our age groups. This multivariate effect is an indication that one or more of the DVs changed with age. We check for a significant effect in the usual way: See if the value for *Sig.* is equal to or less than .05. As you can see, .001 is indeed less than .05. If we fail to get a multivariate effect, then our analysis is finished. We do need to discuss the fact that this table presents four different statistics for the multivariate effect. Each of these can tell us if there is a significant difference for any of our DVs. We choose *Wilk's Lambda* (λ); however, this is another of those circumstances in which you should check with an experienced researcher to see which is the best choice for your data. Additional information needed for an APA-style results section can also be found in this same row. Here is what the APA-style report for the *Wilk's Lamba* should look like: $\lambda = .508$, $F(6, 64) = 4.301$, $p = .001$. All of the values used in this report are circled in the table. So, we rejected the null hypothesis of no difference among any of the DVs. We know that *as a group*, these DVs have something interesting to tell us. Now, we need to see specifically which of the DVs showed a difference among the age groups. We do that in the next step of a multivariate analysis by conducting one-way ANOVAs for each dependent variable.

SPSS presents those results in the next table, *Tests of Between-Subjects Effects.* Look at all of the labels in the column labeled *Source.*

Tests of Between-Subjects Effects

Source	Dependent Variable	Type III Sum of Squares	df	Mean Square	F	Sig.	Partial Eta Squared
Corrected Model	FirstOffer	38.551ᵃ	2	19.276	6.286	.005	.270
	LeastAcceptedOffer	13.779ᵇ	2	6.890	1.976	.154	.104
	SecondOffer	13.955ᶜ	2	6.978	1.939	.159	.102
Intercept	FirstOffer	663.112	1	663.112	216.247	.000	.864
	LeastAcceptedOffer	175.163	1	175.163	50.239	.000	.596
	SecondOffer	845.684	1	845.684	234.971	.000	.874
age_group	FirstOffer	38.551	2	19.276	6.286	.005	.270
	LeastAcceptedOffer	13.779	2	6.890	1.976	.154	.104
	SecondOffer	13.955	2	6.978	1.939	.159	.102
Error	FirstOffer	104.259	34	3.066			
	LeastAcceptedOffer	118.545	34	3.487			
	SecondOffer	122.369	34	3.599			
Total	FirstOffer	809.000	37				
	LeastAcceptedOffer	301.000	37				
	SecondOffer	1012.000	37				
Corrected Total	FirstOffer	142.811	36				
	LeastAcceptedOffer	132.324	36				
	SecondOffer	136.324	36				

a. R Squared = .270 (Adjusted R Squared = .227)

b. R Squared = .104 (Adjusted R Squared = .051)

c. R Squared = .102 (Adjusted R Squared = .050)

You likely have an intuition that many of these will not be useful to you because you do not remember them from other ANOVA tables. If so, your intuition is correct; you can ignore the rows labeled *Corrected Model, Intercept, Total,* and *Corrected Total.*

The inferential statistics that we need are found in the remaining two rows. Look at the block of rows next to the name of our IV ("age_group") and notice that there is a row for each our DVs. Each of these rows offers the *F*-ratio and other values for the separate one-way between-groups ANOVA for each of the three variables. As before, you scan across a row to the column labeled *Sig.* to find values equal to or less than .05 (we hope). "First offer" has a *p*-value of .005, so there is a significant difference in the mean number of marshmallows in the first offer. In other words, children of different ages offered significantly different numbers of marshmallows in their first offer. Our remaining two DVs have *p*-values of .154 and .159. Because these values are not less than or equal to the all-important .05 value, we cannot reject the null hypothesis for least acceptable number of marshmallows or number of marshmallows in the second offer. That is, children of different ages did not reliably differ across these two DVs.

Now that we know something interesting is happening across age groups when it comes to their first offer of marshmallows, we need to explore that effect to see exactly which age groups differ from each other. Time again to look at *post hoc* analyses included in the output file.

The *Multiple Comparisons* table presents the *post hoc* analysis for each of the one-way ANOVAs.

Multiple Comparisons

Tukey HSD

Dependent Variable	(I) age_group	(J) age_group	Mean Difference (I-J)	Std. Error	Sig.	95% Confidence Interval Lower Bound	95% Confidence Interval Upper Bound
FirstOffer	3 - 5	6 - 9	-2.3901*	.67447	.003	-4.0429	-.7374
		10 - 12	-1.2286	.72504	.222	-3.0052	.5481
	6 - 9	3 - 5	2.3901*	.67447	.003	.7374	4.0429
		10 - 12	1.1615	.73656	.269	-.6434	2.9664
	10 - 12	3 - 5	1.2286	.72504	.222	-.5481	3.0052
		6 - 9	-1.1615	.73656	.269	-2.9664	.6434
LeastAcceptedOffer	3 - 5	6 - 9	-1.1813	.71920	.242	-2.9437	.5810
		10 - 12	-1.3429	.77311	.206	-3.2373	.5516
	6 - 9	3 - 5	1.1813	.71920	.242	-.5810	2.9437
		10 - 12	-.1615	.78541	.977	-2.0861	1.7630
	10 - 12	3 - 5	1.3429	.77311	.206	-.5516	3.2373
		6 - 9	.1615	.78541	.977	-1.7630	2.0861
SecondOffer	3 - 5	6 - 9	-1.1923	.73071	.246	-2.9829	.5982
		10 - 12	.2000	.78549	.965	-1.7248	2.1248
	6 - 9	3 - 5	1.1923	.73071	.246	-.5982	2.9829
		10 - 12	1.3923	.79797	.204	-.5631	3.3477
	10 - 12	3 - 5	-.2000	.78549	.965	-2.1248	1.7248
		6 - 9	-1.3923	.79797	.204	-3.3477	.5631

Based on observed means.

The error term is Mean Square(Error) = 3.599.

*. The mean difference is significant at the .05 level.

Again, this SPSS table has a lot of information that is not useful to us. In this case, you might anticipate why that happened. We asked for the *post hoc* analyses, but we did not specify which DVs should be included; we allowed SPSS to run all *post hoc* tests even though we are only interested in the *post hoc* analysis for a the one significant effect. In other words, SPSS conducted *post hoc* analyses for the two DVs that did not reveal significant age differences. However, given our ANOVA results, we will ignore those and only consider the part of the table that includes the analysis of the first offer of marshmallows. Remember, that was the DV with significant results in the *Tests of Between-Subjects Effects* table. When we look at the *Multiple Comparisons* table, we find that there is only one significant difference: The 3–5 year-olds made significantly lower offers than the 6–9 year-olds. Now we need to summarize all of these results in APA style. We think that since there are so many means it is best to include a table along with the results section.

Writing an APA-Style Results Section

Results

The mean numbers of marshmallows offered or accepted with standard deviations for each age group are presented in Table 1. The one-way between-groups multivariate analysis revealed a significant overall effect, $\lambda = .51$, $F(6, 64) = 4.30$, $p = .002$. Individual one-way between groups ANOVAs showed that there was a difference among age groups for the number of marshmallows offered in the first trial, $F(2, 34) = 6.29$, $p = .005$, $\eta^2 = .27$. However, there was not a significant difference among age groups for smallest accepted offer, $p = .15$, or for the number of marshmallows offered on the second trial, $p = .16$. Finally, *post hoc* analyses (Tukey) showed that the youngest group (3–5 year-olds) offered significantly fewer marshmallows than the (6–9 year-olds). None of the other differences were statistically meaningful (all p's > .05).

Table 1 Mean Number of Marshmallows Offered or Accepted With Standard Deviations in Parentheses for the Three Age Groups

	Age Groups		
	3–5 years	**6–9 years**	**10–11 years**
Offer	$n = 14$	$n = 13$	$n = 10$
First	3.1 (1.3)	5.5 (2.3)	4.3 (1.6)
Least Accepted	1.4 (1.3)	2.5 (2.5)	2.7 (1.6)
Second	4.5 (2.2)	5.7 (2.0)	4.3 (1.2)

So, it turns out that the youngest kids playing the Dictator Game offered fewer marshmallows on the first trials than the next older age group. Likely, they wanted more for themselves and did not fully understand the nature of the game in that first trial. With a second chance, they acted like older kids.

Remember that the multivariate design can be expanded in the same ways as an ordinary research design. The term *multivariate* only means that we measure several dependent variables. We can manipulate variables between groups, and we can manipulate more than one variable while taking several measures. We can do similar manipulations but make them repeated measures for a repeated-measures design. And, as you saw in the beginning of this chapter, you can mix those two basic designs to produce a mixed-design.

You and our student both know that the difference in number of marshmallows first offered was not the result of age but rather of some change that was associated with differences in ages. It would be interesting to get a measure of understanding of numbers or compassion and see if changes in those capacities "explain" the age differences. In that case, one of these measures would serve as a covariate to age; we take up that kind of research design in the next section.

ANCOVA

The third research design we promised in this chapter allows you to include a covariate. Including a covariate variable allows you to control for unwanted variability that might overshadow the effect of your IV. A research design has a covariate when you measure an existing variable across all of your participants (something like IQ scores or a personality factor) because you think it might add fluctuations to your DV. As an example, imagine we would like to evaluate two different learning techniques, our IV (e.g., a lecture-based class compared to a discussion-based class). Here, our DV will be test grades. We have two sections of Introduction to Psychology that we can use for this experiment; one meets at 8:00 am MWF, and the other meets at 9:00 am MWF. We might flip a coin to decide which section experiences the lecture and which the discussion. So far, you will recognize this design as a simple between-groups design with two levels. It will not take you long to think of many differences between the two sections that might affect the outcome of our experiment—not just lecture versus discussion!

Before reading on: What are some of those differences that come to mind?

One possible difference is "college preparedness" of the people in the two classes. We will not know until we collect our data if there is any difference between the two classes on this variable, but if there is, it could confound our results. In addition, variation in college preparedness within each class will affect individual performance on the tests and make it more difficult to find a difference between the two kinds of class when there is one. We could use scores on a college entrance test like the ACT or SAT to measure these individual differences in college preparedness. (Yes, we are aware of the controversy about such measures.) When we conduct our analysis, we would use these scores to "control" for individual differences both within and between our two groups. This type of secondary variable is called a covariate. We now have a one-way between-groups design with score on a college entrance test as a covariate. By including this additional measure, the design will allow us to remove some of the variability based on college preparedness and more clearly examine what is really going on with lecture- versus discussion-based courses.

You might be thinking, "Wait a minute, could I divide my participants into two or three groups based on their college entrance exam scores. I would then have a factorial design like the one described in Chapter 8." The short answer is, "Yes, you could." When you do that you lose some power in your statistical analysis. There are also times when your covariate is more of a nuisance variable than a confounding variable. In these cases you should take advantage of the whole range of possible values in your covariate.

When you encounter covariate designs in journal articles, they are often referred to in terms of the statistical analysis; the shorthand for that analysis is **ANCOVA**, which stands for **analysis of covariance**. With this design, you will often analyze your data in two steps (one without the covariate and a second with the covariate). A comparison between the two results will inform you about the strength of the covariate in your research project. You can think of this whole process as showing that the covariate has not interfered with the effects of the IV on the DV.

We hope you noticed that we kept the design simple in this example. We chose one IV with only two levels (of teaching technique). The study contained a manipulated between-groups variable, which defines a true IV, and one DV (number of questions answered correctly), *plus* one covariate (entrance exam scores). Just like other designs we have covered, you can expand this design in almost any way that you would like.

- You could include more than one IV or pseudo-IV if not manipulated.
- You could have more than two levels for variables.
- You could have more than one DV (which would make the design a MANCOVA for multivariate analysis of covariance).
- Finally, if you are really daring, you could have a mixed design with a covariate.

Let us look at an example of a covariate design. Have you ever noticed that some people seem to overestimate their height while others underestimate it? Duguid and Concalo (2012) demonstrated that a simple social interaction can cause individuals to do just that. In one of those experiments, participants were invited to the laboratory in pairs. One member of the pair was randomly assigned to be the manager (high-power condition), while the other was assigned to be the employee (low-power condition) in a simulated work environment. Both participants were then asked to complete surveys as part of "another experiment" (but it was really part of the same study). Imbedded in those surveys was the following question, "How tall are you?" The basic hypothesis was that people in the high-power condition would overestimate their own height, and individuals in the low-power condition would not. In other words, the researchers predicted a significant difference in height estimates between the two groups. Wisely, the experimenters were concerned that participants' actual height might influence the estimates of their own height, so at the end of the experiment, they measured actual height of each participant and used it as a covariate in their study. Their study used a between-groups design with a single covariate. As a result, the analysis of covariance (ANCOVA) was the most appropriate analysis.

Using SPSS

In the following example, we generated some data to mimic the results reported by Duguid and Concalo (2012). The SPSS data file has three columns (the names of the variables are circled in the next screenshot): The first identifies **experimental group** (0 for low power and 1 for high power), the second represents height of the participant (measured_height), and the third column contains estimated height (reported_height).

To conduct the ANCOVA, you would create a data file as we have in this screenshot. To start the analysis, you would click on the *Analyze* option, select *General Linear Model*, and then select the *Univariate* option. This sequence is visible in the next screenshot.

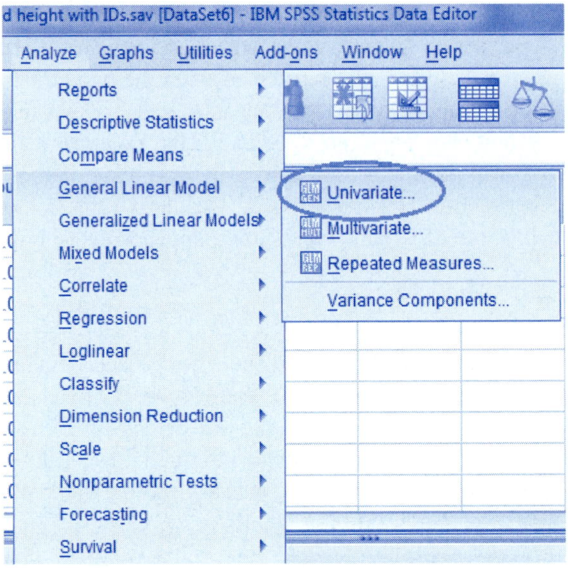

Each of the other options in the *General Linear Model* menu (*Multivariate* and *Repeated Measures*) could also be used for an ANCOVA. We chose the *Univariate* option because it provides the most direct approach to our analysis. If you had a within-groups factor, you would need the *Repeated Measures* procedure and if you had more than one DV you would need the *Multivariate* procedure.

A dialogue box that looks like the one in the following screenshot will open. When this dialogue box opens, all of our variable names are listed in the box on the left.

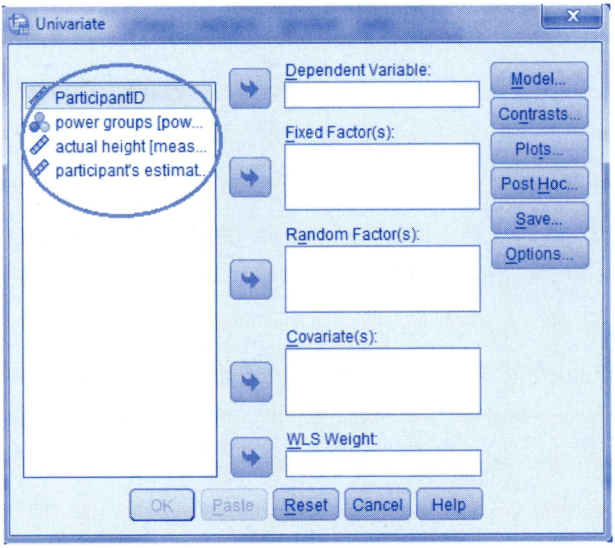

Your job is to move them to the appropriate boxes in the right part of the screen. Can you anticipate which variable names belong in which of those boxes? Take a look at the next screenshot to see where they belong.

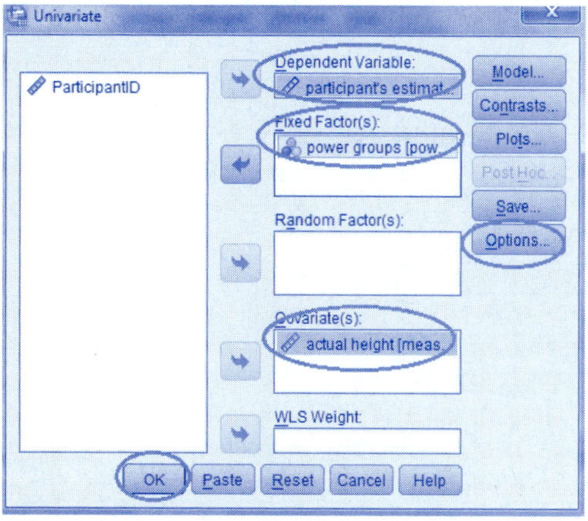

Our DV is the "reported_height" of our participants, so it goes in the *Dependent Variable* box. The IV, "power_groups," is placed in the *Fixed Factor(s)* box. Finally, "measured_height" serves as our *Covariate*. In this case, the covariate is a statistical control condition to give us confidence that the participants' actual heights have not interfered with the effects of the power conditions on estimates of their own heights.

When you are doing this kind of analysis, you will want to include some SPSS options in your output. Click on *Options* to open the following dialogue box. In this case, we want our *Descriptive statistics* and *Estimates of effect size,* so we have checked those boxes. Clicking on the *Continue* button takes us back to the first dialogue box where we can click *OK*.

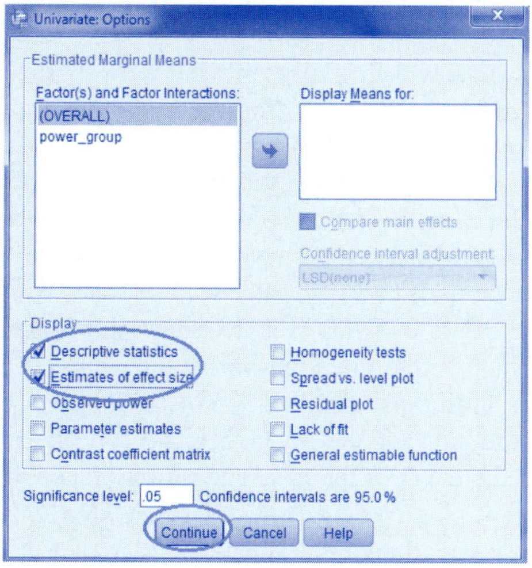

SPSS did its magic, and the entire output screen is included in the following screenshot.

Between-Subjects Factors

		Value Label	N
power groups	.00	low power	20
	1.00	high power	20

Descriptive Statistics

Dependent Variable:participant's estimate of their own height

power groups	Mean	Std. Deviation	N
low power	65.3500	3.78744	20
high power	66.6500	3.39155	20
Total	66.0000	3.60911	40

Tests of Between-Subjects Effects

Dependent Variable:participant's estimate of their own height

Source	Type III Sum of Squares	df	Mean Square	F	Sig.	Partial Eta Squared
Corrected Model	463.700[a]	2	231.850	193.645	.000	.913
Intercept	.000	1	.000	.000	.985	.000
measured_height	446.800	1	446.800	373.174	.000	.910
power_group	25.546	1	25.546	21.337	.000	.366
Error	44.300	37	1.197			
Total	174748.000	40				
Corrected Total	508.000	39				

a. R Squared = .913 (Adjusted R Squared = .908)

The first table in this output simply identifies the two groups and lets us know that there were 20 observations in each. The second table presents the descriptive statistics that we requested. We see that the low-power group estimated their heights with a mean of 65.4 inches, and the high-power group estimated their heights with a mean of 66.6 inches. You can find the standard deviation and sample size for each group in this table too. The most interesting table in our output is the ANOVA table, in this output called *Tests of Between-Subjects Effects*. We say "most interesting" because the ANOVA table tells us if our two groups differ in their estimates of height. We did find a significant difference between the two power groups. We would use the circled values to construct the following report, $F(1, 37) = 21.34, p < .01, \eta^2 = .37$.

We often conduct an ANCOVA in two steps. Showing you the results of those two steps will help you to understand what the inclusion of a covariate can add to our analysis. In the first step, we conduct a simple ANOVA, that is, without the covariate, and then add the covariate in a second step. Comparing these two results tells us the effect of the covariate on our data. On the next page is the output from the one-way between-groups ANOVA without the covariate (see Chapter 8 for a description of this analysis).

Tests of Between-Subjects Effects

Dependent Variable:reported_height

Source	Type III Sum of Squares	df	Mean Square	F	Sig.	Partial Eta Squared
Corrected Model	16.900[a]	1	16.900	1.308	.260	.033
Intercept	174240.000	1	174240.000	13482.224	.000	.997
power_group	16.900	1	16.900	1.308	.260	.033
Error	491.100	38	12.924			
Total	174748.000	40				
Corrected Total	508.000	39				

a. R Squared = .033 (Adjusted R Squared = .008)

The *Test of Between-Subjects Effects* table from the one-way between-groups analysis shows that there is not a significant difference between the two groups ($p = .260$). The values needed for our APA-style report of this result are circled in the table and this is what the report looks like, $F(1, 38) = 1.308, p = .260, \eta^2 = .03$.

You might want to look at the reports of the *F*-ratios from these two analyses where you can directly compare them. Take a moment to compare these two results.

$$\text{ANOVA: } F(1, 38) = 1.31, p = .26, \eta^2 = .03$$

$$\text{ANCOVA: } F(1, 37) = 21.34, p < .01, \eta^2 = .37$$

The analysis without the covariate (first *F*-ratio) did not produce a significant result; however, when the covariate of measured height was included (second *F*-ratio), we found a significant difference between the estimated heights of people in the two power groups. Another way of thinking about this is that when we statistically controlled for the actual height of our participants, the small difference in estimated heights of the two power groups was revealed as statistically significant. Here is how we would present these results.

Writing an APA-Style Results Section

Results

We conducted a between-groups ANCOVA on estimated height with power group as the independent variable and actual height as a covariate. As expected, the high-power group estimated their height as taller ($M = 66.4$ cm, $SD = 3.4$, $n = 20$) than the low-power group ($M = 65.4$ cm, $SD = 3.8$, $n = 20$.) This difference was statistically significant only when actual height was included as a covariate, $F(1,37) = 21.34, p < .01, \eta^2 = .37$.

So, our made-up data showed essentially the same thing that Duguid and Concalo (2012) found. When people are placed in a position of power, they tend to overestimate their heights, see themselves as taller than they in fact are. This difference would be hidden if we did not use actually height as a covariate in this analysis.

Summary

In this chapter, you learned how to analyze three complex designs that we often see in our students' research projects. You learned about the mixed research design with at least one variable that is manipulated between groups and at least one variable that is manipulated within groups. Next, we presented the multivariate design that includes multiple dependent measures. Finally, you learned about the covariate design. Remember that each of these designs can be expanded and that they are very flexible. In the next chapter, you will learn the analysis of correlational designs.

How Do I Know If That Relationship Is Real? **11**

Correlations

Welcome to a chapter on everything you need to know about relationships—data relationships, that is. In this chapter, we will share with you how to analyze a study that examines whether or not two variables are related. Further, if two variables are related, you should be able to predict one variable from the other. Whether you merely want to see if two variables are related or predict one from another is a matter of purpose. Choose your goal or purpose, design your study, then analyze the data as needed. In this chapter, we will explore several examples to make the material clearer to you.

Correlational Design: Two Variables

The word *correlation* already gives away the goal of this type of design. *Co* indicates two variables, and *relation* suggests that you will examine potential relationships. Correlation seeks relationships between two variables. But you will not be limited to studying only two variables in a study; you can examine as many as you would like. Mathematically, you can only correlate two variables at a time, but you can pair up as many as you want. To keep life simple, we will begin with a design using only two variables.

Recall from Chapter 2 the important distinction between correlation as a design and correlation as a statistic. Because these are very different issues, you might want to review Chapter 2 before continuing this chapter. Remember that a correlational design means one thing: no manipulation. With no manipulation, you cannot know cause and effect. You will only learn whether or not two variables are related. Likewise, in Chapter 8, you learned that a *t*-test or ANOVA can only tell you about relationships if the pseudo-IV was not manipulated (which is why we cannot call the variable an IV). Please know that *any study without manipulation is a correlational design*. When you finish a study with no manipulation, analyze your data, and find a significant outcome, celebrate that your results are significant, because you will know that the variables are *related*. Nothing is wrong with merely knowing that two variables are related; that is good information to have and perfectly reasonable to share with the world. But please be careful not to talk about cause and effect!

We should say this again: Any study without manipulation is correlational. So, even though in this chapter we explain correlation as a statistical analysis, you already know about some correlational designs because you read Chapter 2.

We know that if a pseudo-IV is used in your study, you have not manipulated anything, so you only know that your pseudo-IV is *related* to your DV. As an alternative correlational design, instead of having separate groups (not manipulated) and an outcome (called *dependent variable* in prior chapters), you could have two variables, with neither one of them separated into groups. The most popular type of design contains two variables—at least—that offer interval or ratio data (see Chapter 3 for a review of types of data).

Let us look at an example. Imagine you wanted to know if number of Facebook friends relates to number of close in-person friends. You ask participants to tell you the number of Facebook friends they have as well as the number of in-person friends they see regularly. Notice that numbers of Facebook and in-person friends are ratio variables. Imagine these are your data:

Number of Facebook Friends and Number of Close In-Person Friends		
Participant Number	**FB Friends**	**Close In-Person Friends**
1	241	50
2	78	25
3	367	58
4	57	20
5	126	15
6	192	39
7	335	62

Participant Number	FB Friends	Close In-Person Friends
8	270	75
9	103	37
10	150	40

Note that the Participant Number is not a crucial variable; it is offered here to clarify the design.

Before we get ahead of ourselves, we should pause and discuss what we expect from these data. Our design is correlational, not experimental, because we did not manipulate anything in this study. Remember, we merely asked people to report information. That means each row of these data represents one participant, and this data set contains 10 participants.

Before we collected data, we would have read recent research on friendship and online social networks such as Facebook. When asked to conduct research, you want to avoid simply repeating research that has already been done. Instead, you should attempt to address a question not yet answered or at least address the same question using different methods. After reading literature in the area, we might have an idea of whether or not these two variables might be related to each other and, if so, in what way.

Before collecting your data, you need to choose a statistic. When you have two interval or ratio variables in your design, you can examine a potential relationship using Pearson's r (also called the **correlation coefficient**). Remember from Chapter 2 that r is a symbol for the **inferential statistic** we are about to use, just as the t was used for the t-test and F was used for ANOVA. Pearson's r measures the extent to which two variables are related in a linear (straight-line) way. From our example, Pearson's r could capture a significant relationship between number of Facebook friends and number of in-person friends, as long as they are linearly related.

Before calculating the r-value, we can get a feel for the data by sorting numbers on the first variable (number of Facebook friends) from lowest to highest or highest to lowest; make sure when arranging the numbers that each in-person number stays linked with the Facebook value since each row is data from a specific participant. Sometimes rearranging allows people to examine their variables and decide if they look linearly related. If numbers on both variables go in the same direction, the relationship is positive. But if numbers on the variables go in opposite directions (e.g., numbers on one variable increase while numbers of the second variable decrease), then the relationship is negative. In our example, numbers on the two variables go in the same direction, indicating a positive relationship.

Number of Facebook Friends and Number of Close In-Person Friends, Sorted by Number of Facebook Friends		
Participant Number	**FB Friends**	**Close In-Person Friends**
4	57	20
2	78	25
9	103	37
5	126	15
10	150	40
6	192	39
1	241	50
8	270	75
7	335	62
3	367	58

Another way to get a feel for the data is to create a **scatterplot** of the values to see if the points appear to fall in a line-like pattern. Simply label the X-axis with the first variable (FB friends) and the Y-axis with the second variable (in-person friends). Create a scatterplot, with each data point representing one participant. Any graphing program will work; here we have used Excel.

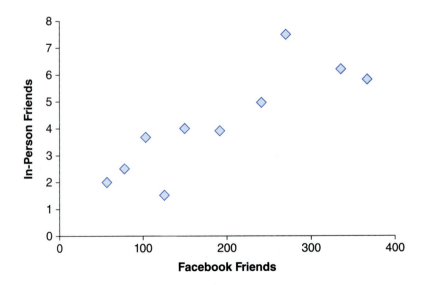

Notice that the dots look like they represent a linear relationship; they fall in approximately a line pattern. Because the line increases (gets higher) across (from left to right) the graph, the data are positively related. If the line had started at the top left and ended near the bottom right of the graph, the data would have been negatively related. For these data, the direction of the line pattern indicates that the two variables are positively correlated, and our chosen statistic should reveal a relationship.

Note that if a scatterplot showed a non-linear pattern such as a U-shaped relationship, Pearson's r would not be a good statistics choice. In fact, a U-shaped function would result in an r-value near zero. It is a good idea to explore your data with a scatterplot to see if a lovely but non-linear relationship exists. In such a case, a scatterplot would indicate the need to learn a statistic other than Pearson's r; additional correlation calculations are explained in an upper-level statistics course.

Interpreting Pearson's r

Mathematically, Pearson's r ranges from −1.00 to +1.00. Of course, the middle of this range is 0. A zero correlation means no relationship at all between the two variables. As the absolute value (remove the sign) of r moves closer to 1.00, the relationship between the two variables is stronger. In fact, an r-value of 1.00 (positive or negative) means a perfect relationship between the two variables. For example, as values on one variable increase by 1, values on the other variable increase by exactly the same amount every time. In the real world, perfect relationships rarely exist. But theoretically, Pearson's r can range from −1.00 to +1.00.

The closer the value is to +/−1.00, the stronger the relationship between two variables. Even though you are not likely to find a perfect relationship, you could find a strong relationship, such as .93, −.85, or even .57. Specifically, a strong relationship is declared if Pearson's r is +/−.50 or beyond; a moderate relationship is depicted by a Pearson's r-value of approximately +/−.30; a weak relationship is illustrated by an r-value of about +/−.10 (and, of course, anything closer to 0, since 0 is the complete lack of a relationship between two variables).

We can go a step further and actually calculate the strength of the relationship by squaring Pearson's r. Why do you need to know this? Because APA style requires you to report the size of an effect if one exists. This effect-size value is called the **coefficient of determination**, a fancy term that simply tells us how much the variables relate with each other, or overlap. An effect size of .01 (and lower) is weak; .09 is moderate; .25 is strong. As a reminder, an effect size of .25 reflects an r-value of .50, which is considered to be a strong relationship.

Analyzing Your Data

We are finally ready to analyze our data using the appropriate statistic, Pearson's *r*, to see if number of Facebook and in-person friends are related. Based on looking at our numbers and a scatterplot, we expect to find a positive *r*-value (to reflect a positive relationship). Further, you might be able to make a guess about the strength of the relationship. Look again at the scatterplot. Most data points fall very close to a straight-line pattern rather than scattered all over the graph with little pattern at all. Based on a clear linear trend, we might expect a fairly strong relationship. However, to talk about whether the relationship is significant, you need to calculate the precise value of *r*.

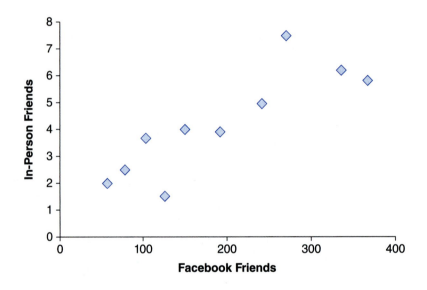

Using SPSS

Enter the data into SPSS exactly as they appear in this book. Remember that each row is one participant, and this study contains 10 participants. Be sure to label your variables as well (see prior chapters).

Type in your data as shown on the next page. We did not enter Participant number because that column is not analyzed. Feel free to enter participant numbers into your SPSS dataset if you would like.

You should also get in the habit of asking for descriptive statistics for variables, so go ahead and ask now. Click *Analyze*, *Descriptive Statistics*, then *Descriptives*.

When the next box opens, you will see your variables on the left.

Move the two variables to the right side. Click *Options*, then make sure a check is beside *Mean, Standard Deviation, Minimum,* and *Maximum*.

Click *Continue* then *OK*. The output file will open at this point, but we still need to analyze these data for a potential correlation. So, minimize the output and return to *Variable View*.

Click *Analyze*, *Correlate*, then *Bivariate*, as shown below.

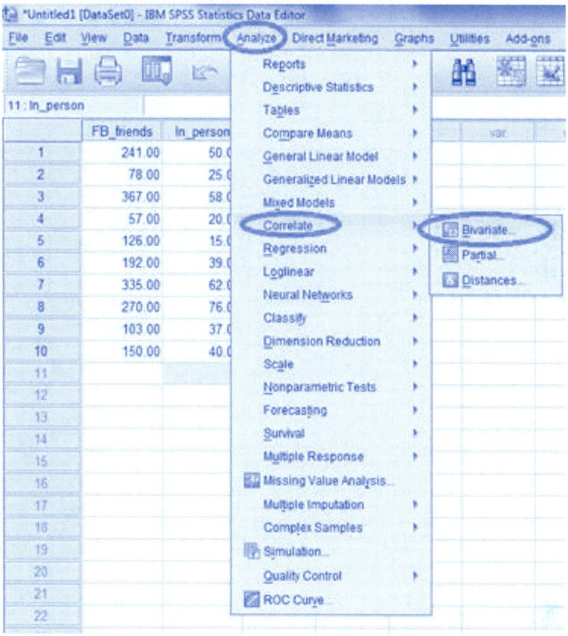

When the following box appears, using the arrow move the two variables that appear in the left box from this data set to the right box and then click *OK*.

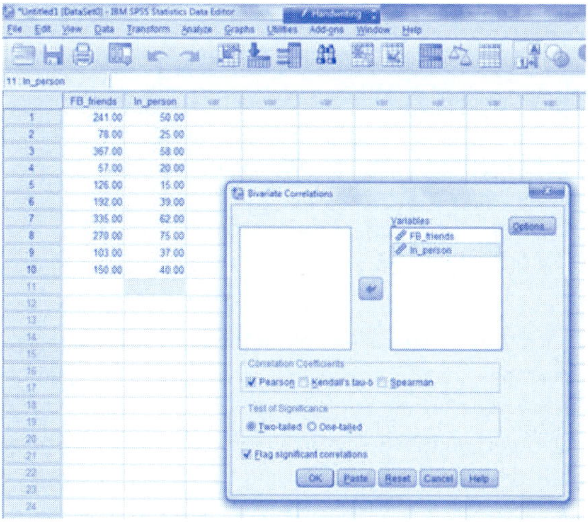

When the output appears, notice in the next screenshot that the **correlation matrix** offers a correlation between a variable and itself, which of course is a 1.00 and not at all useful to us. Instead, we need to focus on the correlation between the two different variables. But even this information is offered twice, and we only need to see it once. Look at either the upper right-side box (which we chose) or the lower left-side box to find *r* for the linear relationship we are analyzing. Because the *p*-value (*Sig.*) is less than .05, we know the *r*-value of .85 is meaningful, and our two variables are related.

Notice that we do not have a section in this screenshot labeled "effect size." To calculate effect size, or the coefficient of determination, simply square the *r*-value (.846) to get .72. Now we can type an APA-style results section by pulling from the output our descriptive statistics (variable means and standard deviations), the *r*-value, the significance value, and the degrees of freedom as $N - 2 = 8$ in this example.

Writing an APA-Style Results Section

Results

We analyzed the potential correlation between number of Facebook friends and number of close in-person friends using Pearson's *r*. The two variables correlated at $r(8) = .85$, $p < .01$, $r^2 = .72$. Number of Facebook friends ranged from 57 to 367 ($M = 191.90$, $SD = 107.92$, $n = 10$). Number of close friends seen on a regular basis ranged from 15 to 75 ($M = 42.10$, $SD = 19.29$, $n = 10$).

For fun, let us consider a new example. Imagine we wanted to know if number of Facebook friends is related to general life happiness. Of course, we must operationally define happiness, and we can use a scale from 1 to 7, with higher numbers indicating more happiness. We can ask each of our participants to give us a rating of happiness. The data might resemble these values:

FB Friends	Happiness
241	4
78	7
367	5
57	3
126	6
192	7
335	2
270	6
103	5
150	4

Notice that we omitted the column for Participant Number, but remember that each row represents data from one participant.

Would you expect number of Facebook friends and happiness to be related positively? Negatively? If you were conducting this study, your review of the available literature published on happiness or similar measures, as well as your reading of articles concerning online social sites, would guide your expectations. If you read that number of Facebook friends sometimes positively relates with happiness but is often negatively related with happiness, you would have reason to expect either type of relationship, positive or negative. If published studies support the notion that either type of relationship might exist, it is not a problem to say you are not sure which way it will go. You would predict a relationship, but you would have trouble predicting the direction of the relationship. Therefore, you will be asking SPSS to conduct a two-tailed test, which simply means you are unsure of the type of relationship you will find.

Likewise, in this example, you might not have a good idea of the strength of the expected relationship. That is okay, too, but you should at least ask yourself about potential direction and strength of a relationship when designing a study. A well-researched and thought-out study tends to be run with more focus and takes away a lot of guesswork after data have been collected.

Remember from the previous example, when your study is complete, you can get a feel for your data by creating a scatterplot. For our most recent example, the scatterplot looks like the one below.

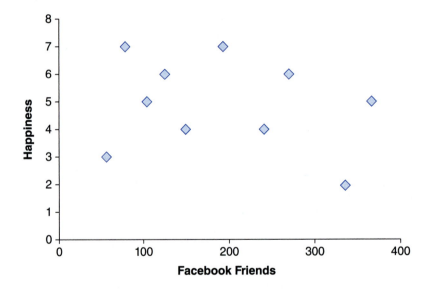

Do you see an indication of a linear relationship? If so, does it look positive or negative? What is your guess about the strength of the relationship?

Using SPSS

Just as in the last example, choose *Analyze, Descriptive Statistics*, then *Descriptives*.

In the box that opens, move your two variables to the right and ask for *Means* and *Std. deviations*.

Click *Continue* and *OK* for the first half of the needed output. Minimize the output and continue with your analysis by clicking *Correlate* and *Bivariate*, as shown below.

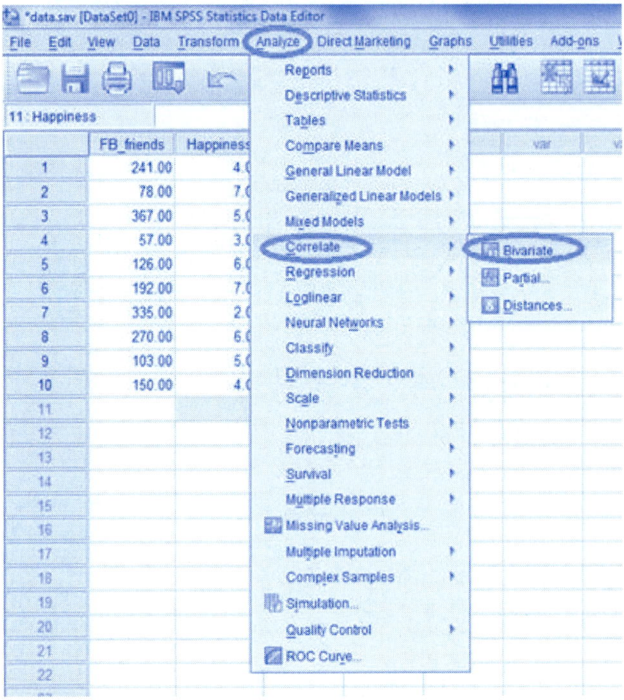

In the box that opens, move variables to the right.

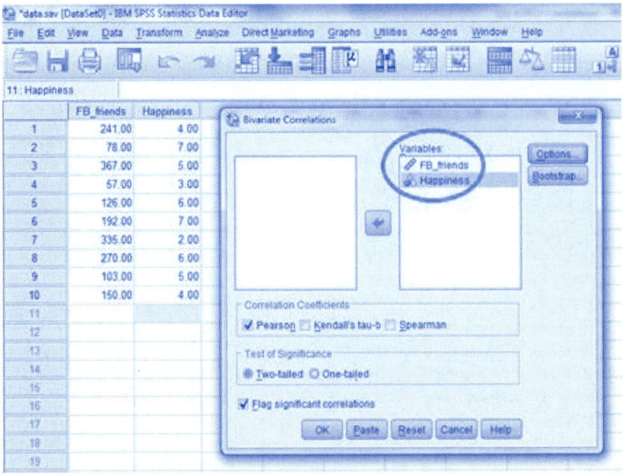

Click *OK* and view the entire output as shown below.

```
DESCRIPTIVES VARIABLES=FB_friends Happiness
  /STATISTICS=MEAN STDDEV MIN MAX.
```

Descriptives

[DataSet0]

Descriptive Statistics

		Minimum	Maximum	Mean	Std. Deviation
FB_friends	10	57.00	367.00	191.9000	107.92019
Happiness	10	2.00	7.00	4.9000	1.66333
Valid N (listwise)	10				

```
CORRELATIONS
  /VARIABLES=FB_friends Happiness
  /PRINT=TWOTAIL NOSIG
  /MISSING=PAIRWISE.
```

Correlations

[DataSet0]

Correlations

		FB_friends	Happiness
FB_friends	Pearson Correlation	1	-.237
	Sig. (2-tailed)		.511
	N	10	10
Happiness	Pearson Correlation	-.237	1
	Sig. (2-tailed)	.511	
	N	10	10

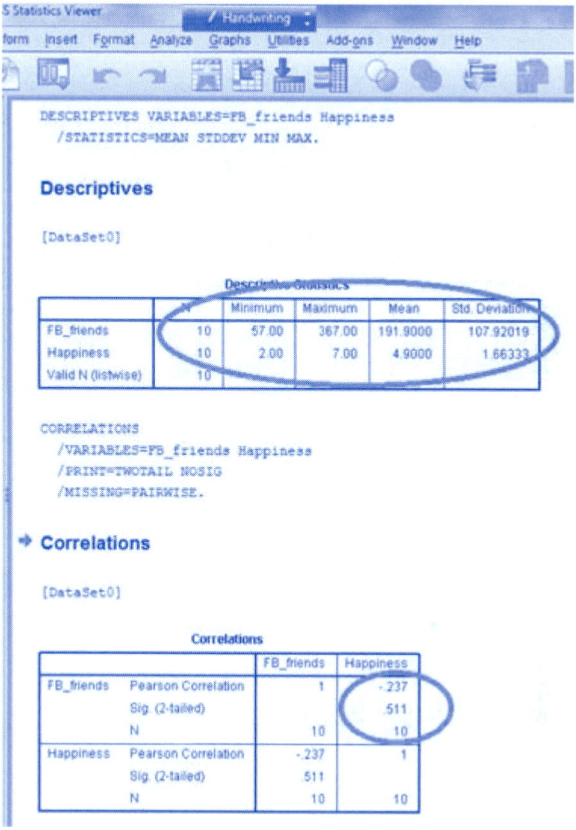

Using this output, we can produce an APA-style results section. Please notice that the *p*-value is greater than .05; you cannot offer an effect size with no meaningful effect! Only calculate effect size when you have an effect in the first place. From the output, pull means and standard deviations for each variable, the *r*-value, the significance value, and $N - 2 = 8$ for degrees of freedom.

Writing an APA-Style Results Section

Results

We analyzed the potential correlation between number of Facebook friends and happiness using Pearson's *r*. The two variables failed to correlate, $r(8) = -.24$, $p = .51$. Number of Facebook friends ranged from 57 to 367 ($M = 191.90$, $SD = 107.92$, $n = 10$). Ratings of happiness ranged from 2 to 7 ($M = 4.90$, $SD = 1.66$, $n = 10$).

As one final example, we could examine the potential relationship between number of close in-person friends and happiness. We could ask 12 people to give us those two pieces of information and perhaps record the following data.

Close Friends	Happiness
6	5
10	6
2	3
3	4
12	7
8	4
1	1
5	4
2	1
10	7
9	6
5	6

We might expect a strong social network to be tied to happiness. (Of course, we would review the literature to form our hypothesis.) Numbers should go in the same direction, with happiness increasing as number of close friends increases; in other words, we would expect a positive relationship. Strength of the relationship would be harder to hypothesize, but we can guess moderate just for the fun of guessing.

Using SPSS

Now we turn to SPSS for data analysis using Pearson's r. Recall that analysis after data input requires *Analyze, Descriptive Statistics*, then *Descriptives*, followed by *Analyze, Correlate*, then *Bivariate*. Refer to earlier examples in this chapter if you need step-by-step details.

```
S Statistics Viewer
form  Insert  Format  Analyze  Graphs  Utilities  Add-ons  Window  Help

DESCRIPTIVES VARIABLES=Close_friends Happiness
    /STATISTICS=MEAN STDDEV MIN MAX.
```

Descriptives

[DataSet0]

Descriptive Statistics

	N	Minimum	Maximum	Mean	Std. Deviation
Close_friends	12	1.00	12.00	6.0833	3.67939
Happiness	12	1.00	7.00	4.5000	2.06706
Valid N (listwise)	12				

```
CORRELATIONS
    /VARIABLES=Close_friends Happiness
    /PRINT=TWOTAIL NOSIG
    /MISSING=PAIRWISE.
```

➡ Correlations

[DataSet0]

Correlations

		Close_friends	Happiness
Close_friends	Pearson Correlation	1	.867**
	Sig. (2-tailed)		.000
	N	12	12
Happiness	Pearson Correlation	.867**	1
	Sig. (2-tailed)	.000	
	N	12	12

** Correlation is significant at the 0.01 level (2-tailed).

The output offers variable means and standard deviations (descriptive statistics) as well as the r-value, significance value, and $N - 2 = 10$ degrees of freedom. Effect size is r^2, which you must calculate and add to the following APA-style results section.

Writing an APA-Style Results Section

Results

We analyzed the potential correlation between number of close friends and happiness using Pearson's r. The two variables correlated at $r(10) = .87$, $p < .01$, $r^2 = .75$. Number of Facebook friends ranged from 1 to 12 ($M = 6.08$, $SD = 3.68$, $n = 12$). Happiness ratings ranged from 1 to 7 ($M = 4.50$, $SD = 2.07$, $n = 12$).

Prediction With Two Variables: Simple Linear Regression

Now that we know that number of close friends and happiness are related in a meaningful way, we can take one more step and predict happiness from number of close friends. With prediction, we will be able to tell the world how many close friends are typically associated with a happiness rating of 6, for example. Let us point out that if number of close friends and happiness were not related, we certainly could not predict one from the other. Correlation and prediction go hand in hand. Sure, sometimes you may only be interested in whether or not two variables are related, but other times you might want to be able to predict, too.

Prediction is called **regression**. In this book, we will stick with **linear regression**, which is based on variables being related in a linear way. After all, linear relationships have been the basis for our entire discussion of correlation so far. In fact, when we discussed scatterplots, the main goal was to see if the data points fell in a straight-line pattern. Regression simply identifies the equation for the best line we could draw through the data points on the scatterplot. The general equation for a line is

$$Y' = bX + a$$

The symbol b represents the slope of the line—how slanted the line is, and in which direction it slants. As you probably guessed, a positive value for Pearson's r represents a positive relationship, an upward slant to the line, and a positive slope (b). A negative r-value indicates a negative relationship, a downward slant to the line, and a negative slope. The symbol a represents where the line crosses the Y-axis of a graph. You need this part, too, because without it, you would not know where to anchor the regression line. For examples, the three graphs below have regression lines with the same slope but different Y-intercepts.

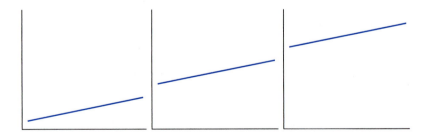

Knowing where to anchor the line (where it crosses the Y-axis) completes the picture. With these two pieces of information, we can draw an accurate line of prediction.

With the slope and Y-intercept calculated and written into the line equation, we are left only with X and Y' to explain. The X symbol represents any X-value we want to plug in (look at the X-axis on the graph for which variable is the X-variable; in this example, X is number of close friends). The symbol Y' is what we are trying to predict. We are using an X-value in the equation to predict a Y-value, which is happiness rating.

When we collect data on number of close friends and happiness, we have a sample that allows us to create a regression line for future prediction—as long as the two variables are significantly correlated in the first place. That is, we use our sample to calculate a prediction line, then we can share that valuable prediction tool with the rest of the world. People who read our study will be able to predict happiness for a person based on his or her number of close friends.

Will prediction be perfect? No. Life is messy, and data reflect life. Lack of perfection when predicting is called error, or more formally, the standard error of the estimate. The error term will tell you (and the world) about how far off the prediction will be, on average, when using a given prediction equation.

SPSS will provide the necessary information. All we have to do is enter the data, analyze it, and make sense of the output. The data are pictured again here for your convenience.

Close Friends	Happiness
6	5
10	6
2	3
3	4
12	7
8	4
1	1
5	4
2	1
10	7
9	6
5	6

Using SPSS

After data are entered into SPSS, click *Analyze, Regression,* then *Linear.*

Move the **predictor variable** (Close_friends) under *Independent(s)*, in the box; then move the outcome variable (Happiness) under *Dependent*. Then click *Statistics* for a second box to open. *Estimates* and *Model fit* probably are checked already. Check *Descriptives*. You will also need the correlation between these two variables, but SPSS will automatically do this based on default settings.

Click *Continue* and *OK* on the boxes to get your full output. The correlation output table looks a bit different from what you saw earlier in this chapter (i.e., prior examples that only involved correlation), but all the pieces are available. In the first two tables, notice that the output contains descriptive statistics as well as Pearson's correlation between the two variables (circled below). In the Correlations table, Pearson's *r*-values appear first, and significance values appear in the next row of the table.

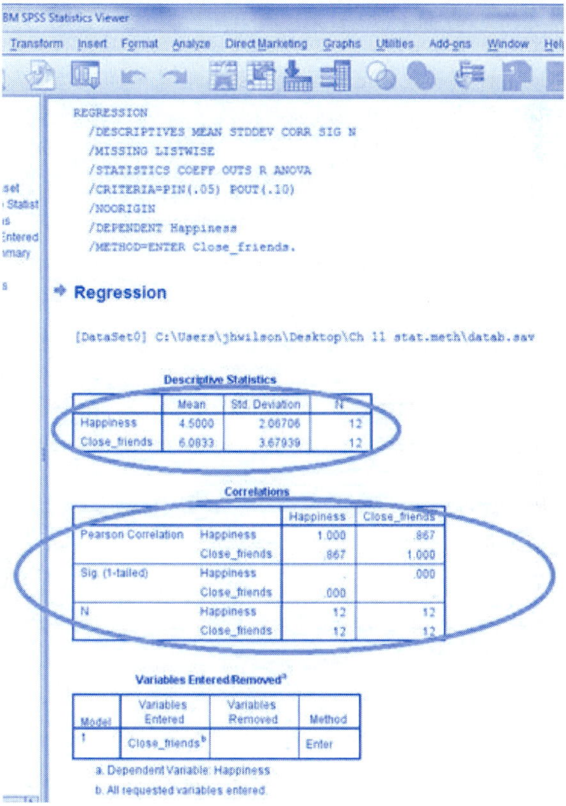

The next screenshot illustrates the second half of the output, which offers new information for prediction. Try not to be overwhelmed by the bulleted list below; look over the example output that follows and notice each piece mentioned here.

- R represents Pearson's *r* (for this simple regression).
- R square represents effect size, or the coefficient of determination.
- In the ANOVA table, a significant *F*-value means the predictor meaningfully predicts happiness. Do not let an ANOVA table bother you; it merely offers an overall test of prediction.

- In the Coefficients table, the B column reveals the Y-intercept and slope of the predictor, respectively. (Note that the Y-intercept is to the right of "Constant" on the output.)
- Also in the Coefficients table, under the *t*-column, the predictor of close friends is a significant predictor, based on a significance value of less than .05.
- Finally, when predicting happiness from number of close friends, prediction will not be perfect; the standard error of the estimate illustrates approximately how far off the prediction will be based on this prediction equation.

The ANOVA summary table above says your predictor or predictors work (if a significant value is found in that table). In this example, looking at the *p*-value in the *Sig.* column, we know that number of close friends predicts happiness (ANOVA table). In the next table (Coefficients), you can see exactly which predictors are useful, much like a *post hoc* test that gives you additional valuable information. In this case, you only have one predictor, and the overall ANOVA test already told you it was significant! Notice that both the ANOVA table and the specific test of close friends (under Coefficients) tell you the same news: Number of close friends predicts happiness. When you only have one predictor, the information is indeed redundant.

Writing an APA-Style Results Section

An APA-style results section would be similar to the one below.

Results

We analyzed the potential correlation between number of close friends and happiness using Pearson's r. The two variables correlated at $r(10) = .87$, $p < .01$, $r^2 = .75$. Number of Facebook friends ranged from 1 to 12 ($M = 6.08$, $SD = 3.68$, $n = 12$). Happiness ratings ranged from 1 to 7 ($M = 4.50$, $SD = 2.07$, $n = 12$).

Linear regression analysis allowed us to predict happiness from number of close friends, $F(1, 10) = 30.16$, $p < .01$, with a slope of .49 and a Y-intercept of 1.54. The variable of close friends significantly predicted happiness ($p < .01$). When predicting happiness from number of close friends, we will err by 1.08 happiness rating points.

If we wanted to add a graph with a prediction line (below), we would be sure to refer to Figure 1 in the results section. For the graph, we relied on Excel to add a regression line by clicking for a *Line of Prediction* in Excel graphing. Click *Chart Tools, Layout, Trendline,* then *Linear Trendline.* Again, use any program you generally use for graphing and locate the command to add a trendline.

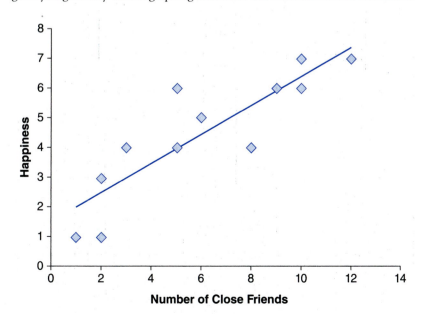

Prediction With Several Variables: Multiple Linear Regression

Just as you can predict one outcome from one predictor, you can predict one outcome from several **predictors**. Usually, prediction from several variables improves prediction, and error is reduced because you are explaining variability based on several different approaches (variables). For example, if you wanted to understand college grades, you could predict simply from number of hours studied, but you would do a better job of understanding (predicting) grades if you also looked at predictors such as student intelligence, hours of sleep, stress, and so on. Note that an individual equation allows only one outcome; one variable can be predicted. You can have many predictors and one outcome per equation.

We can expand the prior example of predicting happiness from number of close friends. Imagine that we also wanted to know if number of events with friends per month (an estimate of the average) and duration of an average social event (in hours) would enhance prediction of happiness. When entering data, researchers generally put predictors in the first columns (left) and the outcome (predicted) variable in the final column to the right.

Close Friends	Number Events	Duration Events	Happiness
6	9	3	5
10	16	2	6
2	1	1	3
3	5	1	4
12	14	4	7
8	8	2	4
1	2	4	1
5	10	2	4
2	8	5	1
10	12	2	7
9	6	1	6
5	6	3	6

Using SPSS

These data would be entered into SPSS using the same format as prior examples, with one row representing data from each participant.

The only difference in multiple regression is to move three variables into the *Independent(s)* box. Do not forget to ask for *Descriptives* in the second box. If you do not recall the steps, refer to earlier sections in this chapter. The next screenshot illustrates how to set up the analysis.

After clicking *Continue* then *OK*, output should look like this:

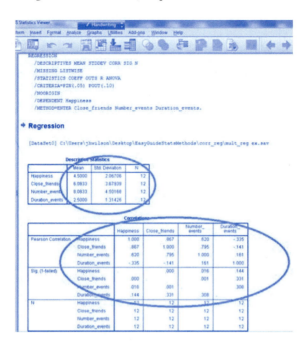

Note that descriptive statistics and correlations among pairs of variables appear in the first half of the output.

As before, an ANOVA examines the overall predictive power of the predictors in the regression equation. With three predictors in this example, we do need to know first if anything is happening with all three as a group. The significant F-value above (.004) in the ANOVA table tells us that the three predictors *as a group* do predict happiness. In fact, as a group, they predict 80% ($R^2 = .797$ on the output in the *Model Summary* table) of the variability in happiness ratings. Notice in the output that we change to R rather than r when we have more than one predictor.

To decide exactly which variables predict happiness well, we turn to the Coefficients table, the last table on the output file, to see that only number of close friends can remain as a viable predictor of happiness ($p = .019$ on the output). The remaining two variables fail to predict happiness ($p > .05$)—or at least *they fail to predict happiness beyond what is already explained well by number of close friends*.

As a caution, you should know that this SPSS analysis will allow the best predictor to get as much overlap with the outcome as possible. A second (third, and so on) variable only gets credit for predictive power that remains after the first variable takes its part. An example might help. Returning to the idea of predicting college grades, suppose hours of studying and intelligence (two predictors) overlap with each other a great deal. If intelligence is a bit more overlapped with grades, SPSS is likely to report intelligence as a significant predictor. If the variable "hours of studying" offers little new explanation of grades, SPSS is likely to report hours of studying as not significant.

In our APA-style results section, we need to report all descriptive statistics, correlations among variables, and results from regression analysis. Researchers often streamline such a results section by referring to a table containing descriptives and correlations.

Writing an APA-Style Results Section

Results

We used linear regression to predict happiness from number of close friends, average number of events with friends per month, and average duration of social events ($N = 12$). Please see Table 1 for descriptive statistics and correlations among variables.

The three variables considered together significantly predicted happiness, $F(3, 8) = 10.49$, $p < .01$, with 80% overlap between the three predictors and the outcome of happiness. When predicting happiness, we will err by approximately 1.09 happiness-rating points based on a scale from 1 to 7. Specifically, number of close friends remained as a significant predictor, with a slope of .49 ($p = .02$); 2.49 quantified the Y-intercept for our regression equation.

To create the following table, we used a word-processing program, then we removed all vertical lines (to follow APA style). Be sure to place the table on a separate page at the end of your document. For more APA-style details on tables, refer to *An EasyGuide to APA Style* (Schwartz, Landrum, & Gurung, 2014).

		Pearson's r		
	M(SD)	**Number Events**	**Duration Events**	**Happiness**
Close Friends	6.08(4.50)	.80*	−.14	.87**
Number Events	8.08(4.50)		.16	.62*
Duration Events	2.50(1.31)			−.34
Happiness	4.50(2.07)			

Table 1 Descriptive Statistics and Correlations Among Variables

*p < .05; **p < .01

Also notice the asterisks in the table. We want to be concise when presenting information, therefore, we use asterisks to denote levels of significance and add a footnote to the bottom of the table to let our readers know what those asterisks mean. Finally, of course, we left some cells blank because there is no good reason to repeat correlations a second time. The correlations in our table show all possible combinations among variables.

As for graphing, we cannot create a figure with many dimensions. Instead, we can choose to share with our readers a scatterplot for each significant predictor and the outcome of happiness. In this example, number of close friends turned out to be the only meaningful predictor, allowing us to offer one useful graph (below).

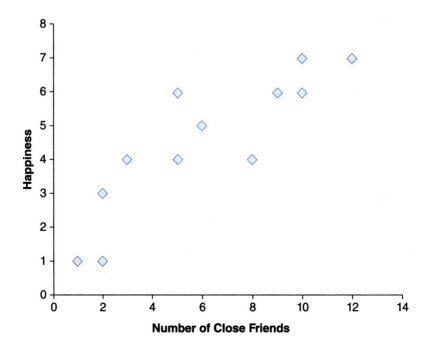

This graph could be included as a figure in an APA-style paper and placed on a separate page toward the end of the manuscript. Once again *An EasyGuide to APA Style* (Schwartz et al., 2014) provides the details needed for figures.

Summary

In this chapter, we discussed correlation and regression as two ways to analyze correlational data. But remember, only your design can tell you if you will learn about cause and effect versus a relationship between variables. If you do *not* manipulate a variable, you will have correlational data *no matter how you analyze it*. If you manipulate a variable (an IV), you *will* know cause and effect, no matter how you analyze it.

This chapter offered two main analyses: Pearson's *r* for interval or ratio data and linear regression for one or more predictors. Use these analyses when your data require it. Otherwise rely on any of the other tools discussed in this book.

Statistics Charades 12

Two Variables, Two Categories
. . . Is It a Chi Square?

Simple frequency data show you how often a value (or behavior) occurs. For example, if we asked everyone in a classroom to raise their hands if they like the taste of asparagus, we could count the number of hands up and have simple frequency data. As you can see, simple frequency data are, well, simple. In this chapter, we will show you how to design a study that merely collects counts or frequencies. We will also show you how to analyze those data, of course, allowing you to gain some information about behavior.

The reason we waited until Chapter 13 to introduce simple frequency is because it is not a very powerful test. Most people will not deliberately design a study that requires only this kind of data. However, it can be done, and we do not want to leave any stone unturned when it comes to your education on design and analysis. The following example should clarify when you might need to analyze simple frequency data.

I Only Have One Question

For our first example, we will consider texting. As a researcher, you might be interested in knowing whether or not college students text while driving a car. Of course, you would have to operationally define your variables, such as sending any text at all and having the car in motion. Imagine a recent survey showed that when adults *of all ages* were asked if they text while driving, 20% said they did, and 80% said they did not. In your study, you only want to know about college students, and you suspect that more than 20% text while driving. In other words, you have an idea of how the data might turn out based on your knowledge of prior research; you have an expectation. Your goal is to lay out these expectations and see if the data fit what you expected. The analysis is called a **goodness of fit test**.

Before you run your study, the only information you have indicates that 20% of adults drive and text, which means you should expect 20% to report texting while driving unless you can show otherwise. If you plan to ask 100 college students to answer your question, 20% would be 20 people. You must begin your analysis assuming that 20 college students will report texting. Next, you will see if any number of people other than 20 is a meaningful (significant) difference from what you expected.

Ask 100 students to answer your question with a "yes" or "no." Then compare the number of people who say yes or no to the expected 20/80 split explained above. In the boxes below, lay out your expectations—**expected frequencies** (f_e)—based on expecting 20% of 100 people to say they text while driving.

Texting while driving	No texting while driving
$f_e = 20$	$f_e = 80$

The numbers you actually collect from your college-student sample are called observed frequencies (f_o). Suppose you found that 50 college students in your sample reported texting while driving, and 50 said they did not. Add your observed frequencies to the table below.

Texting while driving	No texting while driving
$f_e = 20$	$f_e = 80$
$f_o = 50$	$f_o = 50$

Now your job is to see if a 50/50 split is meaningfully different from the 20/80 split you expected (or at least was reported for adults of all ages). To answer this question, you use a statistic called a chi-square analysis, with the symbol χ^2. Specifically, this statistics is called a **one-way** χ^2 because we have one variable of interest (whether or not people text while driving).

Using SPSS

To input these data to SPSS, go to *Variable View.* Label one variable as a general term associated with the study, such as "texting," and go ahead and label the *Values* as 1 = "texts" and 2 = "no texts."

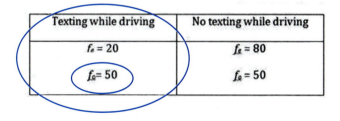

Under *Data View,* enter the number of observed values for the first cell (Texting while driving).

Texting while driving	No texting while driving
$f_e = 20$	$f_e = 80$
$f_o = 50$	$f_o = 50$

In this case, the observed frequency for texts is 50, so enter 50 values of 1 in the first column. Continue under the same column to enter 50 values of 2 as well; these represent the observed frequency for no texts. In the next screenshot, you see a section of the data we entered. Notice that labels appear rather than the numbers entered (1 and 2) because we have asked SPSS to see *Value Labels* under *View.*

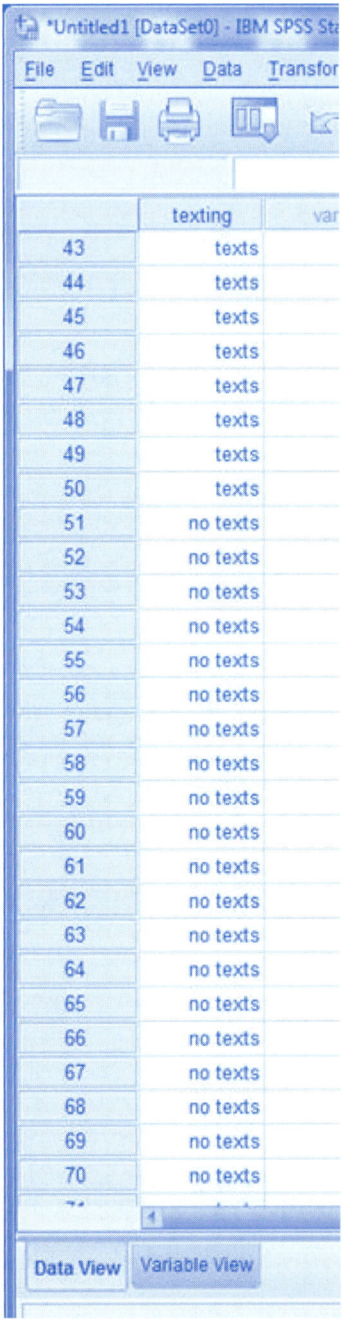

You are now ready to analyze these data. Click *Analyze, Nonparametric Tests, Legacy Dialogs*, and *Chi-square*, as shown in the next screenshot.

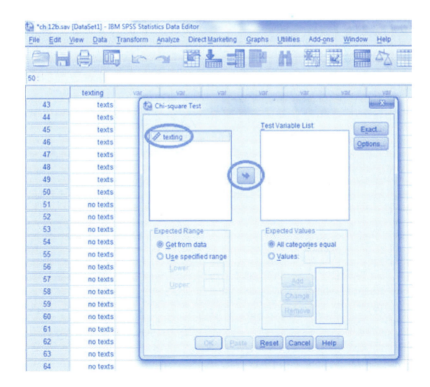

In the box that opens, move "texting" to the right under *Test Variable List*.

Under *Expected Values*, click *Values* (circled below) then type 20 as the first cell's expected value. Next click *Add*.

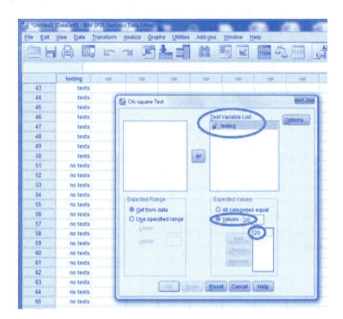

To add the second cell's expected frequency of 80, return to *Values*, remove the 20, and type an 80. Click *Add* again. At this point, both expected values are listed as shown in the next screenshot.

Finally, click *OK* to view your output.

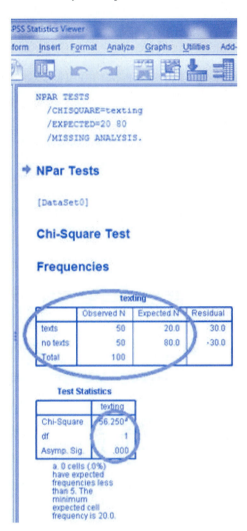

Notice in the above screenshot that you have the chi-square value (56.25), degrees of freedom (1), and a *Sig.* value less than .05, which of course indicates that what you found (observed frequencies) were significantly different from the norm, or what you expected to find (expected frequencies). Before we end this section, we will show you how to put these data into an APA-style results section. But first, we want to share an alternative to SPSS.

The one-way chi square is a simple analysis and a straightforward calculation. Because we promised you SPSS examples, we have offered a way to use SPSS to analyze the one-way chi square. However, we have to admit that we generally calculate the one-way chi square by hand. We will show you how to do the simple calculation in case you prefer it or in situations when you do not have access to SPSS.

The one-way χ^2 formula is below.

$$\chi^2 = \Sigma \left(\frac{(f_o - f_e)^2}{f_e} \right)$$

Just work from the inside of the formula outward, simplifying as you go. First enter the f_o and f_e values from the texting-while-driving box.

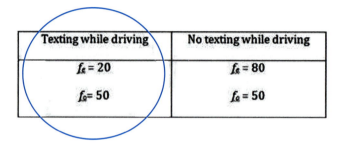

Texting while driving	No texting while driving
$f_e = 20$	$f_e = 80$
$f_o = 50$	$f_o = 50$

$$\left(\frac{(50 - 20)^2}{20} \right)$$

Next, enter the values from the second cell.

Texting while driving	No texting while driving
$f_e = 20$	$f_e = 80$
$f_o = 50$	$f_o = 50$

$$\left(\frac{(50 - 80)^2}{80} \right)$$

Now, notice that the original formula has a sum sign (Σ), which means you have to add up sections for each cell. Because this example only has two cells, the equation has two sections.

$$\chi^2 = \left(\frac{(50-20)^2}{20} \right) + \left(\frac{(50-80)^2}{80} \right)$$

To simplify and solve, add the two sections.

$$\chi^2 = \left(\frac{(50-20)^2}{20} \right) + \left(\frac{(50-80)^2}{80} \right) = 45 + 11.25 = 56.25$$

Your only remaining job is to see if the 56.25 represents a meaningful difference between what you expected to find and what you actually learned from your sample about how many college students text and drive. In other words, you are trying to find out if the 50/50 split you discovered is meaningfully different (significantly different) from the 20/80 split you expected based on prior research with all adults.

You need a chi-square table to show you what number you need to get beyond to say you found something unusual among college students. A chi-square table can be located in a statistics book or on the web. The magic number you need to exceed with your 56.25 is located in the table by first finding *df* based on the number of variable levels (2 in this example, with texting and not texting) and subtracting 1. You always subtract 1 from the number of variable levels to calculate *df*. In this example, *df* = 1. Look up 1 *df* in the chi-square table, slide your finger to the right, and locate the magic number that says this kind of value happens less than 5% of the time normally. In the chi-square table, the comparison number is 3.84 for 1 *df*. Any number beyond 3.84 is considered meaningful. Your result is 56.25, which is wonderfully significant! Based on your findings, this means a 50/50 split is statistically significant and therefore truly different from the expected 20/80 split.

I am sure you would agree with me that we need a bit more information to make sense of what is happening in this data set. We can communicate with people effectively by reporting some percentages. Point out to the reader that although we expected only 20% of college students to text while driving, 50% do! If you feel so inclined, you could also describe the non-texting group: Further, although we expected 80% of college students to say they do not text while driving, only 50% said they do not. You can see how the second sentence is not really needed because you only had two conditions; giving percentages from the first cell indicated what percentages would remain for the second cell.

Writing an APA-Style Results Section

Results

We analyzed our data using a one-way χ^2. We expected 20% of our sample of college students to say they text while driving and 80% to say they do not; however, observed frequencies significantly differed from expected frequencies, χ^2 (1, $N = 100$) = 56.25, $p < .05$. Fifty percent of our sample of college students admitted that they text while driving, and 50% said they do not.

Notice in the above results section that we reported $p < .05$ because we calculated the result by hand (most recently), used a table to look up the critical value (3.84) to exceed for significance, and found that a χ^2 value of 56.25 was significant because it was larger than 3.84. However, if we rely on SPSS to calculate the χ^2 value, as we originally did for this example, we can see a more precise p-value of $p < .001$. If we rely on SPSS output, we can incorporate $p < .001$ in our results section as seen below.

Results

We analyzed our data using a one-way χ^2. We expected 20% of our sample of college students to say they text while driving and 80% to say they do not; however, observed frequencies significantly differed from expected frequencies, χ^2 (1, $N = 100$) = 56.25, $p < .001$. Fifty percent of our sample of college students admitted that they text while driving, and 50% said they do not.

One-Way Chi Square With More Than Two Levels

In the prior example, we kept things simple to get started. But you do not have to restrict your research question to only two groups. You can have as many groups as you want. In the next example, we will use a design with three groups. We will also use a number other than 100 participants so you will need to calculate expected frequencies. Face it, in the prior example, it was pretty easy to calculate 50% of 100 people; you probably figured that out in your head without much effort. We need to make sure a sample size of something like 195 does not cause you problems later. So, we will practice.

We can extend the prior example to help us out here. Imagine you wanted to collect data on cell-phone usage, and you wanted to allow people to choose their answer from three options instead of just two. This time, the choices could be as follows:

1. Yes, I text while driving. I don't even hesitate ("Yes").

2. No, I never text while driving ("No").

3. Sure, I text while driving, but I only text at stoplights or when stuck in standstill traffic ("Sometimes").

Of course, you first need to lay out your expectations based on the plan to collect data from 195 college students. But wait. How do you know what to expect since you just added the "sometimes" category? Make your best guess if you have no prior research to turn to. The good news is that your prior study revealed that 50% of college students text while driving, and 50% do not. You have to assume that students who "sometimes" text must be in the 50% who said they do, so we can break up that 50%. With no idea of how to break it into "yes" and "sometimes" responses, our best approach probably is to expect 25% to fall in the "yes" category and 25% to fall in the "sometimes" category. Our expectations would be 25% in the "yes" category; 50% still in the "no" category; 25% in the "sometimes" category.

Be careful! Do not put 25, 50, and 25 in the cells for expected frequencies! You expect 25 *percent* of a sample of 195 to fall in the "yes" category.

$$.25 \times 195 = 48.75$$

This value represents the expected frequency (number of people expected) in the "yes" category.

The remaining cells need the same attention.

$$.50 \times 195 = 97.50 \text{ for the "no" category}$$

$$.25 \times 195 = 48.75 \text{ for the "sometimes" category}$$

Your data table of expected frequencies might look like this.

Yes	No	Sometimes
$f_e = 48.75$ (25% of 195)	$f_e = 97.50$ (50% of 195)	$f_e = 48.75$ (25% of 195)

Do not be troubled by the expected fractions of people. Sure, there is no such thing as a .50 or .75 of a person, but this is just for the math of the chi square. Fractions of people—as long as we are only talking about hypothetical situations—are fine.

As you know, after your expectations are written, you can collect data and see if the numbers you find (observed frequencies) are different from a 25/50/25 (expected frequencies) split in a meaningful way. For fun, imagine we found that 58 people said "yes," 92 people said "no," and 45 people said "sometimes." We can complete the data table as shown here.

Yes	No	Sometimes
$f_e = 48.75$	$f_e = 97.50$	$f_e = 48.75$
$f_o = 58$	$f_o = 92$	$f_o = 45$

Using SPSS

Next we turn to SPSS, entering our data as we did in the prior example. The only difference in data entry is the use of three categories on the SPSS spreadsheet instead of two. Under *Values*, enter "texting" for the variable name and set Value Labels to 1 = "texts," 2 = "no texts," and 3 = "sometimes."

Under *Data View*, you will enter 1, 2, and 3 for the levels and then click *Value Labels* under *View* to see the labels as seen on the next page.

Choose the appropriate commands: *Analyze, Nonparametric Tests, Legacy Dialogs*, and *Chi-square*.

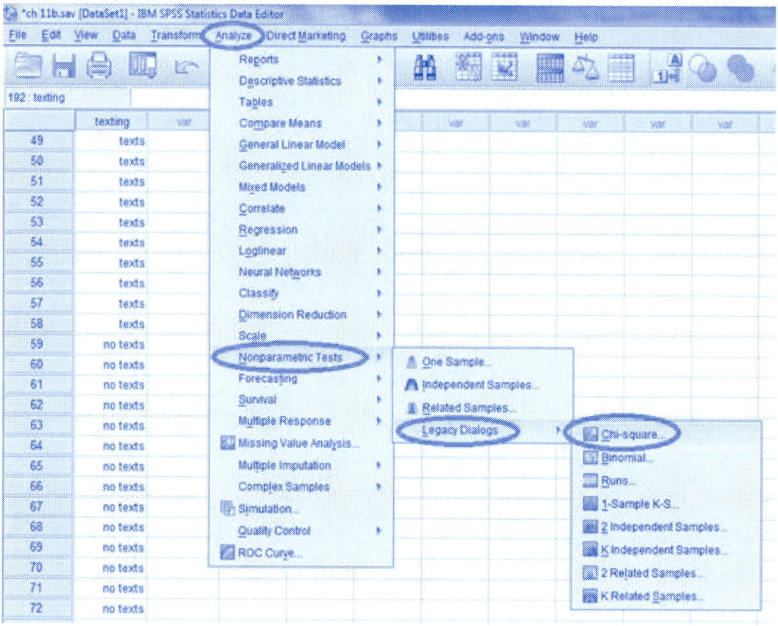

In the box that opens, move "texting" to the right under *Test Variable List*. Then click *Values* on the bottom right and enter *Expected Values:* 48.75, 97.50, and 48.75, clicking *Add* for each value entered until all three expected values are shown as in the next screenshot.

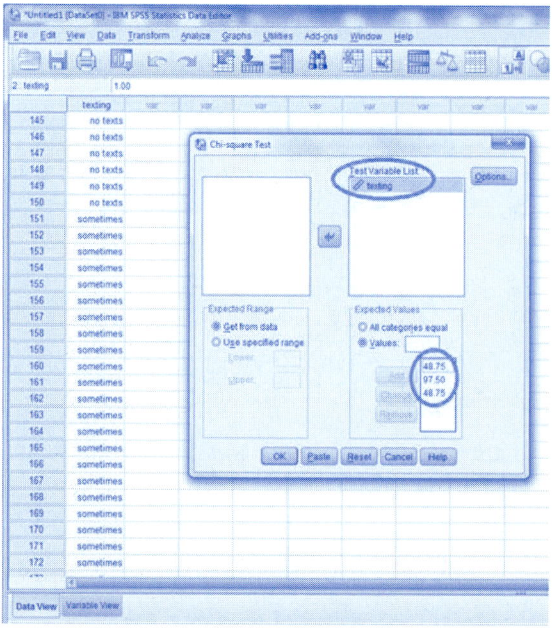

Your output should look like the screenshot below. Notice again that you have the chi-square value, the degrees of freedom, and the significance value.

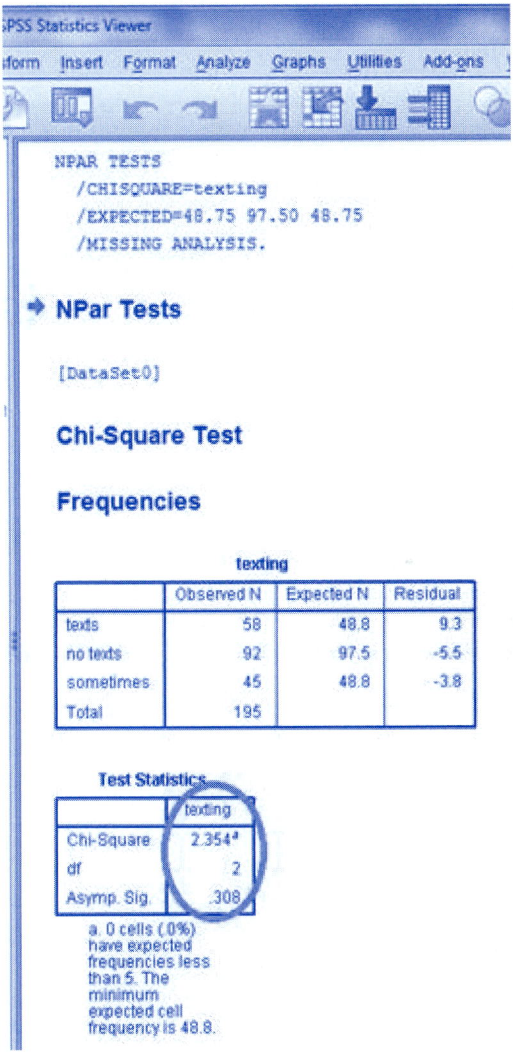

PSS Statistics Viewer
form Insert Format Analyze Graphs Utilities Add-ons
NPAR TESTS
/CHISQUARE=texting
/EXPECTED=48.75 97.50 48.75
/MISSING ANALYSIS.
NPar Tests
[DataSet0]
Chi-Square Test
Frequencies
texting
Observed N Expected N Residual
texts 58 48.8 9.3
no texts 92 97.5 -5.5
sometimes 45 48.8 -3.8
Total 195
Test Statistics
texting
Chi-Square 2.354a
df 2
Asymp. Sig. .308
a. 0 cells (.0%) have expected frequencies less than 5. The minimum expected cell frequency is 48.8.

As an option, we could analyze these data using the now-familiar chi-square formula.

$$\chi^2 = \left(\frac{(58-48.75)^2}{48.75}\right) + \left(\frac{(92-97.50)^2}{97.50}\right) + \left(\frac{(45-48.75)^2}{48.75}\right) = 1.76 + .31 + .29 = 2.36$$

Do not be concerned that SPSS produced a 2.354 value and hand calculations produced 2.36; the slight difference is due to rounding. Importantly, to find out if a 58/92/45 data layout is meaningfully different from the expected 48.75/97.50/48.75 layout, we need to know if $\chi^2 = 2.36$ is beyond the magical (critical) value in a χ^2 table. The critical value of χ^2 with 2 degrees of freedom (number of levels minus 1) is 5.99. Because 2.36 does not reach or exceed the needed value of 5.99, we cannot say that we found anything statistically significant. In other words, what we found is what we expected to find. The outcome was *not* meaningfully different from what we expected to find, but still rather interesting. Although we would be unlikely to publish failure to find anything significantly different from the "norm," we can practice writing another APA-style results section, which of course would need to be included in a research paper. Remember that we rely on percentages to help tell the whole story.

Writing an APA-Style Results Section

> ### Results
>
> We analyzed our data using a one-way χ^2. We expected 25% of our sample of college students to say they regularly text while driving, 50% to say they do not text at all while driving, and 25% to say they text only at stoplights and in standstill traffic. In fact, observed frequencies did not deviate from expectations, χ^2 (2, $N = 195$) = 2.36, $p > .05$.

Our fictional results indicate that about 25% of college students admit that they text while driving without a care in the world. Fifty percent refuse to text at all while driving. Finally, 25% refrain from texting unless the car is completely stopped. Again, we found exactly what we expected to find, which means we found nothing different from normal.

The prior two designs required the researcher to lay out expectations before collecting data. Again, we can get expectations from prior publications (absolutely the best way), personal observations, or logical thought. Then, our goal is to see if what we find in a specific sample is different from what we expected to find. We want to find something different from what is expected because that would be interesting information worthy of sharing with the world. If we only find what we expected in the first place, we have nothing new to report.

The one-way χ^2 is a good tool to use when you have simple frequency data and one variable of interest (with as many levels as you want, as long as people can only fall in *one* of the levels/categories). But wait, the χ^2 also can be used to analyze an entirely different research design. Read on.

Now I Only Have *Two* Questions

When dealing with simple frequency data, we are not limited to one variable; we can have two (or more!) variables with simple frequencies or counts. This merely requires that you design a study where you ask people two questions rather than one. In the first example of texting while driving, we only asked people to answer a single question: Do you text and drive, yes or no? We could add a second question, such as whether or not their parents texted while driving. To keep things simple, we will allow only a "yes" or "no" answer to this question too.

The most interesting characteristic of having two variables instead of one is that your entire research question changes. When you had only one variable, your research question was whether or not what you observed was meaningfully different from what you expected. When you have two variables, your research question is whether or not the two variables are related. In fact, you can think of it like a correlation from Chapter 11 for simple frequency data. The statistic is called a **test of independence** because you are testing to see if the two variables are independent of each other (or, alternatively, related to each other).

Also recall that the chi square with only one variable required you to have some idea of what to expect in the normal population first. In other words, you had to have an idea about expected frequencies before running your study. Without expectations at the beginning, you would have no comparison for the data you collect. A chi square with two variables (**two-way**, or test of independence) follows a much different procedure. You do not worry at all about expected frequencies. Just collect responses from your participants on both variables and be ready to analyze your results. You will quickly know whether or not the two variables are related. If they are related, you will also need to show a measure of effect size.

Suppose we asked college students to report on (1) whether or not they text while driving and (2) whether or not their parents text while driving. With "yes" or "no" options on both, you would set up a table like the one below.

		College students text while driving?	
		Yes	No
Parents text while driving?	Yes		
	No		

Now you are ready to run your study. (Notice that we did not use the word *experiment* because nothing is manipulated. We use the more general term *study* instead.) For this study, suppose you asked these two questions of 250 people.

You might find the following data:

Data Table		College students, do you text while driving?	
		Yes	No
Do your parents text while driving?	Yes	$f_o = 173$	$f_o = 10$
	No	$f_o = 27$	$f_o = 40$

Again, notice that expected frequencies are nowhere to be found. We merely collect observed frequencies, enter the data, and find out whether or not college students' texting while driving is related to whether or not their parents text while driving.

Using SPSS

To enter the data in SPSS, label the first column with either "Students" or "Parents" to represent one of your variables. Here we will use "Students" as the first column heading. Label the second column "Parents," but again, either order is fine. Recall from earlier chapters that you begin in *Variable View*, name your variables, and in this case also label your *Values* as 1= "yes" and 2 = "no" for each variable. The following screenshot of SPSS shows Students and Parents in row form because we are in *Variable View*; clicking to *Data View* will show you column headings.

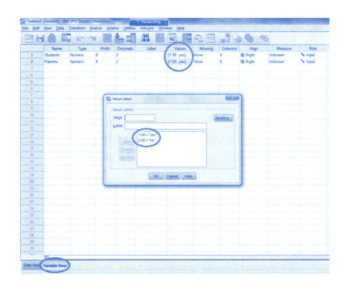

Now comes the part that is so easy it might be tricky. In *Data View*, enter a 1 in the first box to represent "yes," this student texts while driving; enter a 1 in the box to the right for parents texting. Your first row should have two 1 values in it, one in each box. These are the data for the first participant included in the upper left-hand corner of your data table above. This student said yes, (s)he texts while driving, and yes, so do her/his parents. Now you only have 172 more 1, 1 combinations (rows) to enter down these two columns. Hint: Just copy the first row and paste the rest. Make sure you are viewing the data as numbers only by clicking *View* and making sure *Value Labels* is unchecked; you can click to *View Value Labels* after your data are entered. For now we want to make sure you know how to enter data for the two-way chi square, which can sometimes be confusing. Your data file should look like the next screenshot.

	Students	Parents
1	1.00	1.00
2	1.00	1.00
3	1.00	1.00
4	1.00	1.00
5	1.00	1.00
6	1.00	1.00
7	1.00	1.00
8	1.00	1.00
9	1.00	1.00
10	1.00	1.00
11	1.00	1.00
12	1.00	1.00
13	1.00	1.00
14	1.00	1.00
15	1.00	1.00
16	1.00	1.00
17	1.00	1.00
18	1.00	1.00
19	1.00	1.00
20	1.00	1.00
21	1.00	1.00
22	1.00	1.00
23	1.00	1.00
24	1.00	1.00
25	1.00	1.00
26	1.00	1.00
27	1.00	1.00
28	1.00	1.00
29	1.00	1.00

two way chi sq data.sav [DataSet1] - IBM SPSS

File   Edit   View   Data   Transform   Analyz

169:

Data View   Variable View

Although we suggest entering data while *Value Labels* remains unchecked, after data are entered, click *View* and *Value Labels*. Looking at the data here with labels is a bit more reader-friendly.

	Students	Parents
149	yes	yes
150	yes	yes
151	yes	yes
152	yes	yes
153	yes	yes
154	yes	yes
155	yes	yes
156	yes	yes
157	yes	yes
158	yes	yes
159	yes	yes
160	yes	yes
161	yes	yes
162	yes	yes
163	yes	yes
164	yes	yes
165	yes	yes
166	yes	yes
167	yes	yes
168	yes	yes
169	yes	yes
170	yes	yes
171	yes	yes
172	yes	yes
173	yes	yes
174		
175		
176		
177		

*Untitled1 [DataSet0] – IBM SPSS Statistics D.

File Edit View Data Transform Ana

174 : Students

Data View   Variable View

Next, we can enter data for the "student, yes/parents, no" part of the data table. This cell contains 27 people. Sure, you could enter the "no" student texting and "yes" parent texting cell with 10 next; any order for the cells is fine as long as you enter all the observed frequencies in the data table. We will enter the cell with 27 people in it below to represent all the students who text while driving and have parents who do not.

	Students	Parents	
173	yes	yes	
174	yes	no	
175	yes	no	
176	yes	no	
177	yes	no	
178	yes	no	
179	yes	no	
180	yes	no	
181	yes	no	
182	yes	no	
183	yes	no	
184	yes	no	
185	yes	no	
186	yes	no	
187	yes	no	
188	yes	no	
189	yes	no	
190	yes	no	
191	yes	no	
192	yes	no	
193	yes	no	
194	yes	no	
195	yes	no	
196	yes	no	
197	yes	no	
198	yes	no	
199	yes	no	
200	yes	no	
201			

*Untitled1 [DataSet0] - IBM SPSS Statistics Da

File   Edit   View   Data   Transform   Anal

201 : Students

Data View   Variable View

Continuing under the 173 completed rows, begin entering 1, 2 combinations under Students and Parents. Enter that combination 27 times to illustrate all students who said they text and drive, but their parents do not. Of course, next, you will enter data from another cell. In this example, we will enter the "student no/parents, yes" cell with 10 people reporting that they fall in that particular category. Finally, enter data from the bottom, right cell with 40 people. Here is a partial snapshot of those final two cells in our SPSS data file.

*Untitled1 [DataSet0] - IBM SPSS Statistics Dat

File   Edit   View   Data   Transform   Analy

251 : Students

	Students	Parents	
195	yes	no	
196	yes	no	
197	yes	no	
198	yes	no	
199	yes	no	
200	yes	no	
201	no	yes	
202	no	yes	
203	no	yes	
204	no	yes	
205	no	yes	
206	no	yes	
207	no	yes	
208	no	yes	
209	no	yes	
210	no	yes	
211	no	no	
212	no	no	
213	no	no	
214	no	no	
215	no	no	
216	no	no	
217	no	no	
218	no	no	
219	no	no	
220	no	no	
221	no	no	
222	no	no	
223	no	no	

Data View   Variable View

To analyze these data, go to *Analyze, Descriptive Statistics*, then *Crosstabs*. It seems odd to find the chi square under *Descriptive Statistics*, and *Crosstabs* is a term we have not used, but trust us that these menu options will get you to the two-way chi square.

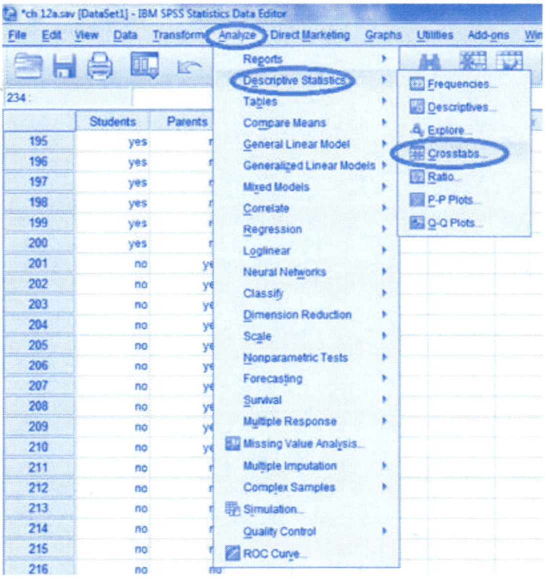

In the *Crosstabs* box shown open in the next screenshot, you have to decide which variable will represent columns in the data table, and which will present rows. We prefer to input the data just as it looked in the original data table, with Student responses as the columns and Parents' responses as the rows.

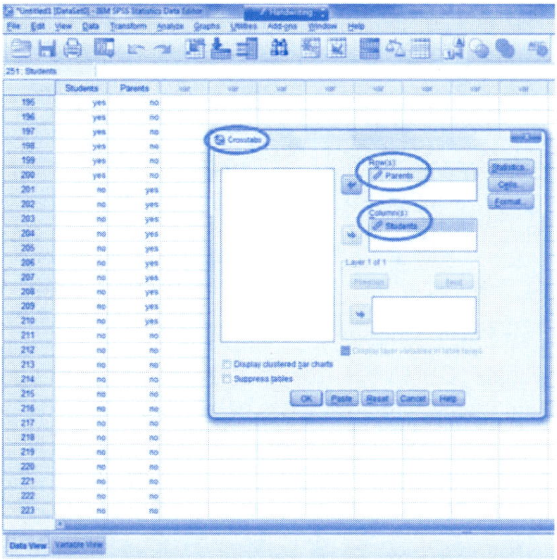

Now we get to move on to the fun part. Let us find out if the two variables are related. Click *Statistics.* When the new box opens, click the box beside *Chi square,* and click the box beside *Phi coefficient (Phi and Cramer's V)* to get the effect size. Remember that you are not allowed to report any effect-size number if there is no effect. But go ahead and set it up just in case you end up needing it.

Now click *Continue,* then *OK* to see the SPSS output. Notice in the third box of the next output file (Chi-Square Tests) that the significance value (Asymp. Sig.) is below the all-important .05. In fact, it is below .01.

Crosstabs

Case Processing Summary

	Cases					
	Valid		Missing		Total	
	N	Percent	N	Percent	N	Percent
Parents * Students	250	100.0%	0	0%	250	100.0%

Parents * Students Crosstabulation

Count

		Students		Total
		yes	no	
Parents	yes	173	10	183
	no	27	40	67
Total		200	50	250

Chi-Square Tests

	Value	df	Asymp. Sig. (2-sided)	Exact Sig. (2-sided)	Exact Sig. (1-sided)
Pearson Chi-Square	90.169	1	.000		
Continuity Correction[b]	86.811	1	.000		
Likelihood Ratio	82.277	1	.000		
Fisher's Exact Test				.000	.000
Linear-by-Linear Association	89.808	1	.000		
N of Valid Cases	250				

a. 0 cells (.0%) have expected count less than 5. The minimum expected count is 13.40.
b. Computed only for a 2x2 table

Symmetric Measures

		Value	Approx. Sig.
Nominal by Nominal	Phi	.601	.000
	Cramer's V	.601	.000
N of Valid Cases		250	

You can safely say that the two variables are significantly, meaningfully related to each other. In other words, you found something interesting to report to the world. Because you have a significant effect, you also need to pull the effect size from the output. The **phi coefficient** (*Phi* of .601 above) measures effect size for a 2 × 2 chi square. Any design larger than a 2 × 2 requires the **contingency coefficient** to measure effect size; the contingency coefficient is one of the options given to you when setting up statistics for the two-way chi square. In your APA results section, the contingency coefficient can be symbolized by a *C*. The phi coefficient can be symbolized by ϕ.

Based on the information circled on the output above and knowledge of your research design, it is time to prepare an APA-style results section. The following results section is a good beginning, and then we will go a bit further with the data to provide a clearer explanation.

Writing an APA-Style Results Section

Results

We analyzed our data using a 2 (students texting and driving or not) × 2 (parents texting while driving or not) χ^2. Whether or not college students texted while driving related to whether or not parents texted while driving, χ^2 (1, $N = 250$) = 90.17, $p < .001$, $\phi = .60$.

Notice that this results section indicates something interesting is happening, but there is not enough information to let the reader know exactly *what* is happening. Recall that chi square relies on percentages to tell the whole story. Of course, you should not mention expected frequencies at all in the two-way chi square because in this statistic, expected frequencies are not part of the theory. But you definitely should tell a story with the observed frequencies (the data you collected from your sample). Using percentages, explain to your reader the categories people fell under, such as students texting and parents also texting.

You have a couple of options when reporting percentages. You can explain what percent of N (in this case, 250 participants) fell in each cell. But that is not a very reader-friendly story. Let us show you: If you merely put each observed frequency over N and multiplied by 100 for percentage, your story would be hard to follow. In this example, you would write that 69% of college students text while driving and have parents who text too; 4% of college students say they do not text, but their parents do; 11% of college students text, but their parents do not; 16% of college students report that they do not text while driving, and neither do their parents. Although technically those percentages are correct, the logic is a bit hard to follow. Readers do not get a clear take-home message.

Instead, choose to discuss percentages either by column or by row. We will discuss percentages by column, examining the first column which is the percent of students who text while driving based on whether or not their parents do. Then, we will discuss the second column—students who do not text while driving—based on whether or not their parents do. See how this approach explains results to the reader in an understandable, logical way.

First, we need to do some simple calculations. Looking only at the first column of data (173/27), divide each value by the column total (200), then multiply by 100 to calculate a percentage in each cell *for that column only.*

Data Table		College students text while driving?	
		Yes	No
Parent text while driving?	Yes	$f_o = 173$ $\frac{173}{200} \times 100 = 86.50\%$	$f_o = 10$ $\frac{10}{50} \times 100 = 20.00\%$
	No	$f_o = 27$ $\frac{27}{200} \times 100 = 13.50\%$	$f_o = 40$ $\frac{40}{50} \times 100 = 80.00$
Column totals		200	50

Using SPSS

If you do not want to calculate these percentages by hand, you can allow SPSS to do it for you. When setting up *Crosstabs*, simply click the *Cells* button and ask for *Observed* under *Counts* and *Column* under *Percentages*.

Click *Continue* and *OK* to allow SPSS to create a table with column percentages. The next output file shows you the same percentages (circled) as our earlier calculations. The column totals are also circled to show you that each should sum to 100%.

Crosstabs

Case Processing Summary

	Cases					
	Valid		Missing		Total	
	N	Percent	N	Percent	N	Percent
Parents * Students	250	100.0%	0	.0%	250	100.0%

Parents * Students Crosstabulation

			Students		Total
			yes	no	
Parents	yes	Count	173	10	183
		% within Students	86.5%	20.0%	73.2%
	no	Count	27	40	67
		% within Students	13.5%	80.0%	26.8%
Total		Count	200	50	250
		% within Students	100.0%	100.0%	100.0%

Chi-Square Tests

	Value	df	Asymp. Sig. (2-sided)	Exact Sig. (2-sided)	Exact Sig. (1-sided)
Pearson Chi-Square	90.169[a]	1	.000		
Continuity Correction[b]	86.811	1	.000		
Likelihood Ratio	82.277	1	.000		
Fisher's Exact Test				.000	.000
Linear-by-Linear Association	89.808	1	.000		
N of Valid Cases	250				

a. 0 cells (.0%) have expected count less than 5. The minimum expected count is 13.40.
b. Computed only for a 2x2 table

Symmetric Measures

		Value	Approx. Sig.
Nominal by Nominal	Phi	.601	.000

We can continue to talk about people in fractions, or we can round the numbers at this point to indicate whole people. We will do the latter to make the story more logical. Below is a complete APA-style results section, using percentages to tell the whole story.

Writing an APA-Style Results Section

Results

We analyzed our data using a 2 (students texting and driving or not) × 2 (parents texting while driving or not) χ^2. Whether or not college students texted while driving related to whether or not parents texted while driving, $\chi^2 (1, N = 250) = 90.17, p < .01, \phi = .60$. Of college students who text while driving, approximately 87% of their parents also text while driving, and only 14% do not. Of students who do not text while driving, only 20% of their parents drive and text; 80% do not.

Notice how much richer the story is with percentages. Now, the reader can understand that college students and their parents pretty much engage in the same behaviors when it comes to texting and driving, at least based on our fictional data. We do not know causation, so we cannot say that college students learn to text and drive from their parents *or* that college students model texting and driving for their parents. But we do know that an interesting relationship exists, and percentages tell us the details of that relationship.

Summary

In this chapter, we discussed how to analyze simple frequency data across categories. The one-way (goodness-of-fit) chi square is used when you have one variable with as many levels as you want. The one-way χ^2 lets you know if what you found in your research matched what you expected based on what is normal in the world. You hope to be able to say what you found was significantly different from what you expected to find. Something interesting and unexpected happened. In the two-way chi square (test of independence), you will learn if two variables are independent of each other or related in some way. Of course, you hope to find a relationship so you can report an interesting result.

SECTION IV

A Summary

This section is so much more than a summary. We start by presenting decision trees, which we believe you will find are invaluable guides to good decisions about design and analysis. We also tie the decision trees to chapters in Section III in case you need more details or a review. Chapter 14, on APA style results sections, is a valuable resource for getting this critical section of a research report right the first time you write one. Here, different parts of the results section are pointed out. Use this chapter to be sure you learn what needs to be included in results paragraphs for different types of statistical tests. Finally, Chapter 15, on advice from experts, can help you avoid mistakes that we have seen over the years. We know these mistakes can easily be avoided if you just take the time to review these essentials. Enjoy!

Mapping Your Decisions 13

You Can Get There From Here

S o here you are near the end of the book and you might be thinking, "How do I remember all of this when I am working on my own research?" This chapter is designed to help you make the correct decisions about matching your research design and statistical analysis. We offer decision trees (flow charts) that will serve as reference tools you can use to ensure that you have a "good" marriage between your methods and statistics. Follow the flow of the branches by answering questions about your design and method. At the end, you will know which analysis to use!

Making Basic Decisions About Your Design

In this chapter, we include three decision trees for you to use that will allow you to make sure you made the correct connection between the design of your research and the type of statistic you use. You can find the three complete decision trees at the end of the chapter. Throughout this chapter, we include parts of the decision trees to illustrate the decision-making process that connects your design and statistic. The first two decision trees (i.e., Decision Trees 1 and 2) follow the decisions made when leading to statistics used with distinct groups when you want to compare the means for those groups or conditions. For example, you have distinct groups in your research when you include grouping variables such as sex or drug condition. Note that when we say *distinct groups*, we mean discrete levels of a variable; we do not mean you have to have different people in the groups. For example, you might have two levels (i.e., groups or conditions) of drug condition, such as a placebo and an antidepressant. You could either randomly assign people to the two conditions or test the same people under each level on different days.

Use Decision Tree 1 for research including just one variable with distinct groups (see Decision Tree 1 at the end of the chapter), and use Decision Tree 2 (also at the end of the chapter) when you decide to include two or more variables with distinct groups. In many cases, the distinct groups are levels of an independent variable (IV), which is the manipulated variable in an experiment. However, even a study with a non-manipulated variable such as participant's sex contains distinct groups; we sometimes refer to this type of variable as a pseudo-IV because it is not an IV that we can manipulate. Throughout this EasyGuide we referred to both manipulated IVs and pseudo-IVs as just variables. Regardless of whether you include a manipulated IV or a pseudo-IV, as you see in the decision trees, the statistic you use is the same. For these two decision trees, your variables can be nominal, ordinal, interval, or ratio (see Chapter 3 for descriptions of each), as long as a few distinct levels are used (e.g., drinking 1, 2, or 3 cans of soda). Importantly, the dependent variable (DV) must be interval or ratio data to allow for the powerful calculations reviewed in this book.

In the third and final decision tree, Decision Tree 3, we show you how to analyze a study with continuous variables that are not separated into distinct groups or categories but rather contain variables with many possible values, such as ounces of soda consumed, and you want to measure the relationship between those variables. The variables in such a study must be at the interval or ratio level to conduct these analyses. Use Decision Tree 3 when your research question relies on variables that do not have a few distinct categories. In such designs, you will analyze the data using either Pearson's r (correlation) or linear regression for prediction, depending on your goals.

In all three of the decision trees, we map out questions you need to ask to identify the components of your design and in turn to identify the type of statistic that your data require. To help you refer back to the appropriate details, the decision trees also include the chapter numbers from this EasyGuide. That way, you can find details on a particular design, the relevant statistic, and how to run the analysis, interpret the output, and write results in APA style. Year after year, we suggest to our students that they laminate these decision trees and keep them handy for any class that requires a research proposal or project. After you have stated your hypotheses and identified the variables you want to investigate, the next steps are easy with the correct decision tree in hand. In this chapter, we also discuss in detail the different components of the decision trees. First, we go over the two decision trees for data with distinct groups (i.e., levels or conditions), and later we explain the components included in the decision tree for data with many values (such as ounces of cola people consume each month). Finally, we include examples to help you understand the differences among the decision trees.

Data With Distinct Groups

Keeping It Simple With One Variable

Let us start with Decision Tree 1 and a design with only one variable. For example, consider the ads you see either on TV or online. Often, advertising agencies use humor to help sell products. Does humor help us remember the product and in turn lead us to buy the product? Or does humor distract our attention away from the product itself, and in the end, we cannot remember what the ad was for because we focused on the humor? Based on the research literature (see Cline & Kellaris, 2007), we might predict that humor will lead to an increase in memory for the product. We could test this hypothesis by creating a design with one factor. In this example, type of ad (presence or absence of humor) would be our variable with two levels. One level would be ads with no humor, and the other level would be ads with humor. Notice on the decision tree below that you have made the choice of including two levels for one variable.

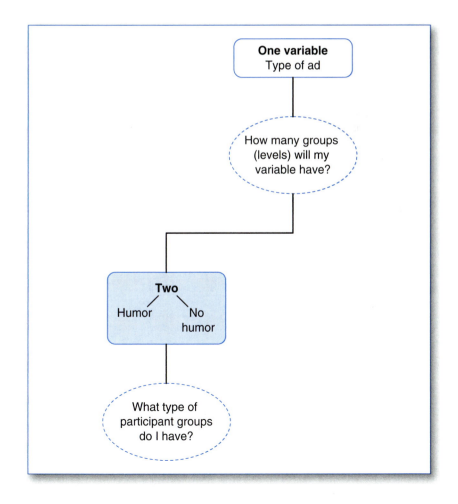

The next decision concerns *how* to present participants with these two levels. As one option, we could choose to have different people see the ad with humor versus the ad without humor. In this case, we would be using a between-groups design because separate groups of participants would experience only one of the two levels of our manipulated IV. As shown in the far left of the decision tree (following the blue highlighted path), this independent-samples design with two groups would require that we use a *t*-test for independent samples. You would use this same approach even with existing groups (a pseudo-IV). For instance, you might be interested in using only ads with humor and comparing memory differences between men and women. You would use all ads that contain humor

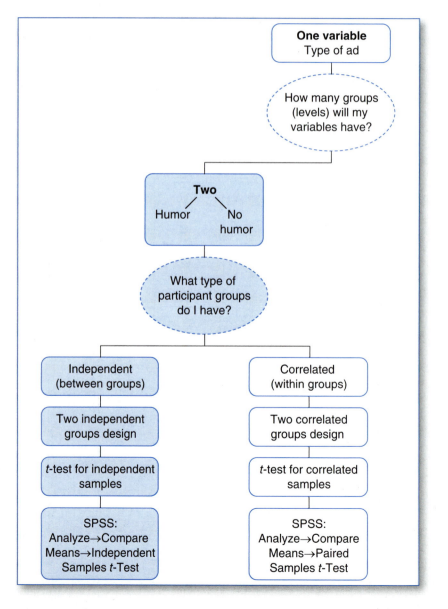

and simply present those ads to both men and women. Then, compare memory for the products between men and women. Chapter 8 provides all the details needed for a between-groups design regardless of whether the variable was manipulated. In Chapter 8, you will also find guidance on how to set up a data file and run an analysis using SPSS as well as write your outcome in APA style.

Now, let us return to the two different types of ads. Imagine that you would like all of your participants to see *both* the humorous and the non-humorous ads. In this case (following the blue highlighted path below), you need to use a **within-groups design** in which the same participants see the two different types of ads. As you see, exposing all participants to both levels of your study changes the design and

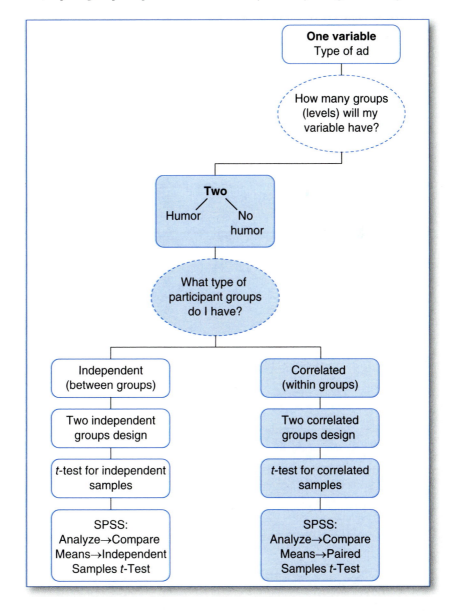

statistic. Remember, if that were the case, you would be comparing the responses of the same participants who were asked to remember details about both types of ads.

There are advantages and disadvantages to choosing a between-groups design versus a within-groups design. When you choose a between-groups design, you do not need to be concerned about carry-over effects. In other words, participants who see the humorous ads are not influenced by previously seeing the non-humorous ads. Why? Because they are presented with only one or the other. That is the advantage of a between-groups design . . . no worries about carry-over effects. So why use a within-groups design when carry-over effects might cause a problem? The answer is all about statistical **power**. Power is the likelihood of accepting your research hypothesis when it is true. Statistically speaking, when you use the same participants in both conditions, variability produced by individual differences has less effect on the analysis because participants serve as their own comparison condition. In this case, if you have significant differences between your conditions, you will be more likely to detect those differences. When you can control for carry-over effects, this increase in power is well worth the effort.

Look at Chapter 9 to learn when to use a within-groups design with only two conditions. Some researchers refer to this design as a *two correlated-groups design*, a *related-samples design*, a *repeated-measures design*, or a *dependent-samples design*. Regardless of what you decide to call it, you analyze this design with a paired-samples *t*-test in SPSS. Chapter 9 will also take you step-by-step through how to set up the data file and what to click in SPSS for this type of design with two levels of the variable.

In the example above, we included only two levels of our variable. However, there are times when we want to compare more than two levels of a variable. For example, the literature might clearly indicate that humor improves attention to the product, but you realize that no one has investigated the impact of *how much* humor. Perhaps a small degree of humor causes a laugh but still allows a consumer to focus on the product, but a large amount of humor actually detracts from remembering the product. In other words, we could compare one ad without humor, one ad with slight humor, and a third ad with a lot of humor. Including

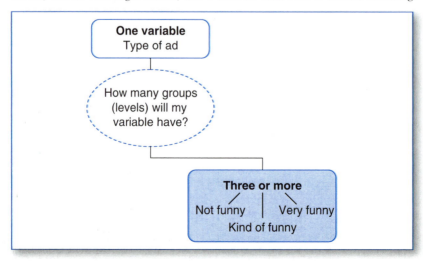

three levels of the humor variable would allow us to test our new hypothesis. When you look at decision tree below, you will see the two different ways we can include additional levels of our variable.

We are now on the right half of Decision Tree 1 (see the full tree at the end of this chapter) where we have three or more levels of a variable. We are still using one variable, degree of humor, but now our design employs three levels of that variable. Because we added another level of the variable, the design name changes slightly from a two-groups design to a multiple-groups design. Just as in the last example, you need to decide if you want to use a between-groups design or a repeated-measures approach to testing participants. When each participant experiences only one of the three levels, you have a between-groups design (Chapter 8). Follow the blue-highlighted section of the next decision tree.

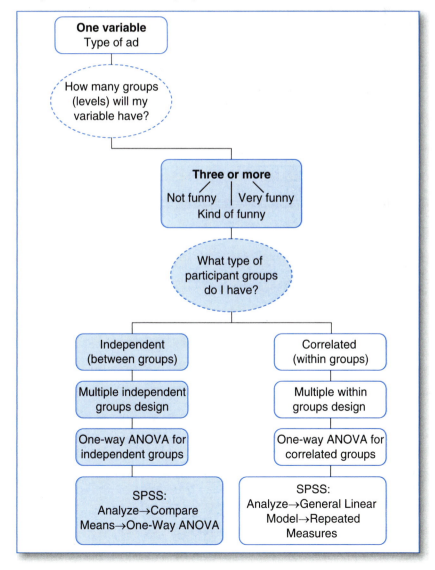

Or, the same participants can view all three ads, which would be a repeated-measures design, sometimes called a *within-groups design* (see Chapter 9). If that is your choice, your design and statistic are highlighted below.

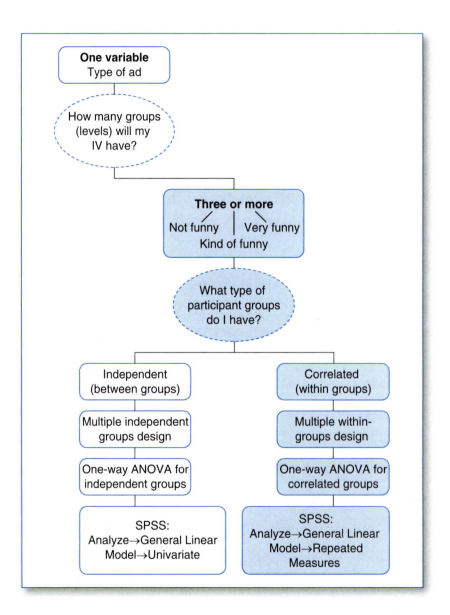

Designs With More Than One Variable

Published articles typically include more than one factor. After all, a researcher learns much more information when using multiple variables. In the humor examples used so far, we bet you could easily think of an additional variable that might increase our understanding of how humor affects memory for products. For example, you might wonder whether the type of product makes a difference when it comes to including humor. Perhaps an ad for a car would benefit more from humor than an ad for life insurance. You can answer this more complex question by including two variables in your research design: amount of humor and type of product. We now move to using Decision Tree 2.

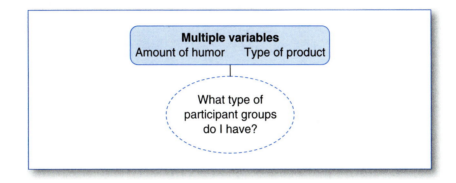

Notice that the difference between the start of this decision tree and the one earlier in the chapter is that we added one more variable to the design. Once again, the decision must be made as to whether to use different participants in your variable levels or the same participants. However, this time the decision needs to be made separately for *each* of the variables included.

You could decide that both variables should be between-groups factors; you would be using a factorial design for between groups. Different participants would be assigned to all four of the different conditions in your research. Notice in the table below that combining the two levels of each of the two different variables leads to four separate conditions.

Type of commercials

	With humor	Without humor
Car ads	Car ad with humor	Car ad without humor
Insurance ads	Insurance ad with humor	Insurance ad without humor

In this factorial between-groups design, some participants would watch an ad for a car with humor, a different group of participants would watch a car commercial without humor, a third group of participants would watch a life insurance commercial with humor, and a fourth group of participants would watch a commercial for life insurance without humor. This follows the highlighted path in the decision tree on the far left as shown below.

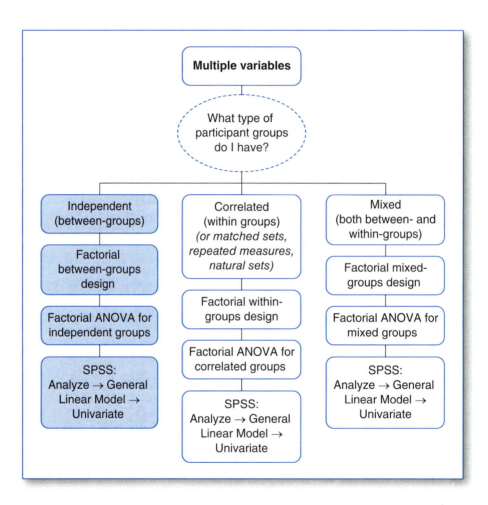

You can find the reasons for making this choice, which statistic to choose, and how to set up the data file and run analyses in Chapter 8.

As an alternative, you could decide that you want all participants to experience the conditions created by the levels of both variables. In that case, the same participants would watch all four types of commercials in your research, and you have a factorial within-groups design. For details, follow the blue pathway in the center of the decision tree on the next page.

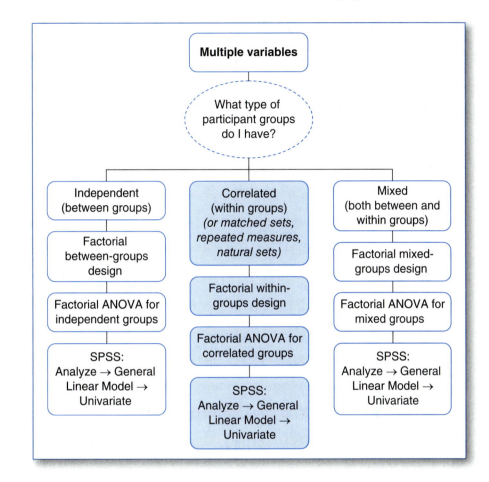

Turn to Chapter 9 for a discussion of when you would want to use a within-groups approach and review how to run the appropriate analyses.

As a third alternative when you have more than one variable, you might decide to include one between-groups variable and one within-groups variable. In that case, you would be using a factorial mixed-groups design. We call it a *mixed* design because the study includes both types of variables: One is between groups, and one is within groups. Perhaps half of your participants watch the humorous commercial for both products, and the other half of your participants watch the non-humorous commercials for both products. In this case, can you figure out which variable is within and which is between? Remember, the within-groups variable is the one that allows all participants to see both levels of your variable (type of product). However, when it comes to the humor in the ad, participants will see either the ads with humor or the ads without humor (a between-groups variables). Your design and analysis choices are highlighted on the far right of the decision tree on the next page.

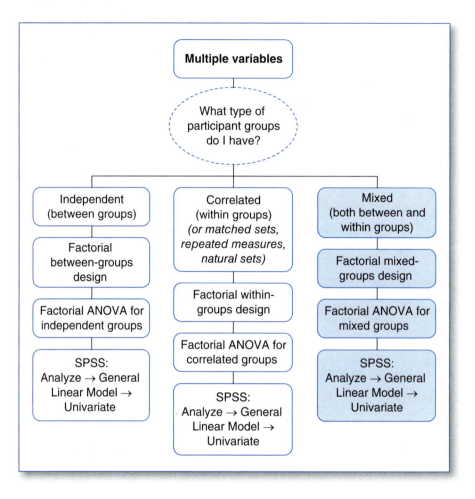

Chapter 10 provides the details you need when using a mixed-groups design and will provide information about what type of statistic to use.

As you can see from our first two decision trees, you can design studies with one or more variables, as many levels as you would like, and you can decide how to assign participants to levels. Follow these decision trees to locate the appropriate statistic. Keep in mind, as discussed earlier, that you can have either manipulated IVs (and show cause and effect) or pseudo-IVs (and know relationships between variables); both types of variables are analyzed the same way.

All of the designs you read about in the previous pages have a single DV. You might be thinking about a research project that will require several dependent measures. For example, you might be thinking about measuring driving ability and desire to measure acceleration from a stop, number of times the fog line is crossed, and stopping distance in both ordinary and emergency circumstances.

Any design that requires more than one dependent measure is called a *multivariate design*. A multivariate design may use any of the experimental designs just described, so it could be a simple within-groups design or a factorial between-groups design. All of them rely on the same statistical procedure, the multivariate analysis of variance, or MANOVA.

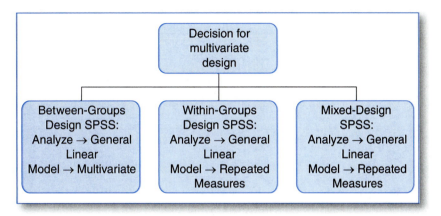

In the next section, we will offer a decision tree to use when you do not have a few distinct levels for your variables.

Interval or Ratio Data With Many Levels

When variables are interval or ratio data with many levels, we often cannot rely on the analyses offered above. Instead, we turn to statistics that can handle a wide range of numbers. You will notice that the statistics include correlation (Pearson's r) and linear regression, but remember that correlational analysis and design mean two different things! Refer to Chapter 2 for a refresher, if needed. In the decision trees, we give you the correct path to a statistical analysis. However, keep in mind that your *design* will dictate whether you talk about cause-and-effect or relationships when you have results in your hand. If you manipulated a variable, you can discuss cause and effect; if you did not, you only can talk about relationships between variables. Either way, you can use Pearson's r to analyze interval or ratio data with numerous levels.

As an example, you might be interested in whether there is a relationship between the number of friends people have and self-esteem. You could ask a large group of people to fill out a survey and indicate how many friends they have (after you define what "friend" means, of course), and then you would measure their self-esteem using an established scale (let us say on a scale from 1 to 10, with higher numbers meaning higher self-esteem). Chapter 11 includes details on how to lay out your data in SPSS, run the appropriate analyses, interpret the results, and finally write up your results in APA style. Because number of friends and values on a self-esteem rating scale have many values in this design, you would analyze these data using Pearson's *r* (correlational statistic). In addition, if you also wanted to predict self-esteem from number of friends, you could go a step beyond Pearson's *r* to prediction with linear regression. In the following section, we offer paths on the decision tree for prediction, *but* if you only want to know whether two variables correlate, simply focus on the correlation branch of the decision tree (far left).

Keeping It Simple With Two Variables

Let us start with a design having only two interval or ratio variables that were not manipulated and have many numbers possible on each variable. For correlational designs (not manipulated), instead of talking about independent variables (IVs), pseudo IVs, or dependent variables (DVs), we talk about plain old variables. If you want to know whether or not two variables are related, you can run Pearson's *r* for correlation as long as the two variables are interval or ratio data and have a wide range of numbers on each variable. Notice that at the top of this decision tree, your first question changes from "How many groups will my variable have?" or "What type of participant groups do I have?" to "How many variables are included?"

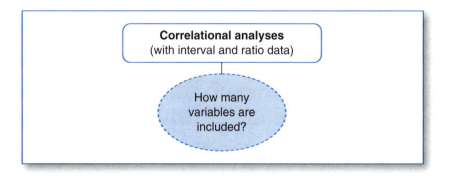

If you decide to include only two variables in your study, then you will follow the far-left path of the next decision tree; this path is for a **bivariate correlation**. A bivariate analysis means you are measuring the relationship between two variables. Sometimes, you merely want to know if two variables are related. If your research question goes a step further, and you want to predict one variable from another, simply look at the middle pathway in the decision tree on the next page, which allows you to test if one variable can predict the second variable. It should come as no surprise that the variable you choose as the predictor is called a *predictor variable*; the predicted variable is called a **criterion variable**. In the decision tree, look at the two blue pathways and notice that even with prediction, you first want to know if the two variables correlate. After all, if two variables are not related to each other, there is not much point in trying to predict one from the other.

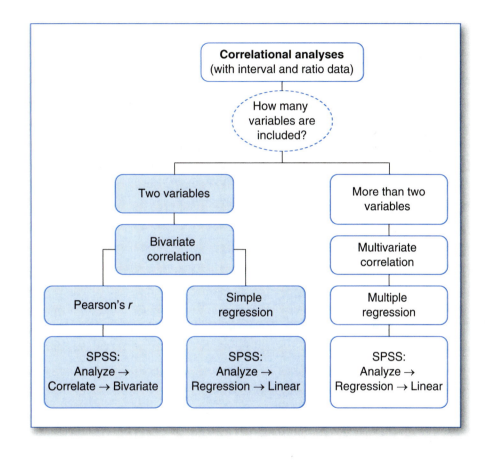

Again, which blue path you choose at this point depends on the goal of your research project. Do you want to measure the potential relationship between two variables? Or are you interested in the ability to predict one variable based on knowing the value of the other variable?

As an example, you might wonder if the amount of chocolate consumption in a country is related to the number of Nobel Laureates produced in that country. This research question might seem odd, but when the relationship was actually measured, many were surprised to find out that the correlation is +.79 (and it was +.86 when Sweden was taken out ☺; Messerli, 2012).

In this example, the findings indicate that the two variables are related to one another, and surprisingly, there is indeed a strong positive relationship between the two. To examine this relationship, you can run a bivariate correlation by using Pearson's *r*. Chapter 11 provides all the details on this type of correlational research, including how to create a scatterplot to visually present your results.

However, sometimes we are interested in more than just estimating the strength of the relationship between two variables. Researchers are also interested in predicting one variable when knowing the value of the other. Using SPSS, a simple regression will provide a regression equation and allow you to understand how well you can predict the outcome of one variable based on knowing the value of your predictor variable. In the chocolate–Nobel example, maybe you have a list of countries and the chocolate consumption of each and want to know if you can predict the number of Nobel Laureates based on chocolate consumption. Simple linear-regression analysis will provide the estimate. In Chapter 11, you can review details on how to set up the data file for both types of bivariate correlations, how to run the analyses using SPSS, how to interpret the SPSS output, and how to write the results up in APA style.

Including More Than Two Variables

After reading the example above and the surprisingly strong relationship between chocolate consumption and number of Nobel Laureates, we hope you realized that correlation does not mean causation. In other words, although chocolate consumption is related to the number of Nobel Laureates, there must be additional factors related to winning a peace prize that will help us better understand why this relationship exists. Posing that type of question brings up the final path on the decision tree. Perhaps you want to include more than one predictor. Maybe countries with more chocolate consumption also are more affluent, or have stronger education systems. Are those variables better predictors of Nobel Laureates than chocolate consumption? You now have multiple predictor variables to include in your design and analysis, so you would need to run a multiple linear regression and follow the path on the far right as highlighted on the next page.

The right side of the next decision tree illustrates the type of design you need to use and the type of statistics to run using SPSS. In the second highlighted box on the far right, *multivariate correlation* is a fancy way of saying you looked at bivariate correlations among all variables. That is, you can only look at two variables at a time when running correlations. Multivariate correlation means you ran Pearson's *r* for every possible pairing of variables in your design. When moving toward predicting, however, multiple predictors are used to predict one criterion (outcome) variable. And all predictors can be analyzed in the same equation, usually allowing better prediction of the outcome variable than using only one predictor. As you can see on the next page, this prediction analysis is called *multiple regression*.

Take a look at the end of Chapter 11 to read about how to run this type of analysis, see what the output will look like, understand how to interpret the output, and learn how to write the results in APA style.

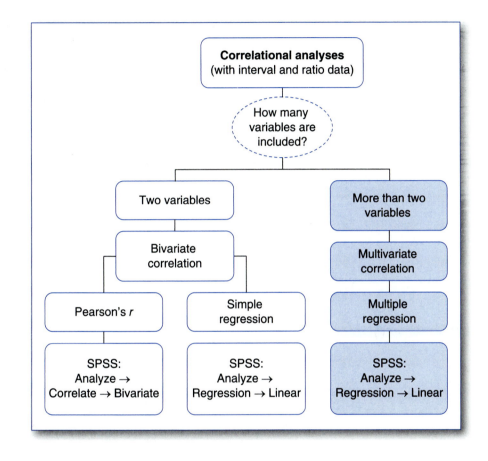

Summary

Throughout this chapter, we have offered examples to demonstrate the different paths to take on the three decision trees. We urge you to copy the complete decision trees included at the end of this chapter and put them up on your wall as a poster. Or simply keep this book handy! Either way, the following pages offer the decision trees in full for your review. As you develop your research ideas, a glance at the decision trees will remind you how each decision you make concerning the design of your research leads to a specific type of design and, in turn, the use of a specific type of analysis and name of statistic to use in SPSS. Remember, the chapters earlier in this EasyGuide cover the design choices and appropriate statistics for each branch of the decision trees. In those chapters, we promise you can find help for each step of the way!

DECISION TREE 1

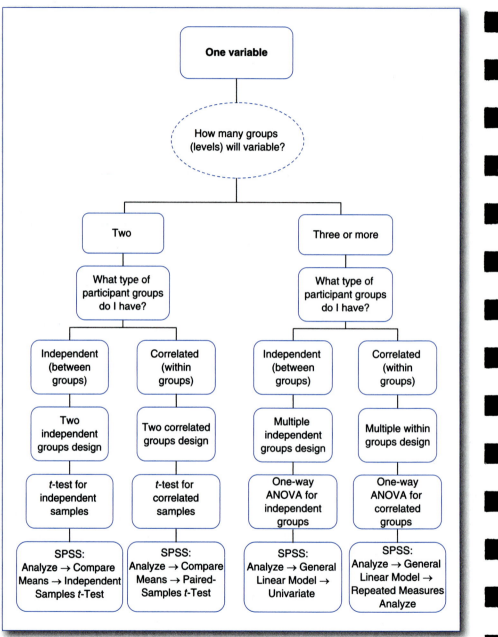

DECISION TREE 2

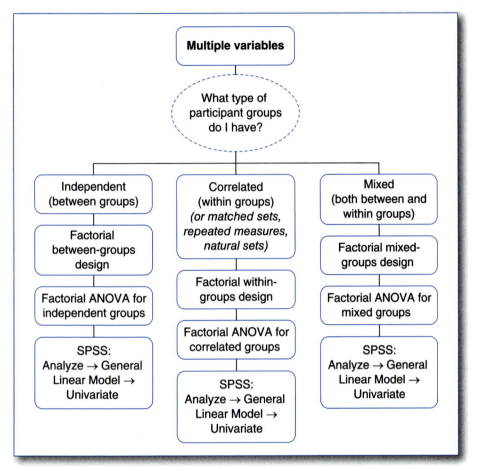

DECISION TREE 3

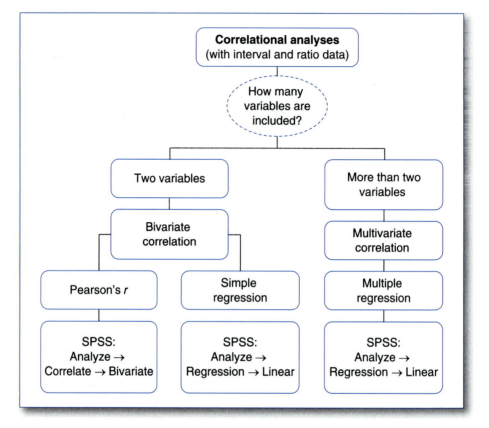

APA Results Sections 14

In this chapter, we include the results sections from previous chapters and provide comments throughout to indicate some important aspects of this section of an APA-style paper. Some of the comments are applicable to *all* results sections, regardless of the type of design and statistic, and other comments are specific to the type of statistic. Keep in mind that APA style requires one-inch margins; however, we made the margins larger throughout this chapter so that we could include the comments that point out important aspects of the results sections. You will notice that at times these comments cover up some text, so we included the page number before each section to let you know where in the other chapters you can find the full paragraph. You will notice that a few of these results sections include tables or figures. We recommend that you use *An EasyGuide to APA Style* (Schwartz et al., 2014) for the details about constructing those to follow APA guidelines.

From Chapter 8 (original found on page 86)

t-Test for Independent Samples (true IV)

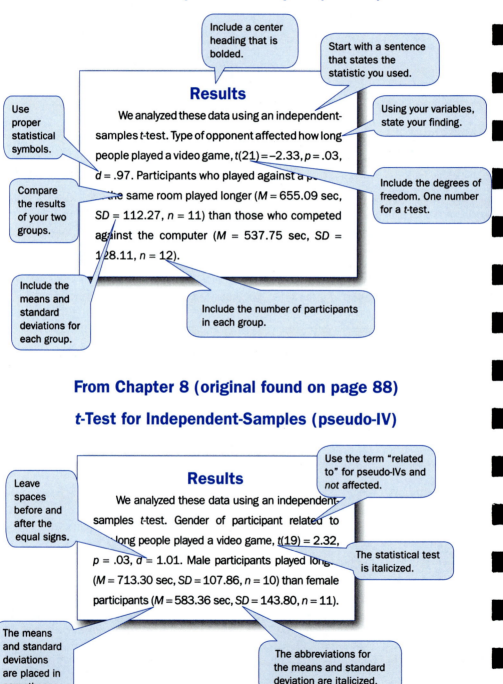

Include a center heading that is bolded.

Start with a sentence that states the statistic you used.

Results

We analyzed these data using an independent-samples *t*-test. Type of opponent affected how long people played a video game, *t*(21) = −2.33, *p* = .03, *d* = .97. Participants who played against a p... the same room played longer (*M* = 655.09 sec, *SD* = 112.27, *n* = 11) than those who competed against the computer (*M* = 537.75 sec, *SD* = 128.11, *n* = 12).

Use proper statistical symbols.

Using your variables, state your finding.

Compare the results of your two groups.

Include the degrees of freedom. One number for a *t*-test.

Include the means and standard deviations for each group.

Include the number of participants in each group.

From Chapter 8 (original found on page 88)

t-Test for Independent-Samples (pseudo-IV)

Results

We analyzed these data using an independent-samples *t*-test. Gender of participant related to long people played a video game, *t*(19) = 2.32, *p* = .03, *d* = 1.01. Male participants played long... (*M* = 713.30 sec, *SD* = 107.86, *n* = 10) than female participants (*M* = 583.36 sec, *SD* = 143.80, *n* = 11).

Leave spaces before and after the equal signs.

Use the term "related to" for pseudo-IVs and *not* affected.

The statistical test is italicized.

The means and standard deviations are placed in parentheses.

The abbreviations for the means and standard deviation are italicized.

From Chapter 8 (original found on page 96)

One-Way, ANOVA for Independent Groups (true IV)

> With more than 2 means you will need a *post hoc* comparison test.

> Include the name of the type of statistic you used.

Results

We used a one way, between-groups ANOVA to analyze these data. Tukey's *post hoc* comparisons examined differences between groups ($p < .05$). Type of opponent affected how long participants played a video game, $F(2, 33) = 6.24$, $p < .01$, $\eta^2 = .27$. Participants who played against another person from a remote location played longer ($M = 710.92$, $SD = 130.24$, $n = 13$) than participants who played against the computer ($M = 537.75$, $SD = 128.11$, $n = 12$). No other group means differed ($p > .05$).

> This is eta squared for the effect size. This is included when you run an ANOVA.

> Use the abbreviation for the type of statistic used.

> Only two places after the decimal point are needed.

From Chapter 9 (original found on page 102)

t-Test for Correlated-Samples

> The type of *t*-test is included in this first sentence.

Results

In this study, we used a paired-samples *t*-test to evaluate differences in typing time in a social and alone condition. We found that typing time was slower in the alone condition ($M = 10.14$ sec, $SD = 5.36$, $n = 20$), compared to the social condition ($M = 8.96$ sec, $SD = 3.98$, $n = 20$). However, this small increase was not statistically significant, $t(19) = -.96$, $p = .18$, $d = -.34$.

> Means are indicated with an italicized capital *M*.

> You can include the test of significance either before *or* after the means. You choose.

> The *t*-value can be a negative number.

> Include Cohen's *d* to indicate the strength of the difference should be included with your report of *t*.

From Chapter 9 (original found on page 112)

One-Way, ANOVA for Correlate Groups (repeated measures)

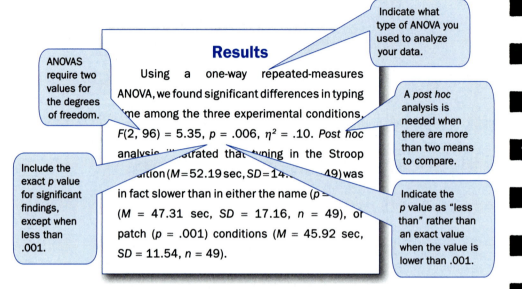

Indicate what type of ANOVA you used to analyze your data.

Results

ANOVAS require two values for the degrees of freedom.

Using a one-way repeated-measures ANOVA, we found significant differences in typing time among the three experimental conditions, $F(2, 96) = 5.35$, $p = .006$, $\eta^2 = .10$. *Post hoc* analysis illustrated that typing in the Stroop condition ($M = 52.19$ sec, $SD = 14.$ ___ 49) was in fact slower than in either the name ($p =$ ___ ($M = 47.31$ sec, $SD = 17.16$, $n = 49$), or patch ($p = .001$) conditions ($M = 45.92$ sec, $SD = 11.54$, $n = 49$).

A *post hoc* analysis is needed when there are more than two means to compare.

Include the exact *p* value for significant findings, except when less than .001.

Indicate the *p* value as "less than" rather than an exact value when the value is lower than .001.

From Chapter 9 (original found on pages 122–123)

Factorial ANOVA for Correlated Groups (repeated measures)

> The variable names are included immediately after the number of levels and without a space.

> Include the names of your variables in parentheses when stating the design of the ANOVA.

> First, write about one variable at a time. Each represents a main effect.

> The second independent variable is included next.

> With two variables, there are too many means to include in the Results section. Instead, include the means of each condition in a table or a figure.

> The third result reported is about whether you found a significant interaction.

> Graphs need error bars. One good option is confidence intervals, which you include here in your Results section.

> End by reporting results of your *post hoc* analyses.

Results

We used a 2(spice) × 2(smoke) within-subjects ... on taste ratings for our soon to be world famous chili. Participants rated the spicy chili (M = 6.4, SD = 2.4, n = 20) significantly more tasty than the mild (M = 5.6, SD = 2.4, n = 20), $F(1, 19)$ = 39.78, p <.001, η^2 = .68. They also significantly preferred the taste of both spice levels of chili when tasting with smoke in the air, $F(1, 19)$ = 47.60, p <.001, η^2 = .71. Most important, the two variables interacted to effect taste ratings, $F(1, 19)$ = 6.78, p <.001, η^2 = .26. We present the mean taste ratings, with 95% confidence intervals, for this interaction between spice and smoke in Figure 1. Our *post hoc* analyses showed that our participants liked both spicy and mild chili significantly more when they were tasted in the presence of smoke; however, the presence of smoke had a stronger effect for the mild chili.

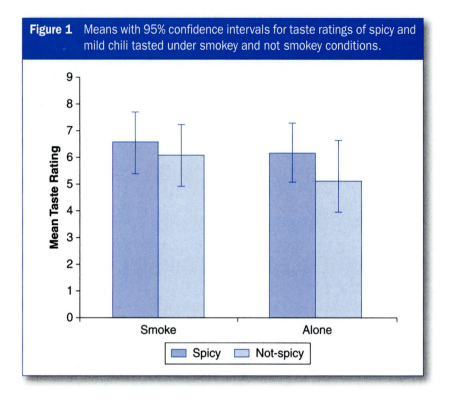

Figure 1 Means with 95% confidence intervals for taste ratings of spicy and mild chili tasted under smokey and not smokey conditions.

From Chapter 10 (original found on page 137)

Factorial ANOVA for Mixed Groups

Start the results section with your design statement.

Results

We conducted a 2 (sex) × 3 (driving conditions) mixed-model ANOVA on stopping distance in simulated driving emergency. Driving conditions served as the within-groups variable. There was a significant difference among the three driving conditions, $F(2, 36) = 579.38$, $p < .01$, $\eta^2 = .97$. As expected, the stopping distance in the phone condition was the longest ($M = 98.65$ ft, $SD = 12.49$, $n = 20$), followed by stopping distance in the music condition ($M = 52.50$ ft, $SD = 10.74$, $n = 20$), and finally the shortest stopping distance was found in the control condition ($M = 47.6$ ft, $SD = 9.8$, $n = 20$). Post hoc analyses showed that all of these means differed from each other, $p < .001$. Females and males did not differ reliably from each other, $F(1, 18) = 1.28$, $p = .24$, $\eta^2 = .067$. Further, there was not a significant interaction between driving condition and sex, $F(2, 36) = 2.48$, $p = .10$, $\eta^2 = .12$.

Indicate which variables served as within-subjects variables.

Remember to include the dimensions of your measurement when you can.

Use eta squared as an effect size statistic with ANOVA.

We needed a *post hoc* analysis because there were three conditions.

As usual we present descriptive statistics for each main effect.

Present the results for your interactions that are not significant.

From Chapter 10 (original found on page 148)

Factorial ANOVA for Independent Groups

Results

The mean numbers of marshmallows offered or accepted with standard deviations for ea~~~ age group are presented in Table 1. Th~ ~e-way between-groups multivariate ar~~sis revealed a significant overall effect, $\lambda = .51$, $F(6, 64) = 4.30$, $p = .002$. Individual one-way between groups ANOVAs showed that there was a difference among age groups for the number of marsh-mallows offered in the first trial, $F(2, 34) = 6.29$, $p = .005$, $\eta^2 = .27$. However, there was not a significant difference among age groups for smallest accepted offer, $p = .15$, or for the number of marshmallows offered on the second trial, $p = .16$. Finally, *post hoc* analyses (Tukey) showed that the youngest group (3–5 year-olds) offered significantly fewer marshmallows than the (6–9 year-olds). None of the other differences were statistically meaningful (all p's > .05).

> Present the multivariate statistic first.

> The usual ANOVA format follows the multivariate statistic.

> Next, report the results for analyses of individual dependent variables.

Table 1   Mean Number of Marshmallows Offered or Accepted With Standard Deviations in Parentheses for the Three Age Groups

	Age Groups		
	3–5 years	6–9 years	10–11 years
Offer	$n = 14$	$n = 13$	$n = 10$
First	3.1 (1.3)	5.5 (2.3)	4.3 (1.6)
Least Accepted	1.4 (1.3)	2.5 (2.5)	2.7 (1.6)
Second	4.5 (2.2)	5.7 (2.0)	4.3 (1.2)

From Chapter 10 (original found on page 155)

Analysis of Covariance

As usual we start the section by identifying the design and analysis.

Results

We conducted a between-groups ANCOVA on estimated height with power group as the independent variable and actual height as a covariate. As expected, the high-power group estimated their height as taller ($M = 66.4$ cm, $SD = 3.4$, $n = 20$) than the low-power group ($M = 65.4$ cm, $SD = 3.8$, $n = 20$.) This difference statistically significant only when actual height was included as a covariate, $F(1,37) = 21.34$, $p < .01$, $\eta^2 = .37$.

Be sure to identify your covariate.

Present your descriptive statistics.

Present the results as you would for any ANOVA.

From Chapter 11 (originals found on pages 167, 171, and 173)

Pearson's *r* Correlation

Pearson's r includes one number for the degrees of freedom.

Results

We analyzed the potential correlation between number of Facebook friends and number of close in-person friends using Pearson's *r*. The two variables correlated at $r(8) = .85$, $p < .01$, $r^2 = .72$. Number of Facebook friends ranged from 57 to 367 ($M = 191.90$, $SD = 107.92$, $n = 10$). Number of close friends seen on a regular basis ranged from 15 to 75 ($M = 42.10$, $SD = 19.29$, $n = 10$).

Start by stating variables you included in the correlation.

You can report r^2 as the effect size statistic for correlations.

Include the range of responses for each variable included in your correlational analyses.

Results

We analyzed the potential correlation between number of Facebook friends and happiness using Pearson's r. The two variables failed to correlate, $r(8) = -.24$, $p = .51$. Number of Facebook friends ranged from 57 to 367 ($M = 191.90$, $SD = 107.92$, $n = 10$). Ratings of happiness ranged from 2 to 7 ($M = 4.90$, $SD = 1.66$, $n = 10$).

Pearson's r includes one number for the degrees of freedom.

Results

We analyzed the potential correlation between number of close friends and happiness using Pearson's r. The two variables correlated at $r(10) = .87$, $p < .01$, $r^2 = .75$. Number of Facebook friends ranged from 1 to 12 ($M = 6.08$, $SD = 3.68$, $n = 12$). Happiness ratings ranged from 1 to 7 ($M = 4.50$, $SD = 2.07$, $n = 12$).

From Chapter 11 (originals found on pages 179 and 183)

Pearson's *r* Correlation and Simple Regression

Results

We analyzed the potential correlation between number of close friends and happiness using Pearson's *r*. The two variables correlated at $r(10) = .87$, $p < .01$, $r^2 = .75$. Number of Facebook friends ranged from 1 to 12 ($M = 6.08$, $SD = 3.68$, $n = 12$). Happiness ratings ranged from 1 to 7 ($M = 4.50$, $SD = 2.07$, $n = 12$).

Linear regression analysis allowed us to predict happiness from number of close friends, $F(1, 10) = 30.16$, $p < .01$, with a slope of .49 and a Y-intercept of 1.54. The variable of close friends significantly predicted happiness ($p < .01$). When predicting happiness from number of close friends, we will err by 1.08 happiness rating points.

For linear regressions, include the variable you included as your predictor.

A linear regression analysis includes an *F* test with two degrees of freedom. The statistical information in your results section will look similar to the statistics from an ANOVA.

When reporting linear regression analysis, you include both the slope and the intercept to indicate the regression equation.

Include a sentence to indicate the error for regression equation.

Results

We used linear regression to predict happiness from number of close friends, average _____ of events with friends per month, and average duration of social events ($N = 12$). Please see Table 1 for descriptive statistics and correlations among variables.

The three variables considered together significantly predicted happiness, $F(3, 8) = 10.49$, $p < .01$, with 80% overlap between the three predictor___ ___d the outcome of happiness. When ____ng happiness, we will err by approximately _.09 happiness-rating points based on a scale from 1 to 7. Specifically, number of close friends remained as a significant predictor, with a slope of .49 ($p = .02$); 2.49 quantified the Y-intercept for our regression equation.

> The first sentence includes all the variables included in the regression analysis.

> With this many variables, the descriptive statistics should be included in a table rather than in the results paragraph.

> With more than two predictor variables, you should include a sentence about the percentage of overlap between them.

From Chapter 12 (originals found on pages 196 and 202)

One-Way χ^2

Results

We analyzed our data using a one-way χ^2. We expected 20% of our sample of college students t_ say they text while driving and 80% to s__ _____ _ not; however, observed freque____ __es significantly differed from expected frequencies, χ^2 (1, $N = 100) = 56.25$, $p < .05$. Fifty percent of our sample of college students admitted that they text while driving, and 50% said they do not.

> Include the Greek letter to indicate you used a chi-square analysis.

> Indicate the expected values first.

> Next you should indicate if the observed frequencies differed significantly from the expected frequencies.

> The observed values are included in a separate sentence.

Indicate the type of chi-square conducted. Here we ran a one-way.

Results

Percentages are reported as values with the percent symbol (%) in the results paragraph.

We analyzed our data using a one-way χ^2. We expected 25% of our sample of college students to say they regularly text while driving, 50% to say they do not text at all while driving, and 25% say they text only at stoplights and in stand still traffic. In fact, observed frequencies did not deviate from expectations, χ^2 (2, $N = 195$) = 2.36, $p > .05$.

If observed did not differ from expected, you do not need to restate the percentages.

Include the number of observation conducted after the degrees of freedom.

State the p value as greater than .05 when the outcome is not statistically significant and you do not know the exact value of p.

From Chapter 12 (original found on page 214)

Two-Way χ^2

For a two-way chi square include the names of the variables.

Results

We analyzed our data using a 2 (students texting and driving or not) × 2 (parents texting while driving or not) χ^2. Whether or not college students texted while driving related to whether or not parents texted while driving, χ^2 (1, $N = 250$) = 90.17, $p < .01$, $\phi = .60$. Of college students who text while driving, approximately 87% of their parents also text while driving, and only 14% do not. Of students who do not text while driving, only 20% of their parents drive and text; 80% do not.

For each variable, include the observed frequencies for the other variable measured.

These percentages are included only when the observed frequencies differ significantly from the expected frequencies.

Did I Do That? 15

Taking Advice From the Experts

The task of designing an experiment, particularly when you are new to the task, is not an easy one. Information you have learned in many courses must be applied to a new situation: your own research project. In this chapter, we want to help you find some of the information you need when you are ready to use it. Below, we address frequently asked questions to present some of the most common types of mistakes you should avoid. Questions are organized within steps of the research process. And, finally, we direct you to the chapter where you can find the details concerning each of these questions.

Questions About Research Design

Did I collect nominal, ordinal, interval, or ratio measurements? Oh my, this question should never be asked in the past tense! If you used the wrong type of measurement, you might not be able to analyze your data at all. When a student asks us this question and indeed cannot analyze the data, we have to say start over from the beginning. Sadly, the entire study has to be rerun. Please review Chapter 3 if you are unsure of the level of measurement for any of your variables. Then, ask a professor or other experienced researcher if your choice of measurement is correct, given you research questions, and if your variables are appropriate for the questions you have in mind.

Should I conduct this experiment with a between-groups or within-groups design? To answer this question, you might ask yourself, "Will my manipulations produce any carry-over effects that are difficult or impossible to reverse?" If the answer to this question is "yes," then you should use a between-groups design. Even when there is a reasonable risk of carry-over effects, you might still prefer a within-groups design if your DV likely has many individual differences. The classic example of a problematic variable is speed of responding. People differ a great deal on response times, and such large individual differences might overwhelm the effect of a manipulation (IV). An explanation of how within-groups designs increase power by reducing error variance is beyond the scope of this book; however, you might want to explore the nuances of within-groups designs at some point in your education. Chapter 8 provides details for between-groups designs, and Chapter 9 focuses on within-groups designs.

How many independent variables (IVs) should I have? You should have as many IVs as it takes to address each of your hypotheses. We suggest using no more than two or three IVs because each IV must have at least two levels. A larger design can become unwieldy and produce results that are difficult to interpret. Take a look at Chapter 4 where we discuss the questions of choosing the number of variables.

Does my independent variable really test my hypothesis? We hope so. Here is an example of what could go wrong. If you are interested in testing the impact of discussing traumatic events with children, you want to be sure that you have two groups that differ according to the variable in question—in this case, discussion of the traumatic event. If you design this study and have half of the children discuss the traumatic event with parents and the other half discuss the event with clinicians, you are not testing the hypothesis because both groups will discuss the event with someone. To test this hypothesis, you need one group of children who discuss the traumatic event with trained mental health professionals and a second group who are not provided with an opportunity for that discussion. Chapter 1 introduces the important connection between your hypothesis and the design of your research.

How many dependent variables should I have? You always need at least one. So the real question is, "Should I have more than one?" For beginning researchers, one DV is typically enough, and as we have said over and over in this book, it is best to keep it simple at first. As you become more proficient at designing research, you might want to add more DVs. Chapter 4 includes a discussion of deciding the number of DVs to include. When you do decide you want to include multiple DVs, make sure that each measure helps you to get a better understanding of potential effects. Do not measure variables that are not at all related to your research questions. For example, if you are interested in how emotions change, you could measure physiological signs of emotion like blood pressure and heart rate, but you would not include attitudes toward abstract art. If you have more than one dependent measure, you should use an analysis called MANOVA (see Chapter 10).

When is a correlational design most appropriate? First of all, be careful about confusing correlational design and analysis (see Chapter 2 for a thorough discussion of the difference). A correlational *design* is defined by use of variables in your study that you did not manipulate. You are merely looking for a relationship between pairs of existing variables, examining as many pairs as you would like. We use correlational designs whenever we want to know the relationship between two existing variables. As an example, researchers have examined height and income and found that as height increases, income increases; the two variables are related to each other. Remember that you must not assume causality when you use a correlational design. No matter how careful you have been in your research, there is always the possibility that an unmeasured variable has affected both of your variables. In our height-and-income example, good nutrition very early in life could increase both height and brain function; therefore, nutrition actually could be the cause of both height and income. Again, Chapter 2 includes information on the distinction between correlation as a design versus correlation as a statistic, and Chapter 11 provides a detailed discussion of Pearson's *r* as a correlation statistic.

Questions About Analyzing Your Data

SPSS has three different kinds of t-test; *which one should I use?* First, know your research design. Each of the *t*-tests corresponds with a different research design (see Chapters 8 and 9). Do you want to look for a difference between two means from the same group of participants? That is, are the same people tested twice (or are participants in the two groups related in some way before they arrive—such as sisters)? Then you should use the *paired-samples* t-*test*. Do you want to find a difference in means from two different groups of participants? Are people in the two groups not related in any way before they arrive? Maybe you even randomly assigned them to levels of the IV. Then you should use the *independent-samples* t-*test*.

These SPSS results do not make any sense. What did I do wrong? Most often when we hear this question, we find that our students have made a mistake when working in SPSS. Some common mistakes are that they have confused the IV and the DV in their one-way ANOVA or have chosen a *paired-samples* t-*test* when they needed an *independent-samples* t-*test*. So, our advice is to be careful. Use the decision trees in this book in Chapter 13 and know your data, especially the variable names you have chosen for all of your variables. When entering variables into SPSS boxes for analysis, be sure to put them in the right locations. That is where the most common mistakes are made—placing the variables in the wrong boxes when setting up your analyses. Chapter 7 provides details needed to set up your SPSS files.

Do I really need to ask for descriptive statistics and effect size when I run my analyses? When analyzing your data, you need to determine more than just statistical significance. In addition to a *p*-value, you should also collect measures of central tendency (e.g., means) and measures of variability (e.g., standard deviations). You will need this information when writing up your results. Descriptive statistics inform your reader what the summary data look like. In addition, effect size communicates how much effect your IV really had on your DV (assuming the effect is significant), or it quantifies the strength of a relationship between variables. In fact, APA style requires effect size if you report a significant effect. Often, in SPSS, obtaining effect size requires a simple check mark in a box, and the output will include the necessary measure. Chapter 7 reviews how to ask SPSS for descriptive statistics when running your analyses and how to include those statistics in your results section.

Questions About Interpreting Your Data and Presenting Your Results

How do I know if my results are meaningful? The simplest answer we can tell you is based on the most popular approach to data analysis: hypothesis testing. When SPSS provides results, look for the appropriate *p*-value on the output. Remember that SPSS labels these values *Sig*. If the value is equal to or less than .05, the chance of the effect happening in a normal population (for example, where nothing is done to people) is less than 5%. That means what you found was a meaningful effect. In other words, the result you found was so rare normally that you must have found a true and meaningful effect. The chapters in Section III provide you with details on how to interpret your data for the specific type of research design you used.

Why do I need to report descriptive statistics? Descriptive statistics offer the best summary of your findings. When presented well, they tell your story clearly and quickly. In addition, your audience wants to know how big any differences were, and they want to compare your results with other published research. Finally, descriptive statistics allow you to create eye-catching figures (graphs) of your data as well as tables. Again, for step-by-step instructions on descriptive statistics, take a look at Chapter 7.

Why do I need to give my measure's dimensions? First, a measure's dimensions simply define what you are measuring (e.g., inches, pounds, or seconds). When you describe your results, your outcomes should be easy to follow. For example, when we report that the experimental group had an average of 7.32, we do not want our readers to have to go back to the methods section to find out what that number means. Instead, we can report that the experimental group completed the task in 7.32 seconds. Our reader then knows exactly what we measured without referring back to earlier parts of the paper. You should avoid requiring readers to go back and find information earlier in your paper to understand what they are reading. How to write results in APA style is included in all the chapters in Section III.

When do I need a table or graph? Here is the short answer: You need a table or graph whenever it will help your reader understand the results. When you have too many values in your results section to easily communicate all the data, it is time to use a graph or table. Graphs or tables might not be needed for a simple *t*-test, but they can be very useful when reporting the results of a more complex design, such as one with two IVs. When you are making the decision between a graph or a table, you should remember that graphs are less precise than tables. If you think your readers need to know the exact values of your means, then a table is a better option. However, if you think your readers need to "see" the pattern of differences among means, then a graph will be more effective. In general, figures engage the reader better than tables. For example, graphs clearly summarize an interaction effect. Graphs are also useful when you want to visually present the means for many conditions or groups; for example, you might want to show measures of heart rate taken at five times during an experiment. Chapters throughout Section III indicate when you might want to consider a table or figure. For instructions on how to create them, you need to take a look at another EasyGuide (Schwartz et al., 2014), which gives you the details on APA-style figures and graphs.

How should I use the term significant? When we report research results, the term *significant* has a highly specific meaning. This term tells your readers that you rejected the null hypothesis and accepted the research hypothesis. It will help if you remember that your hypotheses are either about differences among means or the measured relationships between variables. To be precise, you should report that you found "a significant difference between the means of the two (or more) conditions." Or, if you calculated a correlation coefficient, you might report that you found "a significant positive relationship between two variables." If you conducted an experiment, you might also report that your IV "had a significant effect on" the DV. Or, if you include two IVs, you might also report that a significant interaction emerged between your two variables.

Why can't I interpret my findings in the results section? The purpose of your results section is to report the outcome of your statistical analysis. We know it is tempting to dive into explanations for your results, but do not. Avoid explanations until you get to your discussion section. There you can restate your results and speculate why you believe you found those results. As you see throughout the example results sections included in Chapter 14, a results section is the part of your paper where you simply tell us what you found and not what you think about your findings.

SPSS returned a value for p ***of .15. I know that I do not get to reject the null hypothesis, but how should I report this result?*** The most direct way is to report something like, "The difference between the two means was not significant," or, "A relationship between the two variables was not statistically reliable." The pitfall that captures many beginning researchers is that they report "there was no difference" or "there was no relationship." This kind of phrasing implies that the researcher accepted the null hypothesis, and that should be done only when effect size is very low and power is acceptably high, and we can never know for sure that a relationship does not exist. It simply did not show up in this one study. To read examples of how to report your statistical findings, Chapter 14 includes results sections for the different types of designs included throughout this book.

SPSS returned a value for* p *of .06. May I report that it is "marginally significant"? The answer to this question is controversial. Some researchers argue that determining statistical significance is like determining other yes/no decisions. If the *p*-value is equal to or less than .05, the answer is "yes"; if the *p*-value is more than .05, the answer is "no." However, other researchers argue that .05 is an arbitrary value. We know it means a result is unlikely to happen by chance—so unlikely that it occurs only 5% of the time or less in a "normal" population. But what if a result is so unlikely that it happens only 6% of the time in a normal population? That is still pretty rare! In such cases, many researchers will talk about a result as marginally significant. Using this type of terminology gives the reader knowledge that the general .05 cut-off value was not found, but the *p*-value was pretty darn close. In such cases, you can talk about the result as meaningful in your discussion section as well. Just be transparent about your result so the reader can decide if he or she wants to buy into your way of thinking.

Why should I avoid thinking I proved my hypothesis? Maybe in this one study, this one time, in exactly this circumstance, you were able to reject the null hypothesis. But how do you know for sure that your significant result was not a freak occurrence? Remember from your statistics course that there is always a chance of making one of two types of errors. So there is at least a small risk that we are wrong; no effect really existed. Over time and with replication, we gain confidence that our supported hypotheses are actually true; however, we should always be open to the possibility that someone will come along and show that we were wrong. So, we do not say we proved anything. We must remain humble. All we can do is help the scientific community gain evidence toward proving something.

Should I tell my readers that I used SPSS to analyze my data? No, you do not have to reference SPSS in your results section. People reading about your study will assume that you used appropriate statistical software to analyze your data; in fact, they will likely assume that you used SPSS to run your analyses. We do include details on why we chose to cover SPSS in this book in Chapter 5, but that information is not necessary to include in your paper.

Summary

We cannot *guarantee* that you will be successful in all research endeavors if you follow the advice we offered in this chapter and throughout this book. But we know that you will do a better job of analyzing your data and presenting results if you follow our advice. Review these ideas frequently as you conduct your first few independent research projects and gain expertise in design and analysis.

Glossary

These definitions are brief explanations for these terms. This glossary provides a glimpse into the meaning of many of the terms included in this EasyGuide. If you need additional information, take a look at your research methods or statistics textbooks.

Analysis of covariance An extension of the analysis of variance used for statistically controlling variance associated with a known source, the covariate, and so making it more likely to uncover a statistically significant effect.

Analysis of variance A flexible statistical analysis that allows for multiple factors that may have more than two levels; those factors may be manipulated either within or between groups.

ANCOVA—*see* analysis of covariance.

ANOVA—*see* analysis of variance.

APA style A set of writing rules developed by the American Psychological Association. These rules pertain to formatting, content, paper organization, and writing style.

Between-groups design Different individuals are assigned to the groups included in your experiment (e.g., control group and experimental group).

Bivariate correlation A statistical technique that produces a measure of the strength of the linear association between two variables.

Block randomization Participants are divided into groups, also called *blocks*,

so that the variability within blocks is less than the variability between the blocks. As a result, each group in your research design represents both blocks equally. This type of randomization is believed to control potential confounding variables more effectively than complete randomization.

Carry-over effects A potential problem when using repeated-measures designs. When participants are tested in one condition, the experience can affect how they behave in another condition. If present, these effects could confound your findings.

Causation When one variable influences or causes a change in another variable or variables.

Central tendency Measures, including the mean, median, and mode, that indicate the middle of a distribution.

Chi-square analysis A statistical technique used to compare the distribution of a nominal measure to an expected distribution.

Coefficient of determination Known as R^2, this statistic indicates the "goodness of fit" to illustrate how close your data points fit a line or curve on a scatterplot.

Cohen's *d* An effect size statistic that presents the difference between two means in standard deviation units and is most typically reported with *t*-tests.

Complete randomization When all of your participants have an equal chance of being assigned to any of the groups (e.g., control and experimental) or levels in your experiment. This random assignment is often accomplished by assigning random numbers to participants or flipping a coin.

Confidence intervals A range of values that is very likely (typically 90%, 95%, or 99%) to include the true population mean when the sample is representative of that population.

Confounding variable A variable that, when present, affects the measuring of your DV. As a result, your findings do not illustrate the actual relationship between your IV and DV. This is a type of extraneous variable.

Contingency coefficient This is a statistic sometimes reported with the χ^2 test for independence. It measures the strength of the relationship between the two variables.

Control group This group, sometimes referred to as the *baseline group* for which there is no treatment or a neutral treatment, is included for comparison to all experimental groups receiving a form of treatment.

Correlation coefficient A statistic that measures the strength of the linear relationship between two or more variables.

Correlation is not causation The strength of the relationship among variables does not imply that one variable has a causal influence on the other; it is possible that a third, unmeasured variable has causally influenced both.

Correlation matrix A table that presents each pair of variables and the correlations for each.

Correlational design A research design in which the variables are not manipulated.

The researcher measures each of the variables and examines the relationship or association among the variables included.

Counterbalancing A technique used to avoid order effects for a repeated-measures design. When feasible, all possible order of conditions are included, and participants experience one particular order so that results illustrate the influence of the condition itself and not the order of conditions.

Covariate A variable used in an ANCOVA to statistically control for variance, which might be obscuring the effects of an independent variable.

Criterion variable A variable used in a regression analysis. This is the outcome variable.

Data View The spreadsheet view of a data file in SPSS that includes the raw data from your research.

Degrees of freedom (*df*) A statistical term, typically n-1, where n indicates the sample size. More technically, it is calculated as the number of values that are used to estimate a population's mean minus one.

Dependent variable (DV) In an experimental design, the DV is the measured outcome and usually considered the "effect" in the cause-and-effect relationship examined. The IV is the cause and the DV is the effect.

Descriptive statistics Measures used to summarize a data set. They include measures of central tendency (e.g., mean, mode) and dispersion (e.g., range, standard deviation).

df—*see* degrees of freedom.

Effect size A statistic that indicates how big a difference or how strong an association was found among variables, typically reported in conjunction with the hypothesis testing statistics.

Excel Software developed by Microsoft, used to provide a spreadsheet of information. This is included in the Microsoft Office software suite.

Expected frequencies Values generated based on theoretical assumptions and used as the comparison distribution to observed frequencies in chi-square analyses.

Experimental design A researcher's plan for the number of variables to include how variables are manipulated or measured, and how participants are assigned to conditions.

Experimental group This group, sometimes referred to as a *treatment group*, receives a level of your IV. Results from the experimental group are compared to the control group to examine the influence of the IV on the DV.

Factorial design A research design with two or more IVs (or Pseudo IVs), each with two or more levels. This design allows you to examine the separate influence of each variable (i.e., main effects) as well as the interaction of the variables.

Factorial repeated-measures ANOVA An analysis of variance with at least two independent variables for data that was collected in a within-groups design.

Factorial within-groups design A research design with two or more IVs (or pseudo IVs), with participants exposed to all levels of each IV.

Frequency The number of times that a particular value occurs in a data set.

Goodness of fit test A χ^2 statistic that evaluates how well an observed frequency distribution fits a theoretical or expected distribution.

Hypothesis The stated prediction or answer to your research question. The prediction includes what relationship you expect to find among your variables. These predictions must be testable and as a result can be confirmed or refuted based on results from your research.

Independent-samples *t*-test This test of significance evaluates the difference between the means obtained from two separate groups.

Independent variable (IV) In an experimental design, the IV is the variable manipulated by the researcher and is considered the "cause" in the cause-and-effect relationship examined. The IV can be used to predict the outcome of the DV.

Individual differences A range of variables that can be used to distinguish individuals within a group. They include physical variables like weight and psychological and personality variables like intelligence.

Inferential statistics A group of statistical techniques that help researchers to make judgments about differences among means or strength of relationships in data that they have collected. Examples include *t*-tests and Pearson's *r*.

Institutional review board (IRB) This committee, federally required to be present at all institutions, reviews, approves, and monitors all research before data collection takes place. The reviewers consider all ethical issues concerning the welfare of the participants involved in your research and assess the risk and benefits to decide whether the research should be approved. The committee is sometimes called the *ethical review board*.

Interaction This occurs when the outcome of your DV is dependent on the influence of more than one IV. This effect occurs when the effect of one of your IVs on the DV is dependent on the level of another IV.

Interval A scale of measurement in which there is no absolute zero, but values on the scale are equal in distance from one another. Scores on this type of scale can be meaningfully added or subtracted but not multiplied or divided.

Linear regression A statistical procedure that estimates the straight line that best fits a scatterplot of two variables. The equation for that line can be used to predict values on the criterion variable.

Main effect This occurs when the influence of your IV on the DV does NOT depend on other IVs included in your experiment.

MANOVA—*see* multivariate analysis of variance.

Mean (M) This measure of central tendency might be best characterized as the simple average of the scores (add them up and divide by the number of observations) in a data set.

Median This measure of central tendency indicates the 50th percentile in a data set.

Mixed design An experimental design, sometimes referred to as *mixed-model design*, that includes two types of variables repeated-measures variables and between-subjects variables.

Mode This measure of central tendency is simply the most frequently observed score in a data set.

Multiple regression A regression analysis that includes multiple predictor variables. It produces independent measures of the relationships between each predictor and the criterion variable.

Multivariate analysis of variance The multivariate analysis of variance (MANOVA) is similar to the ANOVA but allows for analysis of more than one dependent variable.

Multivariate design An experimental design that includes more than one variable.

95% confidence interval The most typically reported confidence interval. It is a range of values that is very likely (95%) to include the true population mean when the sample is representative of that population.

Nominal One type of scale of measurement. The numbers for this scale are categorical and therefore have no numerical or value. Instead, this type of scale provides qualitative classifications.

Non-manipulated (pseudo) IV—*see* pseudo-IV.

Non-parametric tests These are statistical tests that do not rely on an estimate of the mean for their calculation. Most commonly, non-parametric tests are used when measures are ordinal or nominal; for example, one might use a Mann-Whitney U to test for the difference between two medians or Spearman's rho to measure the linear relationship between two ordinal variables.

Nuisance variables These variables increase variability in an observation. They are not confounded with an independent or criterion variable, but they can make it more difficult to find a significant difference between the groups you are comparing.

Null hypothesis The opposite of your research hypothesis, which as a researcher you hope to reject based on your findings. When you reject the null hypothesis based on significant findings, you demonstrate evidence for your research hypothesis. Interestingly, you can reject the null but you cannot accept the null.

Observed frequencies These are the values obtained by counting up the number of times each category occurs in a nominal variable for use in a χ^2 analysis.

One-tailed test A statistical test in which the critical area falls under one side of the normal or t distribution. In other words, the .05 value is either at the high or low end of the distribution and not divided between the two. With a one-tailed test, you are testing a directional hypothesis, for which you predict a specific difference between the groups tested.

One-way repeated-measures design A design in which you include one IV that has at least three levels.

One-way within-groups ANOVA An analysis of variance that is used when a design has one independent variable, all levels of that variable have been experienced by all participants, and the researcher has a hypothesis about the differences among the means associated with each level of the independent variable.

One-way χ^2 The goodness of fit statistic applied to a single nominal variable.

Operationalized—*see* operationally define.

Operationally define This is the process through which you define your variables. This includes, for example, exactly how you are manipulating your IV and measuring your DV. As a result, those reading about your research will know exactly what criteria you used when measuring your variables.

Ordinal A scale of measurement that ranks orders. The differences between the ranks are not necessarily equal.

Outliers These are unusually high or low scores in a data set. They can distort the results of a statistical analysis. They are often defined as three or more standard deviations above or below the mean.

p The p-value indicates how likely it is that your data occurred by chance. This value is used to determine your decision as to whether the null hypothesis is true or not.

Paired-samples t-test A statistical test that is used to compare two means that are collected from a single group or from matched pairs (e.g. married couples).

Pairwise comparisons These are typically conducted following an analysis of variance allowing for evaluation of differences among all possible pairs of means—*see post hoc* tests for more information about the statistics used.

Parametric statistics Any statistical test that relies on an estimate of the population's mean.

Partial eta squared (η^2) The effect size statistic typically reported with the analysis of variance. A longer name for this statistic is *proportion of variance accounted for.*

Pearson's r A measure of the linear association between two variables.

Percentages This statistic is sometimes reported in place of simple frequencies or counts. It is obtained by dividing the number of observations for a category by the total number of observations in the data set.

Phi coefficient The effect size statistic reported in χ^2 analysis.

Placebos The treatment given to the control group in an experiment, known to not have an effect. Results from the placebo group provide a baseline measure to compare to an experimental group receiving a therapeutic treatment. Typically, participants are unaware of whether they are in the control or experimental condition.

Population The entire group you wish to study and from which you draw your sample.

Post hoc analysis These analyses are conducted to find differences among specific means following a significant main effect or interaction in an ANOVA.

Post hoc tests Tests conducted when a significant F-ratio is found in an ANOVA. Two of the most commonly used tests are Scheffe and Tukey.

Power—*see* statistical power.

Predictor variable A term more often used for non-experimental research or correlational research to label one of the variables included in the design.

Predictors—*see* predictor variable.

Pseudo-IV An independent variable that lacks random assignment to quasi-experimental conditions. Often, these variables, sometimes referred to as *quasi-IVs*, cannot be manipulated by the experimenter. Instead, assignment to conditions is based on characteristics of the participants (e.g., sex, year in college).

Quasi-experimental design A research design in which you cannot randomly assign participants to your control and experimental groups.

Random assignment A technique used for assigning participants into treatment and control groups to reduce the presence and influence of any extraneous variables and equate the groups prior to collecting data.

Randomly assign The process of using random assignment—*see* random assignment.

Range A measure of dispersion, the spread of a distribution, that includes the lowest and highest observed value in the data set.

Ratio A scale of measurement that includes an absolute zero an d that includes values with equal distance between them. Values on this type of scale can be meaningfully added, subtracted, multiplied, and divided.

Regression A statistical procedure that estimates the line that best fits a scatterplot of two variables. The equation for that line can be used to predict values on the criterion variable.

Repeated-measures designs A research design, sometimes called a *within-subjects design*, in which you measure participants more than one time on your DV.

Therefore, the same participants are in the experimental and control group.

Repeated-measures factorial design—*see* repeated-measures design.

Research hypothesis This hypothesis, also called the *alternative hypothesis*, states your predicted results. A significant finding allows you to support your research hypothesis and refute the null hypothesis.

Sample The group of participants you select to represent the larger population. You analyze the data collected from your sample to draw inferences about the characteristics of the population.

Scatterplot This graph is often created before a correlation or regression analysis is conducted. It plots points for each pair of values on the two variables to be correlated.

Sig. (2-tailed) This is the name used in SPSS for the value of p when it reports the results of a statistical analysis in an output file.

Significance (or *p*-value) The criterion value that p must reach to allow the researcher to the reject the null hypothesis and accept the research hypothesis. It must be set before data are collected and is most typically set at .05, occasionally at .01.

Significant The judgment a researcher makes to reject the null hypothesis and accept the research hypothesis. The basis for the judgment is typically that an observed value of p is less than .05. The judgment is always about differences among means or distributions, or relationships between variables.

Simple frequency The number of observations for each category of a nominal variable.

SPSS A computer program (originally Statistical Package for the Social Sciences) produced by IBM that provides a very wide range of data management and statistical analysis tools.

Standard deviation (SD) A standardized measure of variability in a data set that is typically reported with the mean.

Standard error (SE) The measure of dispersion for a distribution of means. It is calculated by dividing the standard deviation by the square root of the number of observations in a sample. This statistic is used in calculations for the value of t and confidence intervals.

Statistical power This statistic is a measure of the probability that a statistical test will reach the criteria for significance when the research hypothesis is true.

Std. Error Mean—*see* standard error.

t The statistic produced by a t-test.

Test of independence A χ^2 statistic that evaluates whether responses to one nominal variable are dependent on responses to a second nominal variable.

t-test A set of statistical procedures that are used for evaluating hypotheses that propose a difference between two means.

Tukey A *post hoc* test used to evaluate the difference among three or more means following a significant ANOVA.

Two-tailed test A t-test or bivariate correlation that is conducted to evaluate a hypothesis that did not posit a direction for the difference between the means or linear relationship.

Two-way A factorial design that includes two independent variables.

Variability This concept refers to how much scores within a data set differ from each other and from the data set's mean.

Variable View This view of a data set in SPSS that shows the name of the variables along with other information about how each variable is stored in the database.

Within-groups designs—*see* repeated-measures designs.

References

Aron, A., Coups, E. J., & Aron, E. N. (2013). *Statistics for psychology* (6th ed.). Upper-Saddle River, NJ: Prentice-Hall.

Cline, T. W., & Kellaris, J. J. (2007). The influence of humor strength and humor—message relatedness on ad memorability: A dual process model. *Journal of Advertising, 36,* 56–67.

Duguid, M. M., & Goncalo, J. A. (2012). Living large: The powerful overestimate their own height. *Psychological Science, 23*(1), 36–40.

Messerli, F. H. (2012). Chocolate consumption, cognitive function, and Nobel laureates, *New England Journal of Medicine, 367,* 1562–1564. doi:10.1056/NEJMon1211064

Schwartz, B. M., Landrum, R. E., & Gurung, R. A. R. (2014). *An EasyGuide to APA style* (2nd ed.). Thousand Oaks, CA: Sage.

Wilson, J. H., & Schwartz, B. M. (2015). *An EasyGuide to research presentations.* Thousand Oaks, CA: Sage.

Index

⑤SAGE researchmethods

The essential online tool for researchers from the world's leading methods publisher

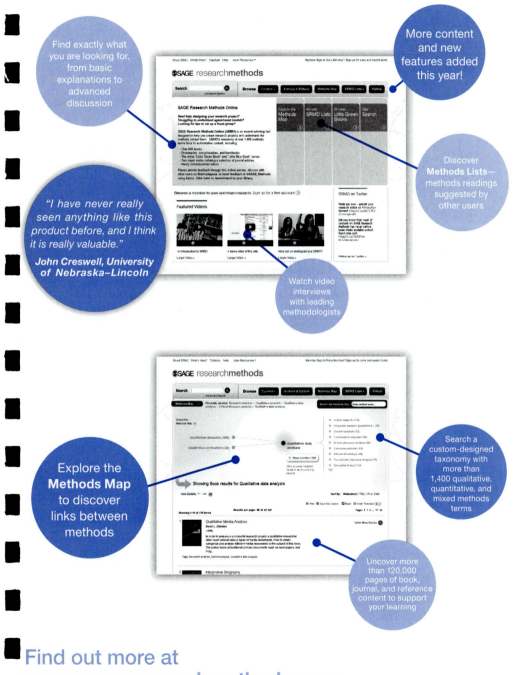

Find exactly what you are looking for, from basic explanations to advanced discussion

More content and new features added this year!

"I have never really seen anything like this product before, and I think it is really valuable."

John Creswell, University of Nebraska–Lincoln

Discover Methods Lists—methods readings suggested by other users

Watch video interviews with leading methodologists

Explore the Methods Map to discover links between methods

Search a custom-designed taxonomy with more than 1,400 qualitative, quantitative, and mixed methods terms

Uncover more than 120,000 pages of book, journal, and reference content to support your learning

Find out more at
www.sageresearchmethods.com